THE TORONTO STAR

OUTDOOR GARDEN BOOK

A COMPREHENSIVE HANDS-ON GUIDE
TO GETTING THE MOST FROM YOUR HOME GARDEN

THE TORONTO STAR
OUTDOOR GARDEN BOOK

THE ART, CRAFT, SCIENCE & DELIGHT OF GARDENING IN SOUTHERN ONTARIO

INTRODUCTION BY
H. FRED DALE
GARDENING EDITOR, THE TORONTO STAR

M&S

First edition

Editor: Tom Main
Design: Dan Diamond
Typesetting: Moveable Type Inc.

McClelland & Stewart Inc.
The Canadian Publishers
481 University Avenue
Toronto, Ontario
M5G 2E9

Canadian Cataloguing in Publication Data
Dale, H. Fred
   The Toronto star outdoor garden book
Includes index

ISBN 0-7710-2528-9

1. Gardening – Canada. I. Title. II. Title;
Outdoor garden book.

SB453.3.C3D34 1989   635.9'0971   C89-094006-1

Printed and bound in Canada by Webcom Limited

THE TORONTO STAR
OUTDOOR GARDEN BOOK

A COMPREHENSIVE HANDS-ON GUIDE
TO GETTING THE MOST FROM YOUR HOME GARDEN

CONTENTS

Lily

THE PLANTS' POINT OF VIEW

Introduction by Fred Dale

Cultivation of plants is synonymous with human civilization. Indeed, in Victorian England horticulture was regarded as one of the highest art forms. And art it certainly is. Growing plants both for sheer pleasure and for aesthetic effect makes our homes, our public buildings and even our factories look more a part of the natural world.

As well, there is something atavistic about us. Some say we evolved from the savannas of Africa and still feel an affinity for grasslands. Certainly, a fine lawn sets off a house as no other ground cover can. Others say we recently descended from tree dwellers and that we still feel safest when surrounded by a canopy of trees. Perhaps both are right.

As farming is to agriculture, so gardening is to horticulture. There is some science involved but, essentially, as the Victorians believed, it is an art form. An old gardener who set me on my course years ago, said that being a gifted gardener was just a matter of seeing things from the plants' point of view. To a large extent, he was right. Possessing a "green thumb" is simply the result of recognizing what plants need and acting accordingly. (Green thumbs were always found on the hands of old-time master gardeners who handled damp clay pots covered with moss which stained their fingers.)

One of the greatest joys in the world is to have a seed sprout before your eyes, to have its seedling take root in your soil and to see it become a mature plant. Gardening rewards its practitioners in different

THE PRESENCE OF GROWING PLANTS MAKES OUR HOMES, PUBLIC BUILDINGS AND FACTORIES LOOK MORE A PART OF THE NATURAL WORLD.

and very special ways. For some, the reward is the flowering of a late-developing perennial; for others it's the basic satisfaction and pride of growing their own food. Anyone who has shelled and eaten peas warm and sweet from the sun, or bitten into a truly vine-ripened tomato has experienced one of life's most wonderful small moments.

But there's much more to it than just being able to produce food that is superior to what you buy at the supermarket. Working in and with the soil provides a reward all its own. It is no accident that gardening workshops have become an important form of therapy for handicapped and institutionalized individuals.

Working in the soil with my bare hands, I feel at peace with myself and with nature. It is while digging in my garden that I feel a contentment that I experience only too rarely on other occasions. I feel immersed in the world around me.

We are almost always self-conscious and aware of our separateness. Digging, cultivating and planting take us out of the shells we live in and bring a calmness that we feel at few other times. Being engaged in a gardening job is a healing experience. And as you get older and the physical work becomes harder to manage, you can watch the plants you set out years before grow on to maturity and old age, too.

Opinion polls show that gardening is the most popular of all hobbies and that more money is spent in its pursuit than on any equivalent pastime. Yet it needn't be costly to stock and maintain a small garden. In terms of pleasure returned per dollar spent, gardening must top the list.

However much we appreciate gardening as art, there are general guidelines and immutable rules – many imposed by our climate – that must be followed. Together, these form the science of gardening.

The science of gardening is knowing the right techniques and the right times to use them. It is knowing how to fertilize, plant and prune and when it is wisest to do so. It is this science that enables busy individuals to garden with a minimum investment of time and it is this same science that steadily increases the satisfaction and enjoyment of the true leisuretime hobbyist.

The information contained in this book can add to all gardeners' enjoyment of their hobby. The concepts (the art) and techniques (the science) described here can improve every garden.

Even if you were fortunate, as I was, to learn the basics of gardening at your grandfather's knee, continued learning about ideas, methods, soil composition and plant characteristics will surely increase the pleasure you derive from working your own garden.

I believe the information that follows can help you do just that.

– H. Fred Dale

CLIMATE

Knowing local climatic conditions is most important for the home gardener. You can change and correct the condition of your soil but you can't do anything about the weather. Living in southern Ontario, we experience moderately hot summers and rather severe winters. Though there might be a period of two to three weeks in July without rain, we receive adequate precipitation year round with an average annual rainfall of approximately 80 cm (31 in.).

TEMPERATURE It is temperature that determines the length of our growing season, which, in southern Ontario, ranges from a maximum of 165 days in the Niagara Peninsula down to a minimum of 125 days or less north of Barrie. Agriculture Canada has divided every region of the country into numbered plant-hardiness zones based on average minimum temperatures. These zones are based on increments of 5.5°C (10°F). The higher the zone number, the warmer the temperature. Each zone is further divided into "a" and "b" sections, with "b" being the warmer of the two. (An important note: the American hardiness classification system is not the same as our own. Subtract one from the American zone number to yield the Canadian equivalent. Zone 6 in the United States corresponds to zone 5 in Canada. The warmest part of southern Ontario, around Point Pelee, is in Canadian zone 7.)

Note your hardiness zone on the map in this chapter. When buying trees, shrubs or any perennials, you will find that these hardiness zones are used to describe their tolerance to winter. For example, a shrub tagged "hardy to zone 4" should survive winters in zone 4 or in any higher-numbered zone. Remember also that other factors such as elevation and wind exposure will affect a plant's ability to overwinter.

EVEN IN THE RELATIVELY SMALL AREA OF SOUTHERN ONTARIO, THE LENGTH OF OUR GROWING SEASON RANGES FROM 125 TO 165 DAYS.

Behaviour of Frost in Southern Ontario

Although the terms "frost" and "freezing" sometimes take on different meanings, both define a condition that exists when the temperature of the air or of the surface of an object drops to the freezing point of water (0°C or 32°F) or lower. For most gardeners in southern Ontario, spring frosts in May or June and autumn frosts in September and October are the main concern.

Freezes (or frosts) may be advective or radiative or a combination of both, depending on the weather conditions under which they occur.

ADVECTIVE FREEZE An advective freeze is caused by the movement of cold air into an area. This usually occurs after a cold front moves through and when the wind shifts counter-clockwise toward the northwest or north, bringing down cold arctic air. Advective freezes are usually widespread, accompanied by moderately strong winds and may persist during the day as well as at night. These freezes can occur under cloudy conditions, although there is usually some clearing due to the cooler, drier air mass.

RADIATIVE FREEZE Radiative freezes occur only on nights with relatively clear skies and calm winds. Under these conditions, heat energy is lost from plant surfaces by longwave radiation. If skies are cloudy, this radiation is reflected back to earth, preventing most of the heat loss. Radiative freezes can be expected when an area is under the influence of a relatively cool dry air mass associated with a high pressure system. During daytime the temperature may be well above freezing, but after sunset, rapid cooling causes the thermometer to dip below freezing levels. A radiative freeze may occur in the early morning just before sunrise, when temperatures are at their lowest and winds are calm. Frost damage can sometimes be prevented by covering plants.

Most crop-damaging freezes that occur in southern Ontario are a combination of the advective and radiative types.

TEMPERATURE INVERSION A temperature inversion occurs in clear calm conditions. In daytime, if the air is very calm, very little mixing occurs between cooler air at the surface and warmer air aloft because the cooler air is heavier. During a calm night, if plant parts or other surfaces are exposed to a clear sky, the radiant heat loss from these surfaces causes their temperature to drop as much as 3°C (6°F) below that of the air around them. Therefore, ground frost can occur even when the "official" temperature does not drop below freezing. A frost warning is usually issued for low-lying areas if the minimum air temperature is expected to drop to around 5°C (41°F) or less under clear calm conditions.

HORIZONTAL TEMPERATURE PATTERNS Frost usually occurs first in low-lying areas because heavy cold air near the surface flows into the hollows creating "frost pockets". However, even a very gradual slope can produce significant differences in temperature. If the cold-air drainage down slopes is partially blocked by dense trees, road embankments or other obstructions, pockets of cold air form on the uphill side. If the obstruction is the result of a stand of trees, this effect can sometimes be reduced by thinning to allow cold air to move through and provide better air drainage.

In areas near large bodies of water such as the Great Lakes, tempera-

ON A CLEAR NIGHT, A FROST WARNING IS ISSUED FOR LOW-LYING AREAS IF THE AIR TEMPERATURE IS EXPECTED TO DROP TO 5°C OR LESS.

tures may be increased by "land breezes" which develop during the night. The air over land cools more quickly than that over water during radiative freezes. This results in a pressure difference which causes an air circulation that flows from land to water. In addition to the mixing effect of land breezes, low-lying land near a large body of water is less prone to frost because cold air moving down slopes can freely move out over the water rather than being trapped in hollows.

Large bodies of water moderate temperatures in areas downwind during an advective freeze particularly in autumn, when the water is considerably warmer than the air.

Plant-hardiness zone map for southern Ontario. Each numbered zone represents an increment of 5.5°C (10°F) in minimum average temperature. Higher zone numbers indicate warmer temperatures. Zones are further divided in half, with "b" being warmer then "a". Major communities that are located in zone 7a include Niagara Falls, St. Catharines, Windsor and Chatham; zone 6b Toronto, London, Sarnia, Hamilton and Welland; zone 6a Kitchener and Goderich; zone 5b Owen Sound, Walkerton, Peterborough, Belleville, Kingston and Cornwall; zone 5a Parry Sound, Barrie, Perth and Ottawa; zone 4b Pembroke; zone 4a North Bay and Haliburton.

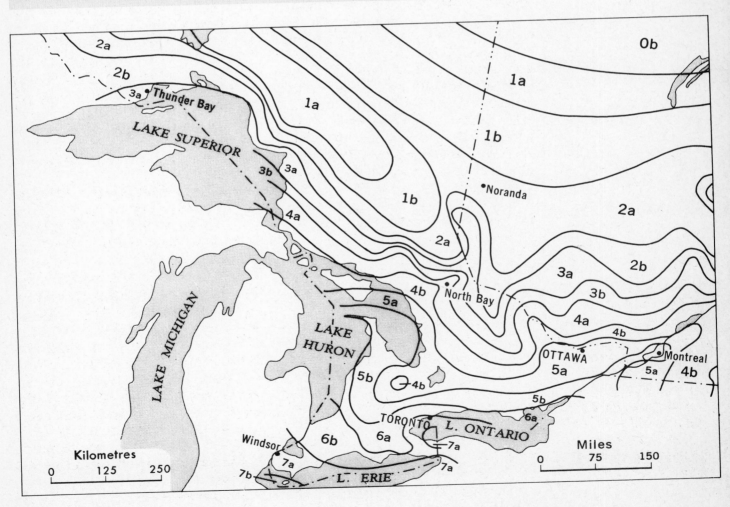

LANDSCAPING: Your Garden Plan

Introduction

Successful landscaping begins by looking at the land around you and at the plants growing there. Whether you are building a new home or living in an existing house, first consider the largest and best established elements of your landscape. These are likely to be some combination of lawns, trees, bushes, driveways, paths, and patios. It is these major elements that you want to design a theme around if at all possible.

There are four main landscaping styles: formal, informal, natural and Oriental. Choosing the styles that suit your taste and your property begins by determining what it is you want out of your surroundings.

A well planned garden provides many benefits. It can:

- beautify your home and increase its value
- provide protection from wind, sun, and cold
- create privacy and reduce noise
- be used as an outdoor room for play and relaxation
- produce fresh food for the table
- add colour, texture, and harmony to the home
- become a healthy, invigorating, and rewarding hobby

With these thoughts in mind, try to visualize the overall theme or style you desire, think only of the end result without concerning yourself with the work required to achieve it. Do you want an intimate private place for entertaining or a large open lawn with a big vegetable garden out back? Do you want the front of the house to blend in with that of your neighbours or do you see it as something different, unique, and separate? It is crucial to have a concept of the completed landscape so that you don't go blindly ahead planting things that later you wished you'd planted else-

IT IS CRUCIAL TO VISUALIZE THE COMPLETED LANDSCAPE BEFORE YOU START TO PLANT. IT'S CHEAPER TO TRY IDEAS ON PAPER THAN IT IS TO UPROOT THEM FROM YOUR GARDEN.

where or not at all.

Most present-day gardeners combine elements from more than one style to create their own theme, but keeping your plans simple is the most prudent course to take. Remember, growing plants need constant care and upkeep. The more complicated you make your garden, the more work you've got ahead of you.

The Formal Garden Formal gardens are rigid, symmetrical and precise. They consist of straight lines and balanced shapes and colour. Sheared hedges, squared plots, even proportions all combine into a geometric perspective inspired by the grand gardens of old Europe.

The Informal Garden As the name suggests, the informal garden breaks all the rules of the formal garden. It is asymmetrical with curved lines and a casual, relaxed feeling. Plants are used in bunches and bold masses to create a striking and dramatic effect.

The Natural Garden Natural gardens are an attempt to recreate the look, feeling, and effect of nature in its own surroundings. Irregular, rambling, and rough textured, a natural garden imitates the nature of a meadow or woodlands or wetlands or rockery. They can be well-kept and controlled or left to go wild and regenerate themselves.

The Oriental Garden In a class by themselves, Oriental gardens are designed with great discipline and concern for the effect produced on the user's state of mind. Serene and natural but neat and orderly, Oriental gardens are a precisely planned union of the inner and outer landscape.

Making Your Landscape Plan

1. Make a rough scale drawing of the property. Use a scale that is both easy to work with and allows you to fit your rough drawing on one sheet of paper. A scale of 1 in. to 4 ft. usually proves convenient to use as does 4 cm to 1 m. Draw in any permanent structures; house, garage, driveways, fences, patios, etc. Indicate north by a directional arrow on the side.

2. Observe sunlight patterns. Determine the time of day each area gets sun. If there are existing trees, how much do they shade the garden?

3. Determine the kind of soil you have; does it vary from back to front? What is the contour of the land? Does it have a natural slope and is there a drainage problem?

4. Are you sheltered or exposed to the prevailing wind? What are the existing views; do you want to hide the ugly garage next door or open up a "window" to view the distant hills?

GARDEN DESIGN Now that you have a rough idea of what you've got and of the kind of landscape you want, it is time to start making plant selections and decide what's going to go where. Make the broad, sweeping decisions first. How large is the lawn space? Are you going to grow vegetables? Where? Are you planning to remove or add trees, hedges or bushes? Do you need a windbreak, etc.?

It is important to bear in mind our southern Ontario climate when making your plans. With prevailing winds from the northwest and relatively severe winters, you must incorporate into your design a year-round approach to your property. There are many trees, hedges and shrubs that retain a beauty and character even through the cold, snowy months.

Sensitive plants such as azaleas and rhododendrons should only be planted in sheltered areas facing north and east so as not to be susceptible to winter sunburn. These sensitive plants will start to respond to sun on warm winter days and, abandoning their natural winter dormancy, will be killed off by frost when a harsh cold descends. Any plant guaranteed to be hardy to Zone 4 should survive the winter.

Most border perennials and annuals need and can take a large amount of direct sunlight, so at this point in your planning place the larger plants, such as trees and bushes, with their shading effect in mind. Leave the flowers for later. To determine the exact price and availability of the kinds of trees, hedges or bushes you might want, your best approach is to obtain a local nursery catalog that describes the plant materials in detail. A word of caution: nurseries are in the business of selling plants and therefore they present their stock, often with pictures, in a overly positive light. Buyer beware: it often isn't that easy!

LOW MAINTENANCE GARDENS The amount of work you are willing to do to maintain the property is an important consideration in the planning stage. Much has been written and said about low maintenance gardens. Low maintence gardens consist of broad lawns, trees, evergreen shrubs, and hedges, well mulched bulb beds and low maintenance perennials and ground covers. These need little to no weeding, minimal pruning and only regular grass cutting.

Contrast this with a high maintenance garden which would include plants such as vegetables, annual and perennial beds that need constant weeding, deciduous hedges that need regular pruning, and any plants that need special attention for watering, fertilizing or preventive treatment for pests and diseases. Again, what you put in is what you get out. Plants are like people. They don't talk back, but they can communicate distress very well and have to be looked after.

PLANT TYPES There are two basic types of plants for gardening purposes: annuals, that go from seed to flowers to seeds again in one season, and perennials that last more than three years. Within perennials, there are two types: woody and herbaceous. Herbaceous plants die back to ground level every year and then send up new foliage the next spring. Woody plants have some woody stem that remains standing above ground throughout the winter. Included are trees that have a single stem or trunk rising out of the ground, shrubs that have many stems, and vines that either cling or twine around a support structure. We tend to think of woody plants as being fairly permanent, so whether it's a rose bush or a full size tree, serious consideration should be given to where each is going to be planted.

PLANT SELECTION Things to consider when selecting plants:
Mature Size Remember that plants grow, so be aware of what the mature size of the plant will be and whether or not it will fit its surroundings when it's full grown.
Growth Rate How long will the plant take to reach full height and breadth?
Spacing A common mistake is to plant too close together. This is natural as the small starter plants bought from nurseries look sparse and inadequate if spaced properly for mature growth. The solution is to find some "disposable" filler plants to use until your prime specimens develop. An example of this approach would be to plant dogwood between blue spruce and then thin them out as the spruce grows.
Size The larger the size of a plant the more it costs and the more likely it is to suffer from transplant shock. On the other hand, if you want

instant results or don't plan to be at the same location for very long, you are forced to go for the most developed plants possible.

Hardiness Plants should be guaranteed hardy to Zone 4 or higher. In certain regions of southern Ontario, mainly around Lakes Ontario and Erie and the Niagara Peninsula, fruit trees and other plants hardy only to Zone 6 will survive the winter.

Sensitivity Some plants are sensitive to sun or shade, certain soils, wind, and moisture (either too much or too little). Some, such as fruit trees, attract pests. Native plants are generally not tolerant of city conditions (salt, wind, air pollution) and others are pH sensitive needing an acid soil.

Unique Characteristics Know the plants that you are buying or ask the person you are buying them from whether they are suitable for the place and purpose intended. For example some trees shed, are sticky or drop fruit. You wouldn't want them overhanging a walk or driveway where cars are parked. Other plants, like hawthorn bushes, are garbage eaters, attracting and holding bits of wind-blown trash. These plants should not be placed in a windy, exposed spot. Some plants are aggressive and seem to spread out and dominate all that is around. This is especially true of some ground covers such as Chinese Lantern, mint, and goutweed.

Composing Plant Arrangements

OVERVIEW Keep it simple. Have a small list of plants. It is better to repeat and arrange in groups than to have a confusion of too many different plants. Choose a few focal points or showcase specimens and offset them with low-lying or useful hedges or windbreaks. Establish

where the primary views are going to be. Draw a straight line along these views on your plan to act as an axis and try for balance on either side. At the front of your house decide how you are going to frame the entrance and other features. Size to scale. The smaller garden needs a more subtle contrast created by smaller, fewer plants.

THE FOUR SEASONS Remember that you have to look at your garden all year round. For bright and lively colour it is not hard to plan for spring and summer, but what about fall and winter? Here are some tips to help plan a year-round garden. Evergreen trees and shrubs look good in winter and maintain their usefulness as windbreaks and snow barriers as well as providing privacy and sound protection.

There are many deciduous trees and shrubs that have beautiful fall colours and, even after they have lost their leaves, have interesting texture and colour to their bark. Others have a striking configuration of branches especially when covered by snow.

Using garden catalogs, select plants with an eye to having continuous blooming throughout summer and into fall. Major catalogs list the time of flowering for annuals, perennials, shrubs, and trees.

Most bulbs are planted in the fall, bloom in the spring, and disappear by the end of June, but there are some spring bulbs that bloom in the fall.

Many plants will bloom all year (except winter) as long as the flowers are diligently picked off before they go to seed. This is called deadheading and should be done weekly throughout the growing season. Only those plants classed as biennials should be left alone so they can re-seed themselves and continually provide new plants. There are some plants that are too

City pollution discoloured and damaged this spruce which was transplanted from the wild.

sensitive to the cold or winds of winter. These should be planted in properly sized containers that are moved inside by the end of October. Indoors, they provide a lush interior landscape throughout the chilly months.

PLANTING NEAR THE HOUSE Be careful not to plant a tree or shrub that will grow so large that its branches or roots will become a nuisance by actually distressing walls or foundations. Avoid forest giants on small lots and plant poplars and willows only on country acreage. Unless shade is particularly desired, don't plant in front of windows. This is particularly true of evergreens which shade windows in the short, dark days of fall and winter. But shrubs and vines can be very useful around a house. They can help tie a house into its setting, provide protection, and can soften or emphasize various features of your building. Many upright evergreens can be used as long as they are regularly pruned to maintain shape and height. Watch for water and snow runoff from the roof so the plants aren't damaged or broken. Vines such as ivy can keep the house cool in the summer and warmer in the winter.

A covering of vines insulates in summer and winter as well as improving the appearance of even the plainest building.

Q&A Landscaping

SELECTING SHADE TREES

Q: We are moving to a new house that is landscaped nicely in the front yard, but is totally bare of trees in the back. It has a southern exposure and a large yard. Could you please suggest some fast-growing shade trees that would thrive in clay soil with a minimum of attention? — *D.D., Oakville*

A: The fastest-growing trees are usually the least desirable in the long run. The western catalpa, Siberian elm, white birch, silver maple, poplars and willows are all fast growing. But most are also short-lived.

For moderate-sized trees good in clay soils and with gorgeous spring bloom, look to crabapples. Makamik, Dolgo and others grow to at least 8 m (26 ft.). But be aware that crabs drop their fruit if you don't pick it first. Even the tartest crabapples can be used to make jelly.

My personal favourite is the native red oak or the scarlet oak. These are among the fastest growing oaks and are the easiest to transplant. They will grow to 15 m (50 ft.). Since oaks are taprooted, they permit gardening underneath and are wind-firm. They have new reddish leaves and bright fall leaf colour.

Among the seedless and thornless honeylocusts are a number of good moderate-to-large trees. These include Moraine, Skyline and Princeton as well as Shademaster, a large, slow-growing tree. In addition, there are smaller varieties with yellow or red leaf colour. Locusts do well on almost any soil and are fairly drought-resistant. As well, by virtue of the fact that they are legumes, they provide their own nitrogen with the aid of bacteria.

The native ash grows to 20 m (60 ft.). It is fast-growing and has good fall leaf colour. Patmore is a popular variety. Ashes thrive in clays. Summit is a seedless cultivar of a different species that is much smaller, though it doesn't offer any special fall colour.

Before you decide on any tree, visit nurseries to see specimens in containers. Compare at least three catalogues, make your choices and plant as directed. If you want instant effect, you can buy what are called caliper-sized trees, and have the nursery dig holes and plant the trees.

Caliper measurements refer to the diameter of the trunk measured 15 cm (6 in.) above the ground. A tree of about 5 cm (2 in.) caliper may run you more than $200. One of 10 cm (4 in.) as much as $600. These prices include delivery and placement in a hole you have already dug, though this hole must be located in a spot that can be reached by the nursery's crane truck. Tree prices are also influenced by the kind of tree and its availability. These instant shade trees are currently known as yuppie trees, but they're worth the money if you have it. You can plant these and other container-grown trees whenever you can ready the planting hole.

Balled and burlapped, this large tree is ready for transplanting.

THE GOOD EARTH

Soil: What kind do you have?

The earth we walk on, dig in and grow our food in is one of nature's miracles. Its structure is complex, infinitely variable and constantly changing. If you treat it well, the earth will respond in kind. If you abuse it, you will reap little from it. So it is extremely important for the gardener to know the kind of soil conditions he or she is dealing with. Every kind of soil has strengths and weaknesses that can be corrected and adjusted. Your relationship with the land around you is best summed up by the old proverb, "you only get out what you put in."

SOIL TEXTURE The basic components of soil are water, air, mineral particles and organic materials. Soil texture is determined by the relative relationships of mineral particles and organic material or humus. Large mineral particles such as gravel or sand do not retain water and are referred to as light soils. Small mineral particles form silt or clay and are called heavy soils. When rained upon, clay retains water and becomes compacted into mud which, when it dries, becomes as hard as brick.

The quick and easy method of determining soil texture is to take a handful of moist soil and squeeze it into a ball. If the soil is sandy it will fall apart and crumble as soon as you open your hand. Clay soil sticks together and forms a compressed ball. Ideal topsoil consists of soil that will mold into your hands, but will easily crumble apart when squeezed. When mixed with lots of organic humus this ideal soil is called loam, and it is this good, dark, crumbly loam that we need for almost all our garden needs.

We are fortunate in southern Ontario to have some of the best topsoil in the world, though there are many areas in our region that have predominately sandy soil and need the addition of humus and

WE ARE FORTUNATE IN SOUTHERN ONTARIO TO HAVE SOME OF THE BEST TOPSOIL IN THE WORLD.

fertilizers. Also note that the top-soil in southern Ontario is only 15–45 cm (6–18 in.) deep and that beneath that slim surface layer there usually lies dense compacted clay, as well as layers of sand, rocks, chalk or limestone.

The bad news for homeowners in new subdivisions is that their builders often scrape off the valu-able natural topsoil, leaving a sub-soil of exposed clay and mud. The best thing to do in this situation is to buy topsoil to mix in with the clay, but make sure all new topsoil is nursery clean, treated, and weed and disease-free or you may be importing more problems than you already have.

SOIL FERTILITY The chemical makeup of your soil is also important to a healthy and productive garden. The first step is to determine whether your soil is acid or alkaline. This is expressed on the pH scale as a num-ber between 1 and 14. Neutral soil, which is neither acid or alkaline, has a pH of 7.0. Anything higher is alkaline or sweet; anything lower is acidic. Most plants thrive on soil in the 5.5 to 7.5 range, though some prefer slightly more extreme condi-tions on either side of the scale.

The primary chemicals necessary for sustaining plant growth are nitrogen, phosphorus and potas-sium. Secondary chemicals include calcium, magnesium and sulphur. There are other micronutrients that are equally important, but only required in very small quantities compared to those mentioned above. (Note that the pH scale is logarithmic: the difference between each whole number is tenfold.)

BE SURE ALL NEW TOP SOIL IS NURSERY CLEAN, TREATED AND WEED AND DISEASE-FREE OR YOU MAY BE IMPORTING MORE PROBLEMS THAN YOU ALREADY HAVE.

Know Your Fertilizers

Plants obtain 13 of the 16 elements essential to their growth from the soil. The other three – carbon, hydro-gen, oxygen – come from water and from carbon dioxide in the air.

These elements are classified in three groups:

Primary – large quantities required
   Nitrogen (N)
   Phosphorus (P, or in fertilizers designated as phosphate, P_2O_5)
   Potassium (K, or in fertilizers designated as potash, K_2O)

Secondary – large quantities required
   Calcium (Ca)
   Magnesium (Mg)
   Sulphur (S)

Micronutrients – small quantities required
   Boron (B)
   Copper (Cu)
   Iron (Fe)
   Manganese (Mn)
   Molybdenum (Mo)
   Zinc (An)
   Chlorine (Cl)

Balanced Fertilizers

Every mixed fertilizer or individual material sold has a guaranteed anal-ysis that is expressed as a three-part number prominently displayed on the bag or container. In order, the three numbers indicate the available nitrogen (N), available phosphorus oxide (P_2O_5), and soluble potash (K_2O). The three numbers reflect the percentage of the total fertilizer product represented by each com-ponent.

In addition to the above, certain secondary minerals and micronutri-ents may also be included and will be listed on the label.

CAUTION: Read the directions that come with the product you buy. Over-application is dangerous. Apply only the amount that is rec-ommended or that you know is desirable from past experience.

Function of Nitrogen (N)

1. Gives dark green colour.
2. Induces rapid growth.
3. Increases yields of leaf, fruit or seed.
4. Improves quality of leaf crops.
5. Increases protein content of food and feed crops.
6. Feeds soil micro-organisms during their decomposition of low nitrogen organic materials.
7. Tends to extend length of maturity period.
8. Will cause plants to fall over (lodge) if too much is applied.

Hunger Signs Indicative of a Lack of Nitrogen

1. A sick yellowish green colour.
2. A distinctly slow and dwarfed growth.
3. Drying up or "firing" of the leaves which starts at the bottom of the plant. In plants like corn and grasses, this firing starts at the top of the bottom leaves and proceeds down the centre.

Function of Phosphorus (P, or in fertilizers as P_2O_5)

1. Stimulates early root functions and growth.
2. Gives quick and vigorous start to plants.
3. Shortens maturity period.
4. Stimulates bloom and helps seed to form.
5. Gives winter hardiness especially to fall-seeded grasses.

Hunger Signs Indicative of a Lack of Phosphorus

1. Plants come up and start off quickly.
2. Purplish leaves, stems, and branches, especially in the seedling stage.
3. Small, slender stalks in corn.
4. Low yield of grain, fruit, and seed.
5. Lack of abundant healthy flower cluster in most annuals, biennials, and perennials.

Function of Potash (K, or in fertilizers as K_2O)

1. Serves as a nutrient regulator.
2. Increases vigour, strength and disease resistance.
3. Makes stalks and stems stiffen.
4. Helps early roots form and grow.
5. Imparts winter hardiness and helps plants harden off for the winter.
6. When found in excess, potash tends to decrease the effectiveness of the plant growth contribution made by nitrogen and magnesium.

Hunger Signs Indicative of a Lack of Potash

1. It "fires up" on bottom leaves of crops like corn, but differs from nitrogen in that the firing goes around the edge of the leaf. Without nitrogen, the firing goes down the centre of the leaf.
2. Legumes "fire up" first in the tip, and then around the edges.
3. Premature loss of leaves and smaller than normal flowers.
4. Plants like corn fall down prior to maturity due to poor root development.
5. Branches and limbs of deciduous trees tend to break off more readily during winter storms.

Composting

The current garbage crisis with its calls for recycling only adds to the need for composting. Whether you live in an apartment building or on a five-hectare lot, you can benefit from this easy practice. Composting is a way to recycle house and garden vegetable waste into a useful additive that will improve the texture of almost any soil. During composting, micro-organisms break down vegetable matter, enabling you to reuse its nutrients in your garden. It is simple, the labour is minimal, and, providing you follow certain guidelines, there is no smell.

Composting can be done in four

A simple compost box

ways: 1) in a heap 2) in a home-made box 3) in a commercial container bin 4) in a store-bought composting tumbler.

COMPOSTING HEAP A heap is probably the least satisfactory. It is difficult to construct neatly, slow to break down and needs to be turned at least once to insure that the outside decomposes. On the other hand, if you have the space, as well as a large amount of hedge clippings, dead plants, fallen leaves or grass clippings, and you are in no hurry, a heap will get the job done eventually.

Do not dig a pit and throw waste into it. Organic materials stored this way will remain soggy and, without access to lots of air, will putrefy and stink. Instead find a well-drained out-of-the-way spot and pile all your garden waste on the top. Each layer of new material of any depth – say every 15 cm (6 in.) – needs a cover of topsoil. This provides most of the the bacteria and fungus spores required for breakdown, while the moving air provides the rest. After two to four years the black loam at the bottom can be removed and used to top dress around your plants. Such a pile requires less effort than bagging the waste and hauling it out to the curb. And if you have been throwing away grass clippings, you have been wasting a valuable source of nitrogen that rots very quickly.

HOMEMADE COMPOST BOX A home-made box is cheap, durable and does a good job. Choose a slightly sheltered semi-shaded spot that is easily accessible. Not much household waste is going to be composted if you have to walk through wet grass or climb a snowbank to reach your composting box. Be sure the location is well drained. A different type of decomposition takes place on a waterlogged site, causing foul-smelling gases. Avoid this by dig-

A composting tumbler

ging the area well or paving it with patio stones spaced to leave drainage channels.

A container of about one cubic metre or 30 cubic feet will be large enough to hold the waste from an average sized urban or suburban family. In rural areas, or if you have a large vegetable garden, increase the size somewhat. You can make the container in many forms and of almost any material that will withstand the weight of the compost. If a solid material is used, drill holes to allow circulation of air. Holes about 3 cm (1½ in.) in diameter and spaced about 15 cm (6 in.) apart should be sufficient. Cracks between logs or rough boards will normally admit enough air. While a single box will normally do the job, a double container will let you use each side in turn, allowing you to leave the material for longer periods and ensuring a greater breakdown.

COMMERCIAL COMPOST CONTAINERS Commercial composters, while expensive initially, are efficient, long-lasting and very suited to decks and apartment balconies where space is limited. They are usually made of plastic and come in different sizes and shapes with pre-cut airholes and a flap at the bottom that you raise to extract the composted material. Neat and tidy, they provide an attractive method of recycling discarded houseplant soil and roots and used kitchen materials such as coffee grounds (including paper filters!), tea bags, eggshells and vegetable peelings. Don't add meat or dairy products as they attract vermin, but you can put in hair, vacuum cleaner contents, pet litter and floor sweepings.

COMPOSTING TUMBLERS A relative newcomer to the scene, commercial tumblers are revolutionizing the image of composting and recycling. A typical tumbler consists of a cylindrical barrel about the size of a large plastic garbage pail standing on a solid, lazy Susan-style base. This allows the tumbler to be rotated and it is this feature that speeds up the decomposing process by aerating the contents. The tumbler has a sealed lid on the top where you put in the material to be composted. You then add about a cup of water a day and give the tumbler a turn.

Remarkably, these composting tumblers create black loam compost within 14 to 21 days. If everyone used one we could solve the garbage crisis and replace the world's topsoil at the same time.

Composting Tips

Organic material needs moisture to decompose. You can add water in dry periods or if your compost area does not get natural rainfall. Do not overwater as this contributes to unpleasant odours.

The composting process is speeded up by turning over the material. This lets air in and prevents the material from becoming overly compacted. Heat also accelerates the process, as do some commercial composting chemicals you can buy at your local garden centre.

Any vegetable material or organic fibres can be used for compost including newspapers, wool and cotton. Do not use animal waste, glass, metal, plastic or synthetic fibres.

The rotting process tends to produce a higher nitrogen level and, especially if oak or chestnut leaves are used, can produce a very acidic loam. It is recommended that you add some alkaline material such as calcium in the form of ground limestone or potassium in the form of hardwood ashes. The easiest way to do this is add a couple of handfuls of ground limestone and/or ashes in every other layer of topsoil covering. Ground limestone can be purchased at your garden centre.

Sprinkling a good source of nitrogen in with the topsoil layer speeds up decomposition. The easiest and cheapest way to do this is to add ammonium nitrate (34:0:0). Organic gardeners can use blood meal (12:0:0). Both are available in 2 kg (4.4 lb.) boxes.

USING THE COMPOST How can you tell when a pile is done? When the material is dark in colour and breaks apart easily in your hand, and when you can no longer distinguish the original materials, it's ready to use. How soon will that be? This depends on your composting container, the nature and size of the original materials, and the outdoor temperatures. Rapid heating under the right conditions can produce ready-to-use compost in a matter of weeks. Lots of leaves, sawdust, or thick woody materials combined with cool weather may take two years or more. Thus it is usually best to compost leaves in separate piles and work your other materials.

WHAT GOOD IS COMPOST? Besides recycling valuable waste materials, compost can supply all your garden's humus and topsoil requirements. In an organic garden, it can be a complete fertilizer. It adds all the trace elements you'll ever need. The composting process creates its own heat, naturally killing weed seeds. You can also sterilize your loam by baking it in an oven or microwave. In both cases the soil should start out damp, as it is steam that sterilizes the soil. In a conventional oven, wrap in tinfoil and bake for 30 minutes at 150–180°F (65–82°C). Use a plastic bag (with no metal ties) in a microwave. Run at high for 2½ minutes for each kilogram (2.2 lbs.) of soil. Let stand for at least five minutes. Do not bake to dryness as this ruins soil structure.

COMPOST TENDS TO BE SLIGHTLY ACIDIC. ADD ALKALINE MATERIAL BY MIXING A COUPLE OF HANDFULS OF GROUND LIMESTONE OR WOOD ASHES IN EVERY OTHER LAYER OF TOPSOIL COVERING.

ANY VEGETABLE OR ORGANIC FIBRES CAN BE USED IN COMPOSTING, INCLUDING NEWSPAPERS, WOOL AND COTTON.

 **Soil**

REVITALIZING TIRED FLOWER BEDS

Q: What can be done to restore health and vigour to flower beds that seem to be tired out? These have perennials that do reasonably well. However, I plant annuals among them each summer and they go nowhere. The soil is clayish in texture and has good drainage.
— *G.L.S., Toronto*

A: You are expecting too much from your soil. The same small beds cannot produce both annual flowers and perennials year after year unless you put something back. Annuals suffer most because they are shallow-rooted, whereas perennials often are able to draw minerals from the subsoil.

To revitalize your flower beds, dig worked or partly-worked compost into the soil, taking care not to damage perennial crowns. Or topdress with sifted compost.

If you don't have a compost heap or box, you can use leaf mould or weed-free manure. Another alternative is to mix in common brown sphagnum peat moss. Spread a 5 cm (2 in.) layer on top of the flower bed and mix into the top 15 cm (6 in.) of soil. Take care not to disturb perennial roots. Add 1 kg (2.2 lbs.) of a tomato-potato fertilizer such as grade 5:10:15.

SOIL ANALYSIS

The Civic Garden Centre, 777 Lawrence Ave. E., North York, Ontario M3C 1P2, offers an inexpensive soil testing service that measures pH and soluble salt levels.

Take samples just before watering or fertilizing. Avoid wet soil. Remove any existing mulch and, using a trowel, dig a hole 15 cm (6 in.) deep. Start at the bottom of the hole and collect a small amount of soil from the sides, placing it in a clean bucket. Repeat this process in four or five locations to get a representative sample.

For trees and shrubs, take soil from several holes at the edge of the branch spread of the plant. For lawns, take soil from the top 5–10 cm (2–4 in.).

Keep a record of the date and location of your sample.

To submit your sample, put 250 g (1 cup) of air-dried pulverized soil in a plastic bag as soon after sampling as possible. Include information on the kinds of plants you plan to grow on the soil, drainage, water source (city, rain, well, etc.) and any fertilizer, manure, herbicide or pesticide that has been added. Mail or deliver your sample to the Civic Garden Centre at the address above along with a cheque (payable to Civic Garden Centre) for $7.00 to cover costs.

Results are available in less than one week.

The Civic Garden Centre's **Horticultural Hotline** is available to answer questions about soil or other gardening topics from noon to 3 p.m., seven days a week. Telephone (416) **445-1552**.

A SOIL TEST WILL DETERMINE IF YOUR GARDEN IS ACID OR ALKALINE. THIS KNOWLEDGE WILL ENABLE YOU TO IMPROVE YOUR SOIL SO THAT IT SUITS THE PLANTS YOU WANT TO GROW.

 **Soil** CONTINUED

POSSIBLE HARDPAN

Q: When we bought our house we spent quite a bit of money on plants, but anything over 250 cm (8 ft.) has either died or not grown. I fertilize in the spring but nothing happens. I have never had my soil tested, but we have a good garden and perennials and shrubs do well.   – *D.R., Fenelon Falls*

A: There are at least two major possibilities. Either there is a hardpan (a thick layer of heavy clay) under your soil or your trees were overmature in containers when you bought them, with girdling roots that effectively cut off expanding outward growth. This is often the case with potted nursery specimens and can be fixed at planting time by trimming off 12 mm (½ in.) all around the rootball or by unwinding the long roots to spread them out in a large planting hole.

   If the trouble is a hardpan underlay, it is very difficult to fix in rocky land. You can test for hardpan and rock underlay by hand digging with a spade, but there's not much you can do about it except replant. One other thought might be to determine if your trees were planted deeper in your garden soil than in their original nursery or container habitats. Buried trees seldom succeed.

COMPOSTING QUERIES

Q: What do you recommend for leaves that have been added to the garden from the previous fall? These have not been composted and are in clumps throughout the soil.

   As well, when making compost, instead of buying limestone and ammonium nitrate, can a person just throw in a handful of fertilizer, say grade 12:4:4? Doesn't it provide the same material to the decomposing matter?

   Finally, my compost heap is located near my garden. I am concerned that it might be leeching the nitrogen out of my garden soil. Is this probable?
                                                                    – *G.P., London*

A: A compost heap cannot remove nitrogen from garden soil. It cannot put out tentacles or roots to absorb it from anywhere but within the pile. Nitrogen is absorbed by the organisms that do the decomposition within the compost heap.

   The fertilizer you suggest would supply extra nitrogen but, like most fertilizing material, tends to make soil acidic. Compost itself contains humic acid, which tends to slow decomposition. Ground limestone (or bone meal or wood ashes) keeps the soil sweet.

   As to the clumps of partly rotted leaves, again a small addition of material that supplies soluble forms of nitrogen compounds would help. The clumps themselves should be broken up and mixed with the soil. This can be done manually, but is much easier to do with a power tiller.

ONE SMALL GARDEN BED CANNOT BE EXPECTED TO PRODUCE BOTH ANNUAL FLOWERS AND PERENNIALS YEAR AFTER YEAR UNLESS YOU PUT SOMETHING BACK.

GETTING STARTED

Garden Tools for Digging and Planting

The novice gardener's tool shed need only contain a small number of tools, but these should be of good quality. As in car repair and home renovation, tools of poor quality require more work to use and don't do as good a job. The best tools are made out of good steel that has been tempered, or heat treated, and are forged rather than stamped out of sheet metal. Look for unpainted handles made of straight-grained ash that has no knots or other flaws. Most tools are designed with a socket that the handle fits into. This socket and the blade of the tool should be fashioned from one piece of steel, rather than from two pieces of metal welded together. The wooden handle must fit tightly into the socket and should be secured with a rivet that goes all the way through both the socket and the handle. There should be no movement between the handle and the socket when pressure is applied in any direction. Test the tool in the store. If there is movement, select another example, for it will only get worse with use.

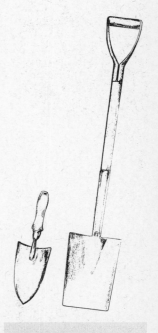

TROWEL A small, semi-scooped, pointed hand tool that is used for everything from digging holes to transplanting seedlings to mixing soil to lifting small plants and potting container plants. Get a solid, forged steel trowel – the cheap, light one-piece aluminum ones will bend with the first rock they hit.

SPADE Another indispensable garden tool, the spade is a shovel with a flat straight digging edge and a very slight scoop for lifting soil. It can be used as an edger, for cutting roots, for lifting and transplanting bigger plants, and for turning over pre-worked soil. A spade should have a "D"-shaped handle and also a lip on

Trowel and spade

the top of the blade that you can place your foot on when digging in stubborn ground. Its height should be above waist level, so you don't get a backache from bending and lifting. Again, a spade should be made of good, heavy, tempered steel and should be kept sharp, clean, and lightly oiled to prevent rust. It is amazing how much easier garden work is when you have a hefty, sharp spade that cuts through thick roots and slices through hard soil.

SHOVEL A gardening shovel is usually a long-handled, round-pointed shovel that is scooped for digging, lifting and carrying earth. As with a spade, it should be of sturdy construction and have a foot lip to assist in digging. This shovel is used when digging deeper and bigger holes, such as those for trees or shrubs, mixing large piles of soil, turning over compost heaps, and loosening and moving rocks and large plants. Again, it should be kept sharp and clean.

DIGGING FORK A digging fork has four flat tines and is the height of a spade with the same kind of "D"-shaped handle. This is the main tool used for soil preparation and is better than a spade for loosening hard packed soils, breaking up clumps of earth, mixing different soils and fertilizer, and generally tilling or aerating the ground. The digging fork is especially useful for lifting out weeds without taking huge clumps of soil with them. When moving perennials or shrubs, it is better to ease them out of the ground with a fork than with a spade or shovel, both of which tend to cut roots. An expensive garden fork is an excellent investment, for the tines on the cheaper ones will bend and break off, and there is nothing more frustrating than to have to go and buy a new one mid-project or mid-season.

Spades, shovels and digging forks can be safely stored in a tub of fine sand that has been sprinkled with oil. The grit of the sand keeps the tools clean; the oil keeps them rust-free.

WHEELBARROW Even if you have a moderately small garden, a wheelbarrow is a wonderful "carryall" and great convenience. A wheelbarrow has great maneuverability, and its built-in leverage enables you to transport heavy loads. It can be used to mix soil, or even concrete for small building jobs. You can load all your tools, fertilizers, pots, plants and stakes in it and move them easily with you around the garden. It is also good for collecting leaves or plant cuttings for the compost pile, or weeds, rocks and other debris for the garbage heap. Buy a sturdy, metal, contractor's wheelbarrow, rather than one that comes as a "gardener's kit" – these are light, have weak joints and braces, and often only last one season. A wide inflatable tire enables the wheelbarrow to cross soft or wet ground. Don't allow water to sit in the barrow for long periods or else the bottom will rust out. Instead, store under cover, tip up against a wall or turn upside down.

HOE There are many sizes and shapes of hoes and each one has a specific purpose. A general purpose standard garden hoe has a flat blade at the end of a long handle. The main uses of a hoe are to break up and move surface soil and to remove weeds. Cultivating your garden with a hoe is beneficial because it allows air and moisture to penetrate into the soil and removes weeds that will tend to sap and suffocate your plants. A hoe can also be used to prepare furrows for seed and to push soil up and around mounded plants. Keep your hoe sharp and you'll expend less energy with heavy weeds.

LAWN RAKE Also called a leaf rake,

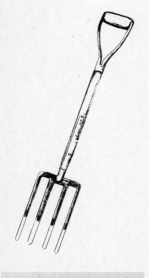

Digging fork

this tool is a must if you have lawns to maintain. It is usually used to rake clippings or leaves and sticks that have fallen from trees, but can also be used to pick up paper and other wind-blown garbage. Lawn rakes have a fan of tines and are made out of bamboo, metal and plastic. Modern plastic lawn rakes are the most durable, especially when used by children. Bamboo rakes are nice, but don't last long, whereas the tines on metal ones are forever bending out of shape or breaking off unless great care is taken in their use and storage.

GARDEN RAKE A level-headed metal garden rake is useful for preparing large garden areas such as vegetable gardens, annual beds or lawn surfaces. It is used for grading and smoothing the ground. Soil can be pulled toward you with the tines facing down, or pushed away from you with the tines facing up. A garden rake is also useful when spreading compost, manure or fertilizer.

HAND CULTIVATOR or **HAND FORK** A hand fork usually has three springy tines and is used for cultivating and weeding between closely planted vegetables and flowers. When using a hand fork it is best to kneel or sit on a flat board placed between the other plants. This distributes your weight evenly and doesn't disturb or compact the soil.

PRUNING SHEARS Though they come in all shapes and sizes, a pair of hand pruning shears is one of a gardener's most important tools and should always be at hand as you work in the garden. Many even come with sheath, holder or belt attachment for convenient access. They are used for pruning roses, shrubs and small branches, cutting back perennials, deadheading flower tops, harvesting vegetables and herbs, and clipping stems for cut flowers. Hedge trimmers have longer blades and are needed if you have a hedge to clip or long grass that needs to be cut back. Strong hedge trimmers, with a sharp notch in one blade, are effective for pruning thicker, woody branches.

WATERING TOOLS All gardens need ready access to water. For an apartment balcony, deck or very small garden, a watering can will do, but for all other gardens and lawns you must have a hose or sprinkler system that reaches to the furthest point of the garden. A rubber hose is easier to handle and more resistant to kinking than a plastic one, but is more expensive. Avoid denting or crushing the couplings, as they can leak, and be sure to drain the hose and store inside in the winter to avoid freezing and cracking. Increasingly popular are hose systems that feature rugged plastic connectors that snap into place without threaded couplings.

There are many styles of nozzles, but one of the most practical is the spray gun type that has a trigger that can be adjusted from a fine spray to a steady stream and can be locked in any position. Better quality ones can be turned off at the nozzle and don't leak.

There are many types of sprinklers and sprinkler systems for lawns and garden and your selection will depend on how much you are willing to spend. There are even automatic timers that give a regular daily watering, whether it's needed or not. There are also soaker hoses that leak water onto the soil without a spray that wets the foliage. Large irrigation systems can be built into your property, but are complicated, expensive and hard to maintain if something goes wrong.

POWER TOOLS The only power garden tool the average homeowner needs is a power lawnmower which

Garden hoe

can be either electric or gas. Electric mowers are quieter and less expensive, but have a range limited by the length of their cords. Gas lawnmowers are available in either rotary or reel types. Reel mowers, which are a motorized version of the standard push mower, are the perfectionists' choice because they make a cleaner cut. They do, however, require professional attention for sharpening and adjustment. They also work best on lawns that are cut regularly. A rotary mower can handle high grass that would choke a reel mower. Rotaries are less expensive to buy and can be sharpened at home with a file. For safety's sake, be sure to disconnect the sparkplug lead on a gas rotary mower before removing the blade for sharpening. Whether you buy rotary or reel, look for a gas mower that is equipped with either a four-cycle engine or a two-cycle engine that automatically mixes gas and oil.

The manual push mower remains an inexpensive and reliable alternative, particularly if your yard is level and not too large. Oiled and sharpened, a push mower can do the job.

Electric or gas edge trimmers that have a nylon cutting thread, which rotates at high speed, are very effective and have become very popular. A rotary tiller is useful if you have a large bed to prepare every year, but if you only need it when you create a brand new garden plot, it makes sense to rent rather than buy.

BECAUSE IT'S USUALLY SAFE TO PLANT OUTDOORS IN SOUTHERN ONTARIO AFTER THE MAY 24TH WEEKEND, SEEDS SHOULD BE STARTED INDOORS AROUND THE BEGINNING OF APRIL.

Planting Techniques

STARTING SEEDS INDOORS Many annuals, perennials, vegetables and herbs should be started indoors about six weeks before transplanting to permanent positions in the garden. Plants that benefit from this indoor start include those that are sensitive to late frost, those that take a long time or need heat to germinate and those that need a long season to fully develop and mature into bloom. Because it is considered safe to plant outdoors after the May 24th weekend in southern Ontario, seeds should be started indoors around the beginning of April. Your alternative is to let your garden centre do this work for you and buy starters or seedlings ready for planting in May. This is, of course, less work but more expensive.

Starting seeds indoors yourself is easy, costs little and gives a great sense of satisfaction. Here is a list of what you need:

- clean potting or topsoil
- peat moss or vermiculite
- planting trays or peat pots with good drainage
- plastic wrap or bags for covers
- strong, regular lighting after germination

Mix the topsoil with peat moss or vermiculite to help retain moisture. Fill the trays or peat pots to just below their top lip with the soil mixture, then tamp down the soil firmly. Do not compact the earth to the point where air spaces are eliminated. Plant your seeds at the depth noted on the seed package. Plant more than one seed per tray compartment or container. You can always thin out the weaker plants after they have germinated. Soak the soil with water and let drain. Do not add fertilizer.

Cover the top of each container with plastic to keep humid and place in a warm spot (room temperature). Do not cover drainage holes and make sure there is enough air circulation so that the seeds do not rot or get mouldy. For plants that have sensitive roots and suffer from transplant shock, be sure to use peat pots, which can be placed whole in the garden.

As soon as seeds have germinated and at least one leaf is showing, remove the plastic and place in a well-lit space. If no sunny window is available, use grow lights which can be purchased at almost every garden centre and most hardware stores. Keep the plants well watered and as close to the lights as possible. Both light and water are crucial at this stage. Insufficient light combined with too much water will result in seedlings that grow so tall and spindly that they fall over. With too much light but not enough water, plants shrivel up, dry out and die. This can happen very quickly to young seedlings, so make sure you keep a close watch on their progress.

COLD FRAMES A cold frame is really a miniature greenhouse that is used to grow seedlings and condition or "harden off" transplants before they go out in the garden. Cold frames can be constructed in many ways, but most are low-lying boxes that have a sloping, hinged transparent roof. The easiest way to build one is to use door hinges, an old storm window for the lid and wood planks for the front, back and sides. Since the coldframe is heated by the sun, angle it to face south. On warm sunny days, raise the hinged top. Close it in late afternoon to collect and store up heat for the evening. By morning, the air inside the cold frame will be down to about the same temperature as the air outside, but will have fallen much more slowly, protecting the plants from the effects of radiant frost and cold winds. A cold frame provides a cozy, humid atmosphere by day and conditions or hardens plants by exposing them to cool temperatures at night. Plants started in a cold frame will be much stronger and hardier when finally planted outdoors in the garden.

PREPARING THE GROUND FOR PLANTING
Having determined the kind of soil in your garden and what you would like to grow, it is then just a matter of preparing the planting bed to the proper depth, texture and composition. You can't control the weather, but you can determine the kind of soil you're planting in. Generally, most garden plants do well in sandy-loam soil with lots of humus. Your soil should have a pH factor between 5.5 and 7.5 and good drainage. Note information on soil testing on page 24.

Your soil should also be well-worked – dug and turned over so that it becomes aerated, clumps of earth are broken up, weeds are smothered and humus, compost or fertilizer is added. Unless your garden is small or you are feeling particularly energetic, rent a rotary tiller to do this work. If you do dig by hand, don't overexert yourself. Working the soil is far harder work than shovelling snow.

Don't begin digging when the soil is wet as it will just form sticky hard clumps. Wait until it crumbles easily. Remove all weeds by hand before using the rotary tiller, as it tends to chop them up and spread them through the soil. This leads to more weeds, rather than less, later on. Rake the completed garden bed so that it is slightly higher in the centre than at its border. This will improve drainage and prevent your garden from turning into a huge puddle after a heavy rain.

If you are creating a new garden bed, it is best to dig it up in the fall and work in a healthy amount of manure or compost. Be sure to dig deep and break up the ground below the topsoil. This is especially important if you have a newly-built house. Developers often scrape off valuable topsoil and sell it to landscapers or nurseries, leaving bare clay that is further compacted by building equipment. After construction is finished, they then add a minimum layer of topsoil that is usually just deep enough to plant grass seed or sod for a lawn. Therefore, it is

Cold frame

very common in southern Ontario to have a thin layer of topsoil on a heavy clay base. If this is the case in your garden, dig deeply, mixing in sand to promote drainage and humus in a form such as peat moss to lighten the soil. In extreme cases of compacted clay subsoil, the whole bed should be excavated to 60 cm (2 ft.) and half-filled with layers of sand and gravel.

If this seems like too much work, it might be easier to construct raised beds. Break up the surface of the ground and then add a topsoil mix to a depth of at least 30 cm (1 ft.). Edge the bed with bricks, cement blocks, railway ties or similar material. Soak the soil before planting so that the earth settles. Raised beds warm up faster in the spring, resulting in earlier crops, but also dry out faster in summer and freeze solid sooner in the winter.

PLANTING SEEDLINGS IN THE GARDEN

Whether they are seedlings you grew yourself or starter plants bought from the nursery, the following rules apply:
- have the garden bed properly prepared
- make sure the time is right for the type or variety of plant
- water the seedlings first so that soil will cling to the roots. If in peat pots, soak the pots thoroughly, then tear sides and bottoms to allow roots to grow through
- dig holes at proper intervals and fill with water
- set in the plants a little deeper than they were in their pots
- cover the roots with loose soil and firm down
- make a small saucer-shaped depression in the soil around each plant to catch rain
- water the soil around plant once again
- protect tender young seedlings from sun, wind and rain

Seedlings can be planted in the garden without removing them from their peat pots. Before transplanting, soak the peat pot and carefully slit its sides and bottom.

PLANTING SEED OUTDOORS

After the soil has been worked and when the weather is warm enough, most seeds can be planted directly into the garden. Cool weather plants such as peas can be planted as soon as the ground can be dug in spring. Be sure that the ground has dried out, for though they can stand a touch of frost, seeds will rot or become mouldy if constantly saturated with water. For other seeds, the May 24th weekend is the accepted outdoor planting date in southern Ontario. In Niagara and around the edges of Lakes Ontario and Erie, including Metropolitan Toronto, you can probably start a couple of weeks earlier if the spring has been warm.

Prepare the soil by raking it into a fine smooth surface which is dry and crumbly. If planting in rows, drive two stakes into the ground, one at each end of the row. Stretch a string tightly between them. This string helps you keep rows straight, making weeding much easier later on. Make a furrow with the edge of a hoe or spade to the planting depth indicated on your seed package. For shallow plantings you may just want to make a slight indentation with the handle of a rake. Water the furrow before planting the seed. Follow seed package directions for proper spacing.

Sow small seed by sprinkling from your hand and then cover with loose earth. For larger seeds, such as beans or peas, make holes with a pencil stub. Put an elastic band around the pencil to indicate the required planting depth and then go down your row poking holes in the soil and popping one seed into each hole. Some seeds, such as cucumbers and squash, can be planted in hills. Dig out a circle about the size of your outstretched hands, fill it with compost, plant four seeds around the edge and one in the middle and then cover with earth. Mound the earth into a shallow saucer shape to collect water.

Water the garden with a fine mist spray after planting, and keep the ground moist until all the seeds have germinated.

MULCHING Mulch is a covering that is laid on the surface of the soil to keep weeds down, conserve moisture, prevent erosion, keep soil cooler in summer and warmer in winter and attract beneficial earthworms. If an organic mulch is used, it will slowly decompose, improving the soil structure and increasing its fertility. A mulched path provides a place to walk and makes the garden more attractive. Mulch should be placed around plants or between rows and hills. Never mulch over top of young plants or seeds. Some organic mulches that are easy to use are hay, straw, shedded bark, wood chips, shavings and sawdust. Hay or straw that comes in bales is probably the best for a garden, for it breaks apart in thick flakes that can be placed like paving stones. It is fairly tidy and easy to clean up and provides good insulation in both summer and winter.

Cedar boughs are another good winter mulch. Cedar holds snow and insulates plants.

A non-organic mulch that is widely used is black plastic sheeting. The plastic is laid over the ground and holes are cut for the plants to grow through, providing very effective weed control. The black colour is unattractive, but it attracts heat and keeps the soil warm.

Many other materials can be used as mulches including newspapers, grass clippings, leaves and nut shells. These have their drawbacks, for they may be messy, ugly, too light, too heavy, etc. Pine needles and cedar chips are probably the nicest-looking mulches for ornamental gardens and are favoured as weed control in attractive, low-maintenance gardens.

Young peach trees benefit from the addition of a heavy layer of mulch with wood shavings (top) and straw (bottom).

LAWNS AND GROUND COVER

Planting Lawns from Seed

Strange as it may seem to home gardeners who are accustomed to a major push in spring and little afterward, late summer and early fall are the best times of the year to grow grass from seed.

Grass plants go to seed in midsummer. Generally, grass seed lies on the surface of the ground until late summer when the nights are longer, there is moderate-to-heavy dew, and the quality of light from the sun favours germination and root growth rather than top growth. As well, there usually are more reliable rains in September.

So if you are considering growing a new lawn from seed, late summer or early fall is the time to prepare the area. Grass needs topsoil to a depth of at least 15 cm (6 in.). The soil bed must not be light sandy silt or heavy clay. If you are faced with either of these two soil conditions, you can improve your soil by mixing in a great deal of humus. Brown sphagnum peat moss is most commonly available, but you can use sifted compost, rotted sawdust, leaf mould or similar material. In clays, also mix in sharp sand.

A fertilizer high in phosphorus and potash is usually recommended for good rooting of new seedlings.

Spread farm grade 6:24:24 or 8:32:16 over the sand or sand/peat material, using about seven kg per 100 square metres or 15 lbs. per 1,000 square feet. If the fertilizer has a higher first figure you'll need less; follow label instructions. You can mix the existing soil and additives by spade, but a power tiller does a better job with less work.

Imported topsoil may be spread to a depth of well over 15 cm (6 in.) loose measure. But first, the undersoil surface should be broken up and graded so that when the new material is added, drainage will be away from buildings and paths. It may be necessary to remove some of

IF YOU HAVE A SOIL BED OF LIGHT SANDY SILT OR HEAVY CLAY, IMPROVE IT BY MIXING IN PEAT MOSS, SIFTED COMPOST, ROTTED SAWDUST OR LEAF MOULD. IN CLAYS, ALSO MIX IN HEAVY SAND.

the undersoil to get the grade you want.

Be sure of your soil sources. Topsoil loaded with weed seeds and roots will bring years of trouble. You shouldn't use farm manure that is not heat-treated and guaranteed weed-free.

Let newly prepared areas sit through a couple of good rains or waterings to settle the soil and show up bumps, hollows and ridges. This also encourages weed seeds to sprout so you can scuff them out. Regrade as necessary. Leave the small furrows a rake makes; these should go across any grade to act as small dams to hold water and seed from washouts.

Choosing Seed

Choose seed from either bluegrass/fescue mixtures, or new lawn-type perennial ryegrasses. For bluegrass/fescue mixtures, use 1 kg (2 1/4 lbs.) of seed for each 93 square metres or 1,000 square feet. For ryegrasses, use 2.26 kg (5 lbs.) for the same area. Use a seed spreader or hand sow as evenly as possible. If you are going to sow by hand, divide the seed in half and go over the area twice, the second time at right angles to the first.

Lightly tamp the new seed into close contact with the soil. An unweighted roller does this job well, particularly if you have seeded a large area. Do not cover grass seed as it needs light to germinate. Then soak with a fog or fine mist nozzle. Where you have water handy, this misting should be done whenever the soil surface becomes dry. Continue regular misting until a green fuzz shows. This can happen in as little as three days with ryegrass or as long as three or four weeks with bluegrass.

The appearance of the first green shoots signals a change in watering techniques. In this second phase,

apply enough water to wet the soil 15 cm (6 in.) deep, and then don't water again for a week or 10 days depending on rain. This encourages deep rooting. Begin mowing as soon as the grass grows higher than your cutting height – 5 cm (2 in.) or more.

Perennial ryegrass will grow into a thick turf the same fall it is planted. It does not, however, spread underground or over the ground to fill in any bare spots. You will have to reseed these. Be sure the seed is in close contact with damp soil. Seed cast over a sodded area is mostly wasted.

Bluegrass and, to a lesser extent, fine fescues may take as long as two years to mature, although they will make a stand the same fall in which they are planted. For this reason, some people like to include ryegrasses in a bluegrass lawn mixture, but the ryes – so-called nurse grasses – may prevent many bluegrass seedlings from reaching adulthood.

In full sun perennial grasses will outgrow and squeeze out most weeds. Crabgrass doesn't get a chance if mowing height is 5 cm (2 in.) or higher.

If your lawn is thin and in heavy shade, particularly over the roots of a forest maple tree, the best you can hope for is to grow grass as a summer annual. For this, it is best to wait for spring. Then topdress and overseed each year, but expect the grass to fade by fall. Maples not only hog the light, they have surface roots that will penetrate the sod for water and minerals.

Planting Lawns from Sod

Whether you are starting a new lawn from seed or sod, the ground should be prepared the same way and to the same depth. It should be prepared at least as deeply as for annual flowers or vegetables.

A well cultivated bed should be allowed to settle for at least a week and through at least one rainfall and/or irrigation. This shows up low or high areas that you can remedy, and lets you remove sprouting weeds.

Sod is a way of getting a fast lawn; it is more expensive than seeding and more labour-intensive to lay. Also, it may not contain the particular type of grass you want or require.

The earth you lay your sod on should be damp, but not so wet that your feet make deep depressions in it. It's a good idea to work from a broad piece of lumber laid flat on the ground. A string-line stretched between stakes helps keep your newly laid sod in straight lines and avoids the problem of being left with a triangular empty spot at the end.

Sod should be laid across a hill, rather than up and down. If necessary, peg each section of sod with short wooden or metal stakes (which must be removed before mowing) to prevent washing out in rain or irrigation.

Tamp each piece of sod as you go; you can use a flat piece of wood nailed on the end of a two-by-four to do this. Lay sod with tightly butting edges so that alternate rows have seams in the middle of the rows above and below, similar to the manner in which bricks are laid.

Edges of rolls and lines should butt but not buckle. Gently tamp or roll sod into intimate contact with the soil, eliminating air bubbles. Work from the spot farthest from the house so you don't have to walk across your new lawn when you've finished. Run a sprinkler to soak the area until water stands briefly on the surface. Repeat every second day for a week, and then water only when rains fail or the soil between the blades is dry. In moderately warm weather, healthy new sod should knit in two weeks – you can tell by

trying lightly to pry up a flap.

Cut seed or sod lawns when the new grass blades grow higher than 5 cm (2 in.). It is best to mow frequently so you never cut off a lot at a time. Let clippings remain on the ground. Fertilize at least once before freezeup.

Lawn Renovation

In renovating an old, thin lawn, you must decide between a complete remake or a fix-up job. Base your decision on how much grass there is. If the sod is covered at least 50 per cent by grass, it's worth renovating. This can be done by digging out bare spots and replacing with new sod you cut to fit, or by digging up the area and reseeding. Fixing the lawn this way means not having to wait to be able to use the grassed area. On hills, peg pieces of sod, or peg burlap over seeded areas. Burlap disintegrates over time, so it needn't be removed.

To thicken old, thin sod, work in stages. First fertilize the whole lawn. Hand weed or spot spray to get rid of weeds. Then aerate with a coring machine. Using a saw-tooth rake, "scarify" or make grooves in the sod of any areas to be seeded. This exposes the soil, allowing seed to come into close contact with the earth and providing somewhere for roots to go when seeds sprout. Follow the frequent light watering method (see "Choosing Seed", page 36) until the new grass is clearly visible.

Maintenance and Upkeep

SPRING As soon as you can work on the grass is the time to take the first steps to maintain your lawn areas for the season.

The brown grass you see on the

surface is last year's above ground growth. It may be safely mowed off with the mower blades set as low as you wish. Such a brush cut allows the first new green blades to be more visible, achieving an effect gardeners used to accomplish by burning off the old brown blades.

On a well-fertilized lawn, it will be worth your while to rake hard to loosen and remove dead blades as well as any accumulated grass clippings from last year that have not rotted down. This material is called thatch; it inhibits the movement of air and water in the soil, sometimes promoting diseases in wet, cold weather. In a rural, cottage or low maintenance lawn anywhere, however, the thatch may remain to break down eventually and add minerals and a little bit of topsoil to the lawn area.

An ordinary common garden rake will do the job on most lawns. A saw-tooth scarifying rake will remove almost all thatch, as well as opening up grooves in the soil to permit newly sprouted seed to gain a purchase. This is required treatment for satisfactory overseeding to thicken up a thin lawn. But bear in mind that most lawns that are thin lack sufficient light, root space, water and/or soluble minerals. Overseeding will produce new seedlings but, in turn, they too will succumb unless growing conditions change.

What about all those home gardeners pushing rollers or spreading black loam?

Unless you have strips of sod or clumps that have come loose, or perhaps brand new sod you've just laid, rollers should not be used. They compact clay soils, reducing air spaces. They do not remove bumps or hollows. These should be fixed by stripping off the sod and removing or adding soil as required; replace the sod and tamp or roll with an unweighted roller.

Topsoil belongs under the sod, not on top of it. Buying and spreading it on top of sod can be harmful as well as expensive and a lot of work. Unreliable suppliers may have incorporated pieces of quack grass root that will sprout to give you years of trouble. Heavy applications of topsoil (including the pile left on lawns by delivery trucks) may kill off parts of a perfectly good lawn. If you must apply it, use only thin coverings, say 60 mm (1/4 in.) at a time. The one place topsoil is invaluable is in lawn areas with heavy shade or competition from maple roots. In such a situation the gardener really is raising grass as an annual because the maples will manage to kill most of the lawn again by fall.

Grass grows best in full sun, with adequate minerals in solution in the soil and with an inch of new water (rain plus irrigation) every week to 10 days depending on temperature and wind.

Of the minerals, nitrogen in soluble nitrate form in early spring when the ground is very cold is in short supply. If you fertilized late last fall (Thanksgiving or later), nitrogen probably is already in place. If not, apply an inexpensive fertilizer with a high first figure. Broadcast it evenly, even on top of a light snow. If you are applying fertilizer over areas with new green showing, water it in even if the ground is damp.

New turf grass cultivars of perennial ryegrass offer nearly immediate results and seed may be sown over even frozen ground. At this time of year, germination may take several weeks but, with any warmth, growth is rapid. These new cultivars blend very well with both bluegrass and fescues and may be mown as soon as they grow above 5 cm (2 in.).

Except for luxury lawns which require high maintenance, leave clippings where they fall over the

UNLESS SOD HAS COME LOOSE OR HAS BEEN FRESHLY LAID, A ROLLER SHOULD NOT BE USED. ROLLERS COMPACT CLAY SOILS AND DO NOT REMOVE BUMPS OR HOLLOWS.

LAWNS AND GROUND COVER

season. Most will rot quickly and, as they break down, will add the equivalent of one fertilizer application, as well as a little bit of humus. A well maintained lawn also makes its own topsoil with sloughed off roots, although this occurs very slowly.

FALL If you are trying to grow a luxurious lawn, late October is the time for the last fertilizer application of the year. In fact, some authorities suggest if you fertilize only once a year, fall is the time to do it.

Grass continues to grow until the soil temperature at root level is just above freezing. Fortunately for those who have to mow, most of the growth consists of new roots for carbohydrate storage over the winter, and tillers (side growth or new shoots).

Rather than low nitrogen and high potassium (first and last figures in the fertilizer grade found on every package label), recent research show grass prefers the same mineral mix advised for the growing season – a product with a high first figure (nitrogen) compared to the others. This could be a 4:1:2 ratio such as 20:5:10.

Most slow-release fertilizers will hold on to their major mineral content until spring, releasing only a little nitrogen during the remainder of this growing season. Research shows that grass plants that go into winter dormancy with a good stock of minerals in roots and crown will be more winter hardy and primed for early spring growth.

As weather warms in spring, the remainder of the minerals in the fertilizer gradually becomes available. To a lesser extent this also is true of organic fertilizers such as those based on Milorganite (Milwaukee sewage sludge). But natural organics can burn grasses, though this is unlikely to happen in cold fall weather. In fact, natural organics are slow to release nitrogen in a form plants can use in cool spring weather too.

While experts and home gardeners argue about the relative merits of various kinds of fertilizer, all agree on the benefit of mowing right till freeze-up. No quality lawn benefits from ending its growing season with long, succulent grass matted over by cold and wet. This long last growth rots on top of the crowns that must survive to produce the green of next spring. Such matted grass or balls of wet clippings thrown out by rotary mowers invite fungus diseases.

Therefore, after mowing late in fall, raking off the clippings should be automatic. Remember, grass is a perennial herb; this year's blades, though they may remain green in colour under the snow, die off and are replaced next spring by fresh shoots.

It is rare that we go into winter with the ground dry, so ordinarily grass (and trees and shrubs) do not need irrigation at the end of the growing season. But if the soil is dry at planting level, newly set-out woody stock and bulbs should be soaked once. Few, if any, garden plants thrive or survive in waterlogged soil.

Upkeep

LUXURY LAWNS require frequent maintenance. Here's a point-by-point guide to make your lawn the best on the block.
- Mow frequently with a sharp mower whenever grass blades are slightly over the cutting height, preferably 5 cm (2 in.) but never lower than 38 mm (1½ in.).
- Fertilize five times a season: in very early spring before any growth is visible; around Victoria Day; and just before Canada Day, Labour Day and Thanksgiving.

- Water with an eye to the weather and soil conditions. The soil should be wetted 15 cm (6 in.) deep; this requires 2.5 cm (1 in.) of water on average soils, more on clays and less in fast-draining soils. Do this whenever the grass blades approach the point of wilting, when they appear bluish and glassy. The average time between such waterings will run about a week in warm weather.
- Rake off, collect and compost all clippings.
- Make daily checks for weeds, hand cutting or spot spraying any that show up. Where crabgrass is a problem, use a pre-emergent herbicide or crabgrass preventer.
- Keep foot traffic to a minimum, especially when the soil is damp.
- Aerate when the soil becomes compacted.
- Topdress by broadcasting or raking sifted compost over the lawn annually, taking care to apply no more than 26 mm (1/4 in.) at a time.

FERTILIZING To maintain a thick turf, follow this feeding schedule (metric measurements are in brackets after the original imperial measures): three to five pounds of ammonium nitrate per 1,000 square feet (1.36 to 2.27 kg per 93 square metres) just as or slightly before the frost comes out. Ten pounds of 10:6:4 or 5 lbs. of 20:5:10 (4.53 or 2.27 kg) around Victoria Day, repeated just before July and again around Labour Day. The application just prior to July 1 can also be of a completely soluble material such as 35:7:7 applied through a hose-siphon bottle according to directions. Three pounds (1.3 kg) will cover 1,000 square feet (93 square metres). Do not use fertilizer in exceedingly hot weather or on dry turf.

Some of the very newest fertilizer products promise a luxury lawn with only one or two applications a season. As well, new liquid and soluble powder products promise a slow release of nitrogen, necessitating fewer applications. These products are more expensive.

Ground Covers

As beautiful as fine lawn may be, there are certain situations where other ground covers are preferred. Lawns will not do well under mature trees that cast too much shade and have many surface roots, or on severe slopes or banks, or on large areas where the soil is too sandy or dry. Also, at cottages or weekend retreats, you might prefer something that does not demand regular maintenance and mowing.

Low maintenance plants may be shrubs, evergreens, vines or herbaceous perennials and are not restricted to any particular grouping of plants. They suppress weeds, recycle nutrients, conserve moisture, prevent soil erosion and contribute to the landscape design in their variety of forms, texture and colour.

When selecting ground cover plants, consider ease of establishment, tenacity, ease of propagation, availability, price and your overall garden design. For instance, on a large property wildflower seed mixtures will provide a relatively cheap cover, whereas a small area in shade can be planted with a number of shade tolerant plants spaced at minimal distances.

To help establish a good ground cover it is essential that perennial weeds be eliminated. Prior to planting, cultivate the area frequently to destroy weeds, or use a chemical eradicant such as glyphosate that can penetrate the weed roots to eliminate infestation. To avoid erosion problems, the latter process is effective for steep banks since the chemical kills grasses and weeds, but leaves the dead roots and crowns in place. Holes can then be dug, plants inserted, watered and mulched with bark or wood chips (which also controls erosion and conserves water on these dry sites). Within three to four years, the plants will be established and take over the function of turf.

For large areas a mixture of trees and shrubs can provide all the design criteria of texture, colour and form required in today's landscape. A few shrubs can cover a large area at a cost that is relatively inexpensive. Evergreens, particularly the spreading types of juniper, are extensively used since they can tolerate hot, sunny sites, provide winter texture and colour, and are relatively free of pests and disease. However, they are slow to fill in and expensive to purchase.

Other ground covers include broad-leaved evergreens such as winter creeper, low-lying shrubs (cotoneaster), vines (English ivy), and herbaceous perennials (creeping cinquefoil).

If allowed to grow to minimum height of 15 cm (6 in.), ground covers will suppress weeds within a few years. Occasional trimming and insect and disease control may be required. Fertilizer similar to that used on lawns may be applied once in the spring.

Some ground covers, such as mock strawberry and crown vetch, tend to become "invasive", taking over your garden. To prevent this, dig in a metal or plastic "edging barrier" to keep roots from spreading outside the plot, and trim back any trailers that try to climb or grow over the top.

Baltic English ivy

Three different ground cover plants: Japanese spurge, front; golden prostrate juniper, centre; Arnold dwarf forsythia, back.

 **Lawns and Ground Cover**

STOPPING CROWN VETCH SPREAD

Q: Due to the very steep incline on my waterfront property, I planted crown vetch. Now, how do I get rid of it? It has taken over my rock garden and is creeping its way up the hill to my vegetable garden. I am afraid to spray as I do not want to harm the birds. Any suggestions? — *D.B., Scarborough*

A: Your plight again proves the definition of a weed as any plant growing where you don't want it. To deal with it, however, you will have to choose between the constant labour of manual control and a herbicide. Perhaps you could erect a root barrier and remove any plant or part of it as it encroaches. Or spot spray with a glyphosate product so that the front line plants of the invading vetches are root killed. Glyphosate is inactivated when touching soil and so shouldn't be dangerous to birds.

BLACK MEDIC

Q: My lawn is infested with a plant with creepy habits, small yellow flowers and leaves that resemble those of white clover. Someone told me it was wild trefoil. Can you advise me on how I can control it? — *I.C.D., Keswick*

A: Your lawn pest is likely *Medicago lupulina*, which is commonly known as black medic. It is also called yellow trefoil or hop clover. Though not a true trefoil, it is indeed a legume and is related to alfalfa. It can even be used for fodder.

It's a Eurasian import that has become naturalized, but has only a negative value in lawns and is difficult to control. It is resistant to 2,4-D alone, except during the seedling stage and uncropped flower heads will produce seed. In lawns, the very minimum treatment is to prevent seed formation by cropping. The Ministry of Agriculture and Food recommends mecoprop, dichlorprop or dicamba, adding that, "the usual 2,4-D mixtures (with other herbicides) work well when applied during periods of rapid growth" which occur primarily in spring.

Used according to instructions, these products should not damage established bluegrass-fine fescue lawns. The Ministry says that mecoprop is safer to use on bent grass than 2,4-D.

Pulling by hand is possible on smaller lawns, especially when the ground is full of moisture. Loosen the roots by wiggling the main shoot base until all the root comes out. Legumes generally compete best with grasses where there is low nitrogen availability in the soil. Fertilize your lawn with a high first figure product to allow the grass to be more competitive. Mow at two inches or higher and water whenever rains fail to deliver 25 mm (1 in.) of water weekly in the prime growing season.

A WEED IS DEFINED AS ANY PLANT GROWING WHERE YOU DON'T WANT IT. STUBBORN LAWN WEEDS OFTEN REQUIRE REPEATED HERBICIDE APPLICATION.

 **Lawns and Ground Cover** CONTINUED

BACKYARD LUMPS

Q: What can I do with my lumpy backyard to make it smooth enough to install a croquet course or badminton court? – *T.M.H., Oakville*

A: There is no magic way of eliminating bumpy sod. Rolling with a weighted roller will only compress the soil under the grass plants. This is not as important in sandy loam as it is in clay. It also does not really level bumps in the soil. All it does for sure is push loose flaps of sod into intimate contact with the earth.

The fastest remedy is to peel back the sod over the area you want to level. Use a sharp, square-mouthed spade or sod-peeling tool to level the bumps on the newly-bared ground. Then relay the sod and roll with an unweighted roller. The sod should be damp when peeled. Water it lightly after relaying and normally afterwards.

Another alternative is to topdress heavily enough so that when rolled with an unweighted roller, the lowest parts of the lawn would be level with the tops of the bumps. Then re-seed over the entire area with a mixture of your choice. A modern perennial ryegrass is best for fast coverage. Some of the old buried grass may survive, but any covered deeply is likely to die. Overseeding the entire topdressed area is insurance. This project will cost more money, but will likely require less labour. If you adopt this approach, be sure of your topsoil supplier. You don't want topsoil loaded with couch grass root parts.

ANNUAL BLUEGRASS

Q: Can you suggest any solution for creeping grass that spreads and covers half of our lawn? It is a lighter green, forms a dense mat and is not unattractive until late August when brown patches begin to appear. We reseeded last year's brown patches this spring, and produced a green turf until browning recurred. – *C.E.D., Agincourt*

A: I think your lawn is suffering from an infestation of annual bluegrass. This is an attractive, light-green patch that appears in spring and dies out in August. This plant can adapt to frequent mowing by flowering and seeding close to the ground. For this reason, all clippings should be removed. Because the plant is an annual, spring seedlings die out in August after again setting seed. It can reproduce in no other way.

Repair dead grass with nursery-grown sod cut to fit. In effect, this removes or buries any seeds on the surface. Treat the whole lawn with a pre-emergent herbicide before seedlings emerge in spring. Repeat as necessary in the following year.

Boston ivy

Ground Cover Guide • SHRUBS AND VINES

NAME	HARDINESS ZONE	HEIGHT	SPREAD	CHARACTERISTICS	OTHER VARIETIES
AMERICAN BITTERSWEET *Celastrus scandens*	Zone 3b	1 m 3 ft.	2 m 6 ft.	• Mound • Native vine • Pale green leaves • Orange-yellow berries • Full sun • Excellent on banks	–
BEARBERRY *Arctostaphylos uva-ursi*	Zone 1	30 cm 1 ft.	1.2 m 4 ft.	• Native broad-leaved evergreen • Purplish-red bark, red berries in fall • Thrives on rocky soil, full sun	A. alpina
CANDYTUFT *Iberis sempervirens*	Zone 5	30 cm 1 ft.	30 cm 1 ft.	• Carpet • Narrow dark green leaves • White flowers • Well-drained soils in full sun	–
SHRUBBY CINQUEFOIL *Potentilla*	Zone 1	1 m 3 ft.	1 m 3 ft.	• Mound • Pale green leaves • Bright yellow flowers • Excellent on banks • Dry with full sun	P. Klondike P. Sutter's Gold P. Katherine Dykes
HANCOCK CORALBERRY *Symphoricarpos c. Hancockii*	Zone 5	1 m 3 ft.	2 m 6 ft.	• Spreader • Dark green leaves • Pink flowers • Rose fruit • Excellent on banks • Full sun to partial shade	–
SKOGHOLM COTONEASTER *Cotoneaster dammeri Skogholm*	Zone 5	30 cm 1 ft.	1 m 3 ft.	• Mound • Small green leaves • Pink flowers • Excellent on banks • Full sun	C. Coral Beauty (red berries)
DWARF EUROPEAN CRANBERRY *Viburnum o. nanum*	Zone 2b	60 cm 2 ft.	60 cm 2 ft.	• Mound • Medium green leaves • Sun or shade on well-drained soils	–
SLENDER DEUTZIA *Deutzia gracilis*	Zone 6	1 m 3 ft.	1.2 m 4 ft.	• Mound • Pale green leaves • White flowers • Well-drained soils in full sun	D. lemoine compacta D. rosea (pink flowers)
DYERS BROOM *Genista tinctoria*	Zone 5	30 cm 1 ft.	45 cm 18 in.	• Mound • Small green leaves • Yellow flowers • Well-drained soils in full sun	G. Lydia G. Vancouver Gold
ARNOLD DWARF FORSYTHIA *Forsythia i. Arnold*	Zone 5	1 m 3 ft.	2 m 6 ft.	• Mound • Pale green leaves • Yellow flowers • Excellent on banks • Dry with full sun	–

Ground Cover Guide • SHRUBS AND VINES

NAME	HARDINESS ZONE	HEIGHT	SPREAD	CHARACTERISTICS	OTHER VARIETIES
HONEYSUCKLE *Lonicera*	Zone 2	1 m 3 ft.	2 m 6 ft.	• Vine with smooth green leaves • Orange trumpet flowers • Excellent on banks • Partial sun to shade	L. Goldflame (Zone 4) L. halliana (Zone 6b)
BALTIC ENGLISH IVY *Hedera helix Baltica*	Zone 6	23 cm 9 in.	45 cm 18 in.	• Vine • Glossy evergreen leaves • Shade-loving	H. Thorndale H. Bulgaria
SPREADING JUNIPER *Juniperus*	Zone 2	1 m 3 ft.	1.2 m 4 ft.	• Mound or spreaders • Grey, green, blue or gold needles • Well-drained soils in full sun	numerous
MUGO PINE *Pinus mugo*	Zone 1	1 m 3 ft.	1.2 m 4 ft.	• Mound • Becomes large without annual shearing • Dry, sunny sites	–
OREGON GRAPE *Mahonia aquifolium*	Zone 5	1 m 3 ft.	1 m 3 ft.	• Mound • Glossy evergreen leaves • Yellow flowers • Shade-loving	M. Forest Green M. Woodland King M. Woodland Queen
PYGMY PEASHRUB *Caragana aurantiaca*	Zone 2	60 cm 2 ft.	60 cm 2 ft.	• Glossy green leaves • Yellow pea-like flowers • Full sun	–
PERIWINKLE *Vinca minor*	Zone 3	30 cm 1 ft.	30 cm 1 ft.	• Carpet • Glossy evergreen leaves • White-purple flowers • Shade-loving	V. Bowles (blue flowers) V. alba (white flowers) V. rubrum (red flowers)
JAPANESE QUINCE *Chaenomeles japonica*	Zone 5b	1 m 3 ft.	1.5 m 5 ft.	• Mound • Glossy green leaves • Orange-red flowers • Edible fruit • Full sun	C. nivalis (white flowers) C. Fire-Dance (red flowers)
SPIREA *Spiraea*	Zone 2b	60 cm 2 ft.	1 m 3 ft.	• Mound • Small green leaves • White-pink flowers • Well-drained soils in full sun	S. Snowhite (white flowers) S. Anthony Waterer (rose flowers)
JAPANESE SPURGE *Pachysandra terminalis*	Zone 3	25 cm 10 in.	30 cm 1 ft.	• Spreader • Glossy evergreen leaves • Shade-loving	–
FRAGRANT SUMAC *Rhus aromatica*	Zone 3	1.5 m 5 ft.	2 m 6 ft.	• Mound • Divided green leaves go red in fall • Excellent for dry, sunny sites	R. Grow-Low (compact)
VIRGINIA CREEPER/ BOSTON IVY *Parthenocissus*	Zone 2b Zone 5b	30 cm 1 ft.	2 m 6 ft.	• Native vine • V. creeper is a rampant grower • Sun or shade	–
BLUE ARCTIC WILLOW *Salix p. Gracilis*	Zone 2b	1 m 3 ft.	2 m 6 ft.	• Mound • Narrow grey-green leaves • Wet moist soils in full sun	–

Ground Cover Guide • SHRUBS AND VINES
CONTINUED

NAME	HARDINESS ZONE	HEIGHT	SPREAD	CHARACTERISTICS	OTHER VARIETIES
WINTER CREEPER *Euonymus fortunel*	Zone 5	20 cm 8 in.	1 m 3 ft.	• Vine-like spreader • Glossy evergreen leaves • Good in full sun to shade	E. coloratus (leaves plum colour in fall)
YEW *Taxus*	Zone 4	1 m 3 ft.	1 m 3 ft.	• Mound • Narrow evergreen needles • Shade to partial sun	T. media Andersonii T. media Brownii

Reptans juniper

Ground Cover Guide • HERBACEOUS PERENNIALS

NAME	HARDINESS ZONE	HEIGHT	SPREAD	CHARACTERISTICS	OTHER VARIETIES
VARIEGATED ARCHANGEL *Lamiastrum g. variegatum*	Zone 5	10 cm 4 in.	1 m 3 ft.	• Spreader • White and green striped leaves • Yellow flowers • Invasive • Shade-loving	–
SILVER MOUND ARTEMISIA *Artemisia Silver Mound*	Zone 4	20 cm 8 in.	60 cm 2 ft.	• Mound • Feathery silver leaves • Well-drained soils in full sun	–
BARRENWORT *Epimedium grandiflora*	Zone 4	1 m 3 ft.	1 m 3 ft.	• Spreader • Glossy green leaves • Pink-red flowers • Shade	E. rubrum (red flowers) E. sulphurenum (yellow flowers)
BASKET-OF-GOLD *Aurinia saxatile*	Zone 5	30 cm 1 ft.	1 m 3 ft.	• Mound • Grey-green leaves • Bright yellow flowers • Well-drained soils in full sun	A. citrinum (lemon yellow flowers) A. compactum
BELLFLOWER *Campanula*	Zone 4	15 cm 6 in.	60 cm 2 ft.	• Mound • Light green leaves • Blue bell-like flowers • Well-drained soils in full sun	–
BERGENIA *Bergenia cordifolia*	Zone 5	30 cm 1 ft.	60 cm 2 ft.	• Mound • Glossy green leaves • Rose flowers • Moist shady locations	B. perfecta (pink flowers) B. Silverlight (white flowers)
BUGLEWEED *Ajuga reptans*	Zone 5	8 cm 3 in.	30 cm 1 ft.	• Spreader • Shiny green leaves • Blue flowers • Shade-loving	A. variegata (green and white leaves) A. atropurpurea (purple leaves)
CATMINT *Nepeta fassenii*	Zone 5	25 cm 10 in.	45 cm 18 in.	• Carpet, grey-green leaves • Can escape and become a weed • Lavender-blue flowers • Well-drained soils in full sun	N. Blue Wonder (blue flowers)
CREEPING CINQUEFOIL *Potentilla r. flore plena*	Zone 3	15 cm 6 in.	30 cm 1 ft.	• Spreader • Green strawberry leaves • Double yellow flowers • Invasive by runners • Well-drained soils in full sun	–
CROWN VETCH *Coronilla varia*	Zone 4	60 cm 2 ft.	1 m 3 ft.	• Spreader • Green pinnate leaves • Lilac-pink flowers • Invasive • Legume used for dry, steep banks	C. v. Penngift C. v. Emerald
DAY-LILY *Hemerocallis*	Zone 2	1 m 3 ft.	30 cm 1 ft.	• Mound • Grassy green leaves • Yellow-crimson flowers • Well-drained soils in full sun	–

Ground Cover Guide • HERBACEOUS PERENNIALS
CONTINUED

NAME	HARDINESS ZONE	HEIGHT	SPREAD	CHARACTERISTICS	OTHER VARIETIES
DEAD-NETTLE *Lamium maculatum*	Zone 5	20 cm 8 in.	60 cm 2 ft.	• Carpet • Silver striped leaves • Mauve flowers • Moist site • Shade-loving	L. Chequers (pink flowers) L. m. alba (white flowers) L. Beacon Silver (silver leaves)
FOAM FLOWER *Tiarella cordifolia*	Zone 5	15 cm 6 in.	30 cm 1 ft.	• Carpet • Green lobed leaves • Creamy-white flowers • Native cover for moist shady site	–
GERANIUM (CRANESBILL) *Geranium*	Zone 5	30 cm 1 ft.	30 cm 1 ft.	• Spreader • Green divided leaves • White, blue or red flowers • Sun or partial shade	G. Sanquineum (magenta flowers) G. Macrohiza (pink flowers) G. Johnson's Blue (blue flowers)
WILD GINGER *Asarum canadense*	Zone 4	15 cm 6 in.	30 cm 1 ft.	• Spreader • Green heart-shaped leaves • Native ground cover for heavy shade	–
GOUTWEED *Aegopodium podagraria*	Zone 3	30 cm 1 ft.	60 cm 2 ft.	• Spreader • Dark green leaves • Can escape and become a weed • Shade-loving	A. p. variegata (green and white leaves)
HOSTA (PLANTAIN-LILY) *Hosta*	Zone 4	45 cm 18 in.	60 cm 2 ft.	• Mound • Green heart-shaped leaves • White-lilac flowers • Shade to partial sun	H. seiboldiana (large blue leaves) H. undulata (variegated leaves)
LAMBS-EAR *Stachys lanata*	Zone 5	10 cm 4 in.	30 cm 1 ft.	• Carpet • Grey woolly leaves • Grey-white flowers • Well-drained soils in full sun	S. Silver Carpet (non-flowering)
LILY-OF-THE-VALLEY *Convallaria majalis*	Zone 3	20 cm 8 in.	30 cm 1 ft.	• Spreader, smooth green leaves • White scented flowers • Invasive • Shade-loving	–
LUNGWORT *Pulmonaria angustifolia*	Zone 3	15 cm 6 in.	30 cm 1 ft.	• Mound • Silver spotted green leaves • Red-blue flowers • Sun or shade	–
MOCK STRAWBERRY *Duchesnea indica*	Zone 4	10 cm 4 in.	60 cm 2 ft.	• Spreader • Strawberry-like leaves • Yellow flowers • Invasive by runners and seeds • Sun or shade	–
MONEYWORT *Lysimachia nummularia*	Zone 4	30 cm 1 ft.	60 cm 2 ft.	• Spreader • Green round leaves • Yellow flowers • Sun to partial shade	L. m. aurea (golden leaves)

Yarrow

Ground Cover Guide • HERBACEOUS PERENNIALS
CONTINUED

NAME	HARDINESS ZONE	HEIGHT	SPREAD	CHARACTERISTICS	OTHER VARIETIES
MOTHER-OF-THYME *Thymus serpyllum*	Zone 3	2.5 cm 1 in.	30 cm 1 ft.	• Spreader • Dark green leaves • Pink-red flowers • Well-drained soils in full sun	T. albus (white flowers) T. languinosus (grey leaves)
PHLOX (MOSS PINK) *Phlox subulata*	Zone 3	10 cm 4 in.	30 cm 1 ft.	• Spreader • Narrow green leaves • White-blue flowers • Well-drained soils in full sun	P. Emerald Blue (blue flowers) P. rosea (pink flowers) P. May Snow (white flowers)
PINKS *Dianthus*	Zone 3	10 cm 4 in.	30 cm 1 ft.	• Spreader • Bluish linear leaves • White-red flowers • Well-drained soils in full sun	D. deltoides (pink flowers) D. Flashing Lights (red flowers)
PURPLE ROCK-CRESS *Aubrieta deltoidea*	Zone 4	20 cm 8 in.	30 cm 1 ft.	• Carpet • Grey-green leaves • Red-purple flowers • Alpine for sunny, well-drained sites	–
ROCK-CRESS *Arabis alpina*	Zone 4	15 cm 6 in.	45 cm 18 in.	• Spreader • Grey-green leaves • White flowers • Well-drained soils in full sun	A. rosea (pink flowers) A. flore-plena (double white)
SNOW-IN-SUMMER *Cerastium tomentosum*	Zone 3	20 cm 8 in.	30 cm 1 ft.	• Spreader • Silver-grey woolly leaves • White flowers • Well-drained soils in full sun	–
ROCK SOAPWORT *Saponaria ocymoides*	Zone 4	15 cm 6 in.	30 cm 1 ft.	• Carpet • Green leaves • Pink flowers • Well-drained soils in full sun	–
SPEEDWELL *Veronica*	Zone 4	15 cm 6 in.	30 cm 1 ft.	• Carpet • Green leaves • Blue flowers • Well-drained soils in full sun	V. Incana (silver-grey leaves)
STONECROP *Sedum*	Zone 3	15 cm 6 in.	30 cm 1 ft.	• Mound, grey-green leaves • Pink-rose red flowers • Invasive • Full sun	S. acre (yellow flowers, invasive) S. Autumn Joy (pink flowers)
SWEET WOODRUFF *Arsperula odorata*	Zone 4	15 cm 6 in.	30 cm 1 ft.	• Spreader • Light green leaves • Aromatic • Shade-loving	–
YARROW *Achillea*	Zone 2	20 cm 8 in.	60 cm 2 ft.	• Mound • Feathery light green leaves • Yellow flowers • Dry sites • Full sun	A. Kelwayi (cerise flowers)

This Norway maple is one of Canada's most famous trees. Located in the east end of Toronto, its falling leaves served as inspiration for Alexander Muir, who, in 1867, composed the unofficial national anthem, *The Maple Leaf Forever.*

TREES AND SHRUBS

Planting for a Good Start

More and more nursery-grown trees, shrubs and evergreens are now grown in containers. This trend makes it possible to plant any time in the growing season that a hole can be dug.

But despite this, these plants still do better in the garden if planted in early spring, the season in which greatest root growth occurs. You should plant literally as soon as you can get a spade in the soil. The sooner the plant is situated, the sooner it can grow new roots that can pick up water and dissolved minerals from your garden soil.

Roots confined to soil in a container are much more subject to drought damage if not watered on time. And with a greater root spread, they can support more leaf growth, which translates into top growth and spread.

It used to be thought that you should prune back new plants, particularly those sold with bare roots. Recent research, however, indicates initial pruning may remove nutrients that are concentrated at branch tips and near buds.

Similarly, preparing special planting soil is now regarded as a waste of time and possibly harmful. It may just turn the planting hole into a dry well that collects water and drowns plant roots.

On the other hand, you won't help the plant adapt and naturalize if you simply jam its rootball (bare or in container soil) into a hole too small for it. Dig the hole so roots can spread downward and outward naturally if the plant is bare root (packaged plants are considered bare root for planting purposes).

If in a container, dig the hole wider and deeper than the container; back fill loosened soil so the plant, when removed and set in the hole, will sit no lower than it was in the nursery row or in container soil – the stain on the lower trunk will

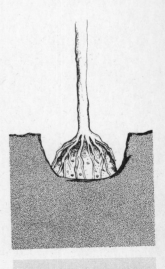

Dig a hole large enough to accommodate the rootball.

indicate this level.

If you have trouble getting the roots out of the container, rap the bottom sharply with a shovel. Holding the container with your feet, try to twist the trunk base around and up. If the plant still refuses to come free, use tin snips or a knife to cut the metal or plastic down one side and pry up the rootball.

If it proves necessary to cut the container to remove the rootball, the plant probably is over-mature, having been in the container too long. Check for roots wound around the outer edge. These should be unwound or pruned off. If the rootball is a solid mass, cut 1.25 cm (1/2 in.) off the bottom and all around before planting – a sharp butcher or chef's knife works well.

You may still find some nurseries selling plants with burlap around the soil and roots – these are called balled and burlapped or "B and B". Treat in the same manner as container plants except do not remove the burlap. Instead, once the rootball has been set at the right depth on loosened soil, untie the burlap and fold it down so that it is covered with garden soil as you back fill.

Occasionally, nurseries offer plants in fibre pots. These do not have to be removed – plant container and all. But you should break off the pot rim above the soil level so it can't act as a wick and draw moisture from the roots after planting. It's also a good idea to slash sides and bottom in several places to allow easy root exits.

Tamp soil lightly in the filled area and add a little more as necessary to maintain the general soil level. Some gardeners like to make a shaped saucer of earth around the planting circle to catch and hold rainwater.

TRANSPLANTER SOLUTION It is better to settle the soil by flushing the planting area with plain tapwater than to use nothing at all. But you'll give the plant a better chance by using a diluted transplanter solution made by dissolving a heaping tablespoon of high phosphorus fertilizer in a gallon of water (5 millilitres in a litre). Grades 10:45:15 or 10:52:10 are very good. 11:52:17 is the highest grade available, but you can also use grade 15:30:15 which often is sold as a geranium food. As well, a new liquid product, grade 5:15:5, contains a synthetic hormone that promotes root growth. Soak the planting area and let drain. Add more earth as necessary – the transplant should not be buried, but sit at the same height as it did in container or nursery, which is shown by a stain mark on the trunk. Then soak with the solution once again. Plants should need no more fertilizer in their first growing season.

If your tree is in a sodded area, edge to keep the sod at least 60 cm (2 ft.) from the trunk.

Keep this area weeded or mulched. The mulch should be of some material that will smother weeds and let rain seep through, or that holds existing moisture in the ground. Bark chips are attractive near dwellings. Partly worked compost is a good choice where neatness is not important. Weighted newspapers make a good weed-suppressing mulch for plants set out at a rural or cottage property.

Water new transplants only when there's a dry spell. Keeping the roots of almost all plants in a wet condition asphyxiates them – they need some air to function. If you are in doubt, excavate with a trowel; if the soil is dry, water to a depth of 15 cm (6 in.).

STAKES Tall shrubs and evergreen trees of any size should be staked for the first year or two to prevent storm and wind damage. Dwarf fruit trees should always be staked. Stake when you plant, thus avoiding root

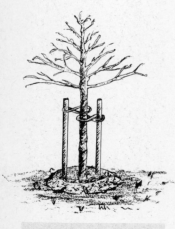

Young trees should be staked to prevent storm damage.

damage that could result if a stake was driven in later. Container saplings often come with a stake in the pot; remove it and drive a new sturdy one (steel fencing T-bars are excellent) through the same hole and well below the bottom of the planting hole, on the windward side of the trunk – in most locations the stake should be on the west side. Soft yet firm ties should be fixed securely – wire fed through old hollow skipping rope or old garden hose will do well; attach in a figure-eight, allowing room to grow.

On bare root plants, note where to drive the stake to avoid root damage. On unstaked container plants try to feel your way through the soil to cause the least damage.

Large evergreens are best secured with three guy wires from a place on the trunk to three pegs (tent pegs will do). To avoid accidents, spray paint pegs a bright, fluorescent orange and perhaps attach some flags.

LOCATION Choose the kind of plant you want with an eye to its eventual height and spread; make sure it is sufficiently far from foundation walls, doors, windows, driveways and paths, and overhead wires. Too often that "cute little evergreen" turns out to be a 60-foot giant that blocks all light from the window facing it in winter as well as in summer. Avoid twinning – setting apparently identical trees (usually evergreens) on either side of a house corner or driveway; they almost never grow at equal rates and often one fails or suffers dieback. By the time you are bothered sufficiently to change the situation, the "good" tree requires commercial tree care people to move it.

TRANSPLANTING FROM THE WILD can be an inexpensive and enjoyable way to acquire young trees, but you are almost sure to get better speci-

mens and plants more suitable to urban or suburban lots by buying from a nursery. If you do transplant from the wild, bear in mind that the relocated plant might not thrive, wasting your time and forcing you to plant again. The suggestions that follow will improve your odds for success.

Early spring is the time to transplant.

Nursery stock is root-pruned so that most of the feeder roots – hair roots – are in the ball of soil under and around the main stem (in a container or burlap ball). Wildlings may have all their roots on one side, depending on root space among all the plants growing in one area.

It is important to get as many of the hair roots as possible, while the heavy, woody roots may be pruned back or cleanly sliced off. A clean cut allows for quick healing, but is difficult to achieve with larger trees. As a result, relatively small trees make the most successful candidates for transplanting from the wild.

Cedars are one of the easiest trees to uproot. If growing in sand and/or gravel, they may sometimes simply be pulled up, hair roots attached. If you are moving a number of cedars, shake soil from the roots and bundle together. Pack wet moss, bog peat or similar material around them. Place in a plastic bag and squeeze out the air. Tie the bag to keep the roots damp. Plant as soon as possible.

Transplanted cedars do best with frequent watering, as they can grow in bogs and swamps. Plant cedars 30–60 cm (1–2 ft.) apart for hedging, depending on size of plants. No special soil preparation is needed, except to break up more than enough to accommodate the rootballs, so soil is loose under and around roots. Some old-fashioned gardeners like to lay down a layer of cattle manure 15 cm (6 in.) below

It is important that the transplanted tree and its rootball are set in a hole no deeper than that of the tree's original location.

the soil on which the cedar roots sit.

Water somewhat more frequently whenever rains fail to deliver 2.5 cm (1 in.) of water; soak the root area. You could scatter a handful of grass fertilizer (high first figure of the grade) around and between cedar plants in June.

Native Birch from cottage country are perhaps the hardest trees to transplant. If you are determined to try, select your tree and then postpone the actual move for a year. Using a sharp spade, pierce the ground to blade depth around half the circle of the base – the circle's diameter should be 30 cm (1 ft) for 60–100 cm (2–3 ft.) high trees, which is about as big as can easily be transported south.

In fall, pierce the other half of the circle. This causes new roots to grow inside the circle. Next spring dig out the rootball, set it on a piece of burlap, canvas or strong sheet plastic, bring ends around to the trunk and tie them in place. Move in a truck or station wagon if possible. Birch plants should be staked for the first year.

Pines and Spruces from the wild are unlikely to have the uniform growth of nursery-grown specimens, with branches evenly spaced and foliage all round. And unless you have a very large lot, it is doubtful you should be planting forest-size pines and spruces. White pines, common in the woods, are not suitable for another reason – they are not tolerant of city pollution or auto exhaust. As well, there are more decorative spruce than the common white one of the forest; consult any good nursery colour catalog.

But if you do bring them back alive, plant them no deeper in your soil than they stood in the bush. Water them initially with transplanter solution (described above), but don't keep them wet; provide

A shaped saucer of earth formed around the planting hole enables a young tree to catch and retain water.

no more fertilizer this year. Stake any plants taller than 1 m (3 ft.).

ORNAMENTAL TREES The container revolution in nursery growing has virtually eliminated the strict limits that were once placed on transplanting trees. Now you can set them into a hole in your garden almost at will. Still, they do grow new roots into the soil better in fall and early spring. But even parks departments now plant in summer and winter when landscaping a road.

It used to be said that you should not plant poplar, willow, birch, magnolia, cherry (Japanese or fruit) or London plane trees in autumn. This stricture still applies to birch, which doesn't grow satisfactorily in pots, and to magnolia, which has tuberous, easily damaged roots that apparently do not heal in autumn.

If you want to be safe, save planting the rest of the no-no list until very early spring as well. However poplar, which used to be very temperamental, no longer is quite that way when available as a grown-in-pot plant.

While spring planting is still preferred, most hardy trees, shrubs and evergreens planted in the fall will be further ahead than those set out next spring. So if you have the time and a hardy specimen available in the fall, go ahead and plant.

It makes sense to choose a shade tree with good fall colour in the fall when you can judge it best.

Bear in mind that nursery plants should be set at the same level they stood in the nursery, so that the garden soil is no higher than the soil in the nursery container. Burying tree roots too deeply has killed many transplants. However, every rule has its exceptions and these include grafted (but standard size) fruit trees, hybrid locusts, grafted lilacs and other man-made plants. These should be planted so the wood above the graft comes in contact with the soil and thus can grow roots of its own.

But if your fruit trees are grafted dwarfs (as distinct from genetic dwarfs), they must be planted shallowly indeed. If the intermediate (stem) wood contacts the soil, it will bypass the dwarfing rootstalks resulting in a 40-foot tree you cannot spray or even pick from the ground.

The sooner you get container-grown plants into your garden soil, the better they will do next year. They will go on growing new roots which will spread out into your garden soil until freeze-up – until the temperature of the soil at the root level drops below 2°C or 35°F.

In fact, container-grown plants may actually be set into the ground even in winter. So if you plan on a live Christmas tree in a pot and wish to keep it, dig the hole before freeze-up and keep some of the excavated soil unfrozen to pack around the plant. All pre-dug holes should be covered securely to prevent accidents.

If your tree is to be dug from nursery rows without a ball of soil intact around the roots, the time to plant it is just as the tree's leaf colours change, usually around Thanksgiving.

Soil at the bottoms and sides of the planting hole should be stabbed repeatedly with a hoe or trowel to open it up for easy root penetration. It is not necessary to use special mixes; new research indicates transplants establish themselves better in garden soil if it is similar to that around the roots. This same research reinforces the practice of using a diluted, high phosphorous fertilizer transplanting solution of the type described earlier.

SHRUBS Few things bought by the homeowner have as many uses, and are as sound a long-term investment, as shrubs. Unlike most trees that require many years to reach maturity, shrubs are fully established in just a few years. With a great assortment of sizes, shapes and colours to choose from, shrubs can be used as privacy screens, border hedges, boundary markers, foundation plantings and as specimen plantings both in the ground and in containers. Branching or the absence of a trunk distinguishes shrubs from trees. The branches of a shrub start near or below ground level, while a tree has a single trunk with branches starting some distance above the ground. Both have permanent, woody branches, flowers of some kind, and seed or fruit.

When selecting shrubs from your garden centre, don't buy an oversized plant in an undersized container, for the roots may not be sufficiently developed to support the topgrowth. Beware, also, of undersized plants in oversized containers, especially if they are sold by the size of the pot. Look for a balanced, healthy plant in a pot that seems to be fairly lightweight for its size. A heavy pot means that the shrub has been overwatered, creating the possibility that the roots are sodden or rotting.

Planting a shrub is a permanent proposition, much like planting a tree, and as much care should be taken in preparing the soil. Make sure you work plenty of peat moss, compost or other organic material into the soil before planting your shrubs. In heavy clay areas or where drainage is poor, you can consider mound planting. Scoop out a hole about three times the size of the container and fill it with good sandy loam. Place the shrub on top and build a mound of humus and topsoil so that the soil surface is about 5 cm (2 in.) higher than the nursery grown surface level.

EVERGREENS Evergreen trees and shrubs are easy to grow and thrive in poor soil. They add colour to your garden year round, maintaining

Potentilla

Blue spruce

their green leaves or needles throughout the winter. There are two basic types of evergreens: narrow-leaved (with needles) and broad-leaved (with flat, wide leaves). Narrow-leaved evergreens can tolerate drier air, more wind, and colder temperatures than broad-leaved varieties. Narrow-leaved foliage ranges from flat and fern-like (arborvitae) to scale-like (false cypress), dark, dense, soft needles (yews), or hard, pointy needles (pine). Some plants, like the juniper, combine scale and needle foliage. Most broad-leaved evergreens prefer full shade and do well on the east and north sides of buildings. They include such plants as boxwood, cotoneaster, holly, azalea and rhododendrons.

Narrow-leaved evergreens like sandy, gravelly soil where their roots can run and ramble. They will cling to rock cliffs and find a home in cracks between boulders. Wherever they are, they must have good drainage. They hate heavy soil, muck and clay. If you are planting in soil that is mainly clay, dig a hole twice as big and deep as required to plant the tree. In the centre of the hole dig a further shaft, or drainage hole, as deep as you can. Then fill that shaft and one-third of the planting hole with a mixture of sand and gravel. Set the new plant into the hole and fill the rest with sandy loam. Press the soil down firmly and cover with cedar-chip mulch. Other than occasional pruning to maintain shape and watering during extremely dry periods, there is not much else you need to do to have a healthy plant.

Broad-leaved evergreens grow best in regions having mild, humid climates and soils that are naturally acidic and high in organic matter. Southern Ontario only partly meets these requirements, but if care is taken to choose the hardiest plants, proper soil and best location, suc-

cess can be achieved. Light shade and protection from wind are preferred. Exposed plants invariably suffer from windburn and desiccation. A site sloping to the north or east is beneficial. Such a site will be less affected by cold, drying winds and rapid changes of temperature in late winter and early spring. In southern Ontario the prevailing winds are westerly, therefore plants should be situated on the east side of buildings or among a dense group of trees or tall shrubs. Full exposure to sun in winter may cause leaf scorch. Avoid low areas which can be both poorly drained and natural frost pockets.

Azaleas and Rhododendrons The name rhododendron is derived from two Greek words meaning "rose" and "tree". These variegated plants range from dwarf shrubs to soaring trees and feature magnificent foliage and beautiful flowers. Both broad-leaved evergreen and deciduous varieties exist, though evergreen rhododendrons are the most popular. Although botanists classify all azaleas as rhododendrons, gardeners continue to use the name azalea for most deciduous or leaf-shedding types. Though azaleas are often thought of as perennials, they have the same requirements and thrive under the same conditions as other broad-leaved evergreens.

Soil for rhododendrons or azaleas should be acidic (pH 4.0 to 5.5), well-drained, coarse-textured and high in organic material. Do not excavate deep beds in heavy clay soils because drainage may not be adequate. Instead build raised beds. Rhododendrons and azaleas are by nature long-lived plants though thorough soil preparation is necessary if they are to survive. Once planted, little can be done to improve the soil around them because they root close to the surface and disturbing their soil damages the

White evergreen azalea blossoms

Above: The colourful Japanese maple turns deep-red in fall. Cultivars with year-round red foliage are also available. Far left: Junipers like this tall vinespire add colour twelve months a year. Left: Lilacs offer deep green leaves and fragrant white, pink or purple flowers.

roots. When properly established they require little care other than a good mulch of pine needles, oak leaves or wood chips to help maintain moisture and protect against temperature extremes. Removal of dead flowerheads in summer will prevent seeds from forming and encourage new growth. In winter, it is advisable to cover with evergreen boughs. Avoid planting rhododendrons and azaleas under or close to shallow-rooted trees such as maple, ash or elm.

Using Trees and Shrubs for Colour

One permanent method of adding interest and colour throughout our active garden season – and beyond into fall and winter – is growing a shrub and tree garden in which plants are carefully chosen to provide a succession of colours.

The idea of using such woody perennials may not work in a very small garden, but certainly it offers a way of enhancing your landscape without much of the labour required to plant and maintain a herbaceous perennial garden.

And unlike annual flowers – which still may have their role to play – shrubs and trees usually need be planted only once in a lifetime. Once established, they require no more than occasional pruning, repairing of storm damage, occasional fertilization and leaf raking in fall.

Different types of shrubs or trees display abundant colour throughout spring, summer or fall.

The native hardy potentilla offers yellow/orange flowers continuously all summer; a new version called Princess has pink flowers. Anthony Waterer spirea is a low-growing shrub with inconspicuous but pinkish-red flowers all season. Various hydrangea shrubs offer flowers from summer through to heavy frost.

Climbing honeysuckles offer white to flaming red flowers intermittently over the summer and can be trained to trellises, walls, and railings.

Shrub roses, hawthorns, sumac, mountain ash, *Elaeagnus* (Russian and autumn olive) and *Shepherdia* (buffaloberry) have colourful fruit and/or colourful leaves that can even appear silvery, as do those of the silver poplar.

Royalty crabapple has glossy, red leaves all season, as does the purple sand cherry; purple-leafed plum has purple leaves, but is not so hardy. Red-leafed European maple cultivars such as Crimson King or Royal Red provide blood-red-coloured leaves most of the season – they darken and lose colour in fall. Another version, the Harlequin maple, has variegated white and green leaves all season.

Tender Japanese shrub maples offer delicately-cut leaves, some with brilliant red colour all season. Much hardier and more vigorous is the Amur River maple with colourful keys (seeds) and brilliant, though brief, fall colour.

The large native Canadian red maple is suitable for sites that are damp or near water. It has young red twigs, red flowers, and bright orange/red fall colour. The native Canadian red oak also offers bright fall leaf colour on a tap-rooted tree of moderately large size.

We don't usually think of evergreens providing colour in our gardens. But in fact many juniper cultivars offer foliage from bronze to blue over the winter. The Oregon grape holly is quite hardy here though it may lose its purplish red leaves in a severe winter – it remains shiny under an early and lasting snow cover. In addition, it has yellow flowers and dark bluish-black fruit.

Hydrangea shrubs flower until heavy frost.

Winter Protection

Winter creates problems for shrubs and trees. Unlike people, trees, shrubs, evergreens and roses cannot be kept warm by wrapping them tightly.

But like people, they may be smothered if wrapped in sheets of plastic that are virtually airtight. Plastic can also promote heat buildup. Plants in such situations cook by day and freeze by night.

This does not mean, however, that other kinds of wrapping are dangerous or of no use. Springy plastic netting that looks like the mesh bags used for onions or of the type used to pack Christmas trees for transportation, can be an ideal way to protect upright-growing evergreens from having branches bent down or broken off by heavy, wet snow or freezing rain.

It usually takes two people to apply plastic netting. One holds the branches upright, while the second slips the mesh over the tree. The holes in the mesh let air pass through freely, but the form and strength of the plastic will keep the tree shapely in most situations.

It stands to reason that you should not shovel snow on to foundation evergreens. Sometimes, however, roof snow will slide down and damage the plants. The only way to avoid this is to erect snow sheds that cover the plants. But this protection is costly and labour-intensive. It's better to take your chances, and prune or replace the evergreen should such damage occur. Plant inside or beyond where the roof snow lands.

Also, it is easy enough to arrange not to shovel snow or machine-blow it on top of shrubs and evergreens. Let the lawn take the mounds. Damage to it, if any, can be fixed much more easily and cheaply.

Do not use salt or calcium chloride where it will be shovelled or drain on to the area above plant roots. Salt itself is most harmful and works in several ways to damage plants. First of all, any direct spray from nearby roads coats bark, twigs and evergreen needles. This, in turn, literally sucks the moisture out of the living plant tissue.

It also damages the soil structure, and when taken up by plant roots, interferes with plant nutrition – it appears that plants absorb it instead of potassium. Try urea or ammonium nitrate as snow melters. But if you have no other choice, a high board fence is probably the most effective barrier.

Some plants are much more susceptible than others. Fortunately for us, many trees and shrubs popular in southern Ontario gardens are salt-hardy, including the seemingly fragile paper birch and Colorado blue spruce.

But plants we grow that have a very low salt tolerance include our native red maple, sugar maple, balsam fir, American hornbeam, shagbark hickory, hackberry, the common red osier dogwood, yellow-twig dogwood, winged euonymous, black walnut, common privet, Hopa crabapple, Norway spruce, red pine, white pine, Douglas fir, American (big leafed) linden, eastern hemlock, and the native high bush cranberry.

These plants are to be avoided or replaced if their location is likely to get salt spray or salt-laden clearings from the walks and drives.

Plants such as yew and some kinds of boxwood and euonymous are perfectly hardy here. But when the ground is frozen their roots cannot take up moisture. So if the plants are exposed to the March winds and sun, their leaves are gradually dried out; they turn brown as they would in a drought, and look dead or actually drop off. Most plants will recover with the new growing season.

DO NOT USE SALT OR CALCIUM CHLORIDE WHERE IT WILL BE SHOVELLED OR DRAIN TO AREAS ABOVE PLANT ROOTS. IT DAMAGES THE SOIL STRUCTURE.

Though Japanese and hybrid yews are less susceptible, many plantings near roads are protected by burlap. This proves effective, but the down side is that you have to look at burlap instead of green needles during the winter months.

Formal hedges may also suffer snow damage. Branches and twigs are brittle in the cold and freezing rain; just a heavy snowfall can cave in sections.

While you can't prevent all damage, appropriate pruning can avert most problems. Rather than having the pruned hedge top a rectangular shape – flat and parallel to the ground – it should be rounded on top, which not only helps shed snow, but also, during the growing season, prevents the lower leaves from being shaded which is the most common reason for hedges to have thin foliage or to be bare near the ground.

Another way to help protect plants against winter desiccation is to make sure they have plenty of water available to their roots as the ground freezes. This is particularly important if the fall has been exceptionally dry or in those locations where plants are growing near a house wall and/or under an overhang.

Pruning

Proper pruning improves the health and appearance of your trees, shrubs, and evergreens.

There are a variety of reasons for pruning:

1. To help plants recover from root injuries following transplanting.
2. To remove or restrict unwanted growth.
3. To encourage or train growth where it is desired.
4. To remove dead or injured wood or to repair damage.
5. To alter the natural form of the plant.
6. To rejuvenate old shrubs.
7. To promote bloom, fruit production, colourful twigs or foliage.

TREES Most deciduous trees should be pruned late in March or early April before their leaves come out. Fruit-bearing trees and vines, usually pruned at this time, have unique pruning requirements (see page 86). As well, maples, birches, walnuts and the rare yellow-wood bleed profusely when the sap is rising in early spring. The time to prune them is when they are in full leaf – usually June in southern Ontario – but ahead of summer's heat. This allows any new sprouts that appear time to harden before killing frost.

Successful pruning requires thought. It is important to visualize the finished tree before you begin. Your object is to remove weak or unattractive branches and to promote balanced growth throughout the plant. It is not good enough just to go out and hack away. Sloppy pruning technique can result in branches splitting and tearing off a strip of bark, sometimes all the way to the ground. Nor should pegs be left on the trunk. These stubs may be a delight to tree-climbing children but are no favour to the tree, which cannot grow healing bark over them. Leave only a very slight protuberance, cleaning away with a sharp knife any signs of rot or torn bark. The latest theory is that you shouldn't paint the wound. It seems that although painting makes the gardener feel better, it doesn't help and may even hinder the tree's ability to heal itself.

Pruning to increase structural strength should start when the tree is young. Narrow or "Y"-angled crotches are weak and should be cut off as soon as possible. The strongest crotch is one in which the branch comes out horizontally from the central leader.

Most pruning techniques for

Shagbark hickory

ornamentals are similar to those for fruit-bearing trees. See "Pruning Rules" on page 89.

SHRUBS When shrubs are neglected for several years, they tend to become ragged looking and have a reduced bloom. Thinning out old, dense and weak wood allows light penetration and improves the plant. Often a three-to-four year program of rejuvenation is required, removing one-third of the old wood each year, until by the fourth year, the shrub is completely renewed and producing a more uniform crop of flowers and fruit. Some shrubs that are vigorous and originate from a crown at soil level can be cut back to a height of 15 cm (6 in.). Forsythia and dogwood fall into this group.

EVERGREENS that accept shearing or shaping should be done in early spring to keep their new growth within bounds. Examples are broadleafed evergreens such as euonymous and boxwood, and needle evergreens such as cedar and yew, which do not normally grow into a cone or single trunk specimen by themselves. Old-fashioned grass clippers work well for this task.

Overgrown foundation plants may be reshaped by removing even big branches underneath the point where a small fresh twig shoot appears. They will look ugly for a few years, but will recover eventually. However, foundation evergreens have a limited lifespan as decorative plants, and many a house would look better with ugly, overgrown old shrubs removed and replaced with shapely, vigorous new ones. These are available in containers and may be replaced at will any time in the growing season.

Prune other decorative pines and spruces by nipping out part of the current year's soft new growth with a thumbnail. Reducing the leader or main new shoot by up to two-thirds of its length reduces the space between annual whorls of branches and thus makes the plant denser.

If you cut out the leader entirely take care to monitor the tree to make sure it doesn't become a two-headed monster. Sometimes this happens naturally. In such a case, either remove the shorter and weaker of the new leaders, or reduce them both by three-quarters so that one dominant centre shoot emerges.

PRUNING TOOLS Hand-held pruning shears work on branches up to 1.5 cm (1/2 in.) in diameter. Long-handled pruners or loppers will allow you to remove branches up to about 5 cm (2 in.) in size. The jaws of a pair of loppers have one sharp and one square edge. The cleanest cuts are achieved by positioning the tool so that the sharp-edged jaw is at the bottom of the branch to be cut.

For larger branches, use a pruning saw with widely spaced teeth that will not bind in wet wood. Cut in three stages. Make a first cut from the bottom up about 2–3 in. from the trunk; make a second cut from the bottom nearby but slightly closer to the trunk. At some point the weight of the branch will snap the wood between the cuts and it will drop. Make a final cut from above as close to the trunk as possible. Large branches should be tied before cutting, so they can be lowered gently and safely to the ground after being cut.

Weeping Nootka falsecypress

 Trees

RED KING MAPLE GOES GREEN

Q: On our front lawn is what used to be a beautiful red king maple. The leaves no longer appear with the dark blood-red colour we have admired for years. The tree is about 30 years old. This change has come about in the last five or six years. The tree is quite a bit larger than the nurseryman who sold it to us predicted. I see other red maples nearby that still have red leaves. What happened to ours? Can we do anything to change the colour back to the original red? – *A.F., Scarborough*

A: I don't think there is anything practical you can do to change the leaf colour again. The so-called Crimson King and Royal Red are grafted versions of the European or Norway maple and aren't close relations of the native red maple. All such grafted trees technically are a part of the original mutation on a cultivar called Schwedler's maple noticed in Orleans, France and first introduced into North America in 1948. Schwedler's, which is closely related to the ordinary green-leafed Norway maple, has new red leaves that turn green in summer.

The mutation discovered on a nursery tree in Orleans had a branch on which leaves kept their blood-red colour all season. Pieces were taken and grafted onto seedling Norway maples. This practice has been continued today. Either your tree reverted to its original and more stable form, or a root sprout from below the graft was allowed to grow up as the main trunk. The green-leafed maples (and Schwedler's) are more vigorous and bigger growing. Sometimes both forms appear as co-existing trunks. Unpruned, the green-leafed form will dominate.

Either enjoy the tree you have or plant a new red-leafed cultivar to replace it, cutting down the older tree as the new one gains size.

TREE ROOTS AND CHANGING GRADES

Q: We have a 5 m (16 ft.) mountain ash that is 14 years old. In spring, its blossoms and tiny green leaves didn't open properly. We wonder if it's a fungus attack. The tree is surrounded by interlocking bricks except for a 45 cm (18 in.) square opening. We punched six holes and filled them with lawn fertilizer (21:12:6) and watered heavily. Any advice?

– *L.N.F., Downsview*

A: You didn't specifically say so, but I gather the bricks are new. They must have been laid on a minimum of 5 cm (2 in.) and preferably 15 cm (6 in.) of soft sand. Presumably this was all done over the existing grade, thus burying hair roots the tree developed to gather water, minerals and oxygen. Heavy watering would only compound the problem. Some mountain ashes grow root sprouts and/or suckers from the base so you may be able to save it.

In general, established tree roots should not have their grade changed. Unless you are prepared to remove the interlocking bricks and sand bed, you can only wait to see if the tree survives into next spring.

Mountain ash

 **Trees** CONTINUED

PUSSYWILLOW TREE

Q: We have a pussywillow tree about 1.5 m (5 ft.) from our foundation wall. It is about 9 m (30 ft.) high. I hear there are problems with the roots of such trees. Can they cause problems to foundations and water and sewage pipes? How high will they grow? – *R.R., Whitby*

A: As a general rule, poplars and willows should not be planted within 15 m (50 ft.) of a foundation wall or underground pipe. Exceptions to this rule include the dwarf Arctic willow and dwarf pussywillow. The pussywillows found at your local florist are *Salix caprea* which have large yellow catkins, but other willows are also given the common name pussy. In any case, 1.5 m (5 ft.) is far too close for a 9 m (30 ft.) shrub with vigorous roots. Confine such plants to the back and/or wet end of the yard if you grow them at all.

RED OAK AND GARDEN YIELD

Q: I planted a red oak about ten years ago that now covers about half my vegetable garden with its leaves. Vegetable production is poor. There is plenty of water, so I assume the oak is draining nutrients. Only early peas do well now. Would things improve if I built a raised vegetable bed? Would this kill the oak's roots? – *A.G.T., West Hill*

A: Oaks normally are taprooted rather than being surface feeders like maples. It is likely that shade is your problem. The fact that early peas do well tends to back this up. You can improve things by removing all but the top branches, but ultimately it is a choice between the shade tree and a good garden. Raising the depth of soil over tree roots can be fatal.

WHITE PINE

Q: We have a white pine tree growing on our front lawn. Last winter we put plastic netting around it, thinking it would protect it from wind and cold temperatures. But much of the tree has turned brown. The buds at the ends of the branches are alive, but the tree is a sad sight. Can you suggest anything to revitalize the tree? – *M.F., Toronto*

A: In a word, no. White pine is rare in the city as it does not do well in exposed situations or with urban pollution, root restriction, poor aeration and all the other ills of a forest tree in the city.
    It is also susceptible to winter burn.

Red oak

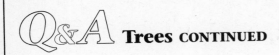

Q&A Trees CONTINUED

TRIMMING MAPLES

Q: I have six hard maples on the front of my lot. They are growing too fast. Can I trim their tops to slow growth and keep them to 6 m (20 ft.)? They are half that now. *– O.N., Sundridge*

A: It is possible using the European practice of pollarding which involves cutting back each year's growth, perhaps to the beheaded top of the trunk at the height you choose. I don't favour this technique because I think the resulting tree is ugly, with the new sprouts resembling reversed umbrellas at the top of a post.

It is far better to plant trees that are naturally small and then remove the sugar maples entirely. They are forest trees unsuitable for building lots.

If you still want a maple, get a nursery grown Amur river maple, which can be grown as a shrub or small tree with a maximum height of 6 m (20 ft.). It has small, deeply-cut leaves that turn a brilliant scarlet briefly in fall. New shoots are reddish in spring; leaves are a medium green with purplish twigs. Flowers are small and white, but fragrant winged seeds (keys) are bright red in summer. Cut out suckers and allow only one trunk to maintain a tree shape.

VANDALIZED SPRUCE

Q: Someone used a knife to cut off the top spike of my 1.5 m (5 ft.) silvery blue spruce. When I noticed the damage, sap was running out of the cut. I painted this with non-oily paint. Can you tell me if the damage will hurt the growth of the tree. Is there anything else I can do? *– P.E.D., Cambridge*

A: The newest information I have says that painting is neither helpful nor necessary. The sap or spruce gum usually seals cuts immediately and oxidizes to form a protective coating. The vandalism likely won't hurt the general health of the tree, but will make it bushier by encouraging more bud growth on lower branches. All such pruning reduces the height the tree will reach.

One or more of the ring of branches closest to where the top spike was cut will bend up and try to replace it. Very often two such branches will compete, producing a double-headed monstrosity. Your job will be to watch and pinch back the weaker one of the two if necessary.

I assume yours is a cultivar of the Colorado spruce, a tree which is extremely tough and hardy. It is unlikely to need any special watering or fertilizing, especially if it is grown in a well-maintained lawn.

Norway maple

Eastern redbud

Deciduous Tree Guide

COMMON NAME	BOTANICAL NAME	HARDINESS ZONE	HEIGHT	NOTES
HEDGE MAPLE	*Acer campestre*	Zone 5b	9 m 30 ft.	• Dense tree • Yellow fall colour • Tolerates heavy pruning • Tolerates alkaline soil • Few pests
AMUR MAPLE	*Acer ginnala*	Zone 2b	9 m 30 ft.	• Dense tree • Red fall colour • Tolerates heavy pruning, most soils • Becomes shrubby unless kept to one stem • Few pests
JAPANESE MAPLE	*Acer Palmatum*	Zone 6	5 m 16 ft.	• Red and cut-leaved cultivars • Red fall colour • Very slow growing • Sun or partial shade • Avoid exposed locations • Moist loam soil
STRIPED MAPLE	*Acer pensylvanicum*	Zone 2b	10 m 33 ft.	• Green and white striped bark • Yellowish fall colour • Thrives in shade
NORWAY MAPLE	*Acer platanoides*	Zone 5	15–23 m 50–75 ft.	• Several forms and leaf colours available • Casts dense shade • Tolerates pollution and most soils
SILVER MAPLE	*Acer saccharinum*	Zone 2b	18–27 m 60–90 ft.	• Cut-leaf variety available • Underside of leaves light green • Fast growing • Thrives in moist to wet soil
SUGAR MAPLE	*Acer saccharum*	Zone 4	18–27 m 60–90 ft.	• Subtle yellow flowers in early spring • Yellow to orange-red fall colour • Casts moderate shade • Not tolerant of pollution • Moist loam soil
ALLEGHANY SERVICEBERRY	*Amelanchier laevis*	Zone 3b	9 m 30 ft.	• White flowers in early May • Tasty red fruit • Orange to red fall colour • Smooth grey bark • Thrives in sun or shade
PAPER BIRCH	*Betula papyrifera*	Zone 2	15–23 m 50–75 ft.	• Distinct white bark • Yellow fall colour • Fast growing • Moderately short-lived • Full sun • Best on moist loam soil
EUROPEAN WHITE BIRCH	*Betula pendula*	Zone 2	9–12 m 30–40 ft.	• Distinct white bark, slightly drooping form • Yellow fall colour • Fast growing • Short-lived • Full sun • Best on moist loam soil

Deciduous Tree Guide
CONTINUED

COMMON NAME	BOTANICAL NAME	HARDINESS ZONE	HEIGHT	NOTES
BLUEBEECH (MUSCLEWOOD)	*Carpinus caroliniana*	Zone 3b	10 m 33 ft.	• Orange to red fall colour • Muscle-like grey bark • Thrives in shade • Very hard wood • Slow to grow after transplanting • Few pests
NORTHERN CATALPA	*Catalpa speciosa*	Zone 5b	12–18 m 40–60 ft.	• Orange-white flowers in late June • Long slender pods • Large heart-shaped leaves, dense shade • Short-lived • Tolerates dry soil but best on moist loam
EASTERN REDBUD	*Cercis canadensis*	Zone 6b	9 m 30 ft.	• Pink flowers in May • Yellow fall colour • Sun or partial shade • Moist loam soil
YELLOWWOOD	*Cladrastis lutea*	Zone 4b	11 m 36 ft.	• White flowers in June • Red fruit • Purple-red fall colour • Horizontal branching • Thrives in sun or filtered shade • Moist loam soil
ALTERNATE-LEAF DOGWOOD	*Cornus alternifolia*	Zone 3b	6 m 20 ft.	• Small purple fruit • Orange to red fall colour • Horizontal branching • Thrives in sun or filtered shade • Moist loam soil
FLOWERING DOGWOOD	*Cornus florida*	Zone 6b	10 m 33 ft.	• White flowers in late May, red fruit • Flowers rare outside Zone 7 • Purple-red fall colour • Horizontal branching • Thrives in sun or filtered shade • Moist loam soil
CORNELIAN-CHERRY DOGWOOD	*Cornus mas*	Zone 5b	7 m 23 ft.	• Small yellow flowers in late April • Red fruit • Large shrub or small tree • Sun or filtered shade
TURKISH HAZEL	*Corylus colurna*	Zone 5	15 m 50 ft.	• Broad pyramid form • Scaly bark • Tolerates pollution and moist soils • Few pests
WASHINGTON HAWTHORN	*Crataegus phaenopyrum*	Zone 5	7 m 23 ft.	• White flowers in June • Red fruit which lasts into winter • Glossy green leaves • Thorns
RUSSIAN OLIVE	*Elaeagnus angustifolia*	Zone 2b	10 m 33 ft.	• Small yellow flowers in June • Silver green leaves and fruit • Grows well in infertile soil • Tolerates pruning and highway salt

Deciduous Tree Guide
CONTINUED

COMMON NAME	BOTANICAL NAME	HARDINESS ZONE	HEIGHT	NOTES
EUROPEAN BEECH	*Fagus sylvatica*	Zone 6	15–24 m 50–80 ft.	• Yellowish-bronze fall colour • Moderately slow growing • Hard to transplant • Smooth grey bark • Tolerates heavy pruning when started young • Moist loam soil
WHITE ASH	*Fraxinus americana*	Zone 3b	15–23 m 50–75 ft.	• Purplish fall colour • Fast growing • Tolerates moist to wet soils
GREEN ASH	*Fraxinus pennsylvanica lanceolata*	Zone 2b	12–15 m 40–50 ft.	• Yellowish fall colour • Fast growing • Tolerates moist to wet soils
GINKGO (MAIDENHAIR)	*Ginkgo biloba*	Zone 4	12–18 m 40–60 ft.	• Fan-shaped leaves • Yellow fall colour • Long lived in its native Orient • Few pests • Purchase a male clone to avoid unsightly fruiting
THORNLESS HONEYLOCUST	*Gleditsia triacanthos inermis*	Zone 4	15–20 m 50–65 ft.	• Yellow fall colour • Fruitless • Casts very light shade • Tolerates dry soil but best on moist loam
WITCH HAZEL	*Hamamelis virginiana*	Zone 4b	5 m 16 ft.	• Yellow flowers in October • Yellow fall colour • Large shrub or small tree • Thrives in sun or shade • Moist loam soil
TULIPTREE	*Liriodendron tulpiifera*	Zone 5b	12–24 m 40–80 ft.	• Greenish-yellow tulip-like flowers • Yellow fall colour • Somewhat hard to transplant in large size • Moist loam soil
STAR MAGNOLIA	*Magnolia stellata*	Zone 5b	5 m 16 ft.	• White, fragrant flowers in early May • Bronze fall colour • Slow growing shrub or small tree • Full sun • Moist loam soil
SAUCER MAGNOLIA	*Magnolia x soulangiana*	Zone 5b	8 m 25 ft.	• White, pink or purple flowers in May • Full sun • Avoid exposure • Moist loam soil
CRABAPPLE	*Malus*	Zones 2–5	3–8 m 10–25 ft.	• Many cultivars with white, pink or red flowers and yellow or red fruit • Select for disease resistance • Rosy Bloom and Dolgo recommended cultivars • Full sun • Moist soils

Deciduous Tree Guide
CONTINUED

COMMON NAME	BOTANICAL NAME	HARDINESS ZONE	HEIGHT	NOTES
HOPHORNBEAM	*Ostrya virginiana*	Zone 3	10 m 33 ft.	• Yellow to orange fall colour • Scaly bark • Thrives in shade • Very hard wood • Slow to grow after transplanting • Few pests
LONDON PLANETREE	*Platanus x acerifolia*	Zone 6	18 m 60 ft.	• Yellowish-brown fall colour • Showy green under bark after peeling • Broad massive tree when old • Tolerates heavy pruning when started young • Tolerates many soils
AMUR CHOKE CHERRY	*Prunus maackii*	Zone 2b	8 m 25 ft.	• White flowers in late May • Small black fruit • Yellow fall colour • Handsome bark • Full sun • Well-drained soil
SARGENT CHERRY	*Prunus sargentii*	Zone 5	8 m 25 ft.	• Pink flowers in May • Orange to red fall colour • Vase-shaped form • Handsome bark • Full sun • Well-drained soil
RED OAK	*Quercus rubra*	Zone 3	12–25 m 40–80 ft.	• Red through brown fall colour • Strong wood • Well-drained soil
LAUREL WILLOW	*Salix pentandra*	Zone 1	12 m 40 ft.	• Glossy green leaves • Tolerates heavy pruning • Fast growing • Thrives in wet soil
JAPANESE PAGODATREE	*Sophora japonica*	Zone 6b	8–18 m 25–60 ft.	• Creamy white, fragrant flowers in August • Green twigs • Casts moderate to light shade • Tolerates urban conditions
MOUNTAIN ASH	*Sorbus*	Zones 3–5	8–11 m 25–35 ft.	• Several species • White flowers in late May • Orange-red fruit • Disease susceptible • Full sun
JAPANESE TREE LILAC	*Syringa reticulata*	Zone 2	8 m 25 ft.	• White flowers in June • Handsome cherry-like bark • Full sun • Tolerates pollution
LITTLELEAF LINDEN	*Tilia cordata*	Zone 3	12–15 m 40–50 ft.	• Yellowish, fragrant flowers • Broad pyramid form, no fall colour • Tolerates heavy pruning when started young • Tolerates pollution

Courtesy of Ontario Ministry of Agriculture and Food

TREES AND SHRUBS

Evergreen Tree Guide

COMMON NAME	BOTANICAL NAME	HARDINESS ZONE	HEIGHT	NOTES
WHITE FIR	Abies concolor	Zone 4	18–30 m 60–100 ft.	• Grey-green needles • Moderate growth rate • Tolerates dry soil but best with adequate moisture • Tolerates moderate pollution
DWARF ARIZONA FIR	Abies lasiocarpa 'Compacta'	Zone 3	6 m 20 ft.	• Blue-green needles • Slow growing • Compact • Tolerates dry soil
WEEPING NOOTKA FALSECYPRESS	Chamaecyparis nootkatensis 'Pendula'	Zone 6b	24–30 m 80–100 ft.	• Medium green needles • Moderate growth rate • Distinctive appearance with weeping lateral branches
JUNIPER	Juniperus	Zones 3–4	5–8 m 15–25 ft.	• Many species and cultivars • Very narrow to broad pyramid shape • Bluish-green needles • Tolerates dry soil and pollution
DAWN REDWOOD	Metasequoia glyptostroboides	Zone 6	18 m 60 ft.	• Medium green needles shed each fall • Fast growing • Fine texture • No insects or pests • Moist loam soil • Tolerates pollution
NORWAY SPRUCE	Picea abies	Zone 2b	20–30 m 65–100 ft.	• Dark green needles • Long cones • Moderately fast growth • Tolerates urban conditions
DWARF ALBERTA SPRUCE	Picea glauca 'Conica'	Zone 4	3 m 10 ft.	• Light green needles • Very compact dwarf pyramid • Very slow growing • May winterburn in very exposed site
SERBIAN SPRUCE	Picea omorika	Zone 3b	20–30 m 65–100 ft.	• Needles dark green above and white below • Moderate growth rate • Narrowest of the spruces • May winterburn in very exposed site
BLUE COLORADO SPRUCE	Picea pungens glauca	Zone 2	15–25 m 50–80 ft.	• Blue-green needles • Several cultivars with bright blue needles • Moderate growth rate • Tolerates dry soil and highway salt
SWISS STONE PINE	Pinus cembra	Zone 2	10–20 m 30–65 ft.	• Dark green needles • Narrow pyramid • Slow growing • Best on loam soil
AUSTRIAN PINE	Pinus nigra	Zone 4	12–20 m 40–65 ft.	• Long, dark green needles • Moderately fast growing • Extremely broad pyramid • Tolerates pollution and highway salt

Blue Colorado spruce

Evergreen Tree Guide
CONTINUED

COMMON NAME	BOTANICAL NAME	HARDINESS ZONE	HEIGHT	NOTES
RED PINE	*Pinus resinosa*	Zone 2b	15–30 m 50–100 ft.	• Needles dark green in summer and lighter in winter • Reddish bark • Moderate growth rate • Thrives on dry sandy soil
WHITE PINE	*Pinus strobus*	Zone 2b	20–30 m 65–100 ft.	• Long, soft needles • Moderately fast growing • Huge tree with long cones • Poor growth on wet alkaline soil • Damaged by pollution and highway salt
SCOTS PINE	*Pinus sylvestris*	Zone 2	10–25 m 30–80 ft.	• Medium green needles • Moderate growth rate • Orange bark when mature • Poor growth in wet soil • Self-seeds prodigiously
WHITE CEDAR	*Thuja occidentalis*	Zone 2	5–13 m 15–40 ft.	• Dark green needles • Moderate growth rate • Narrow form • Tolerates heavy shearing • Not tolerant of highway salt, dog urine
EASTERN HEMLOCK	*Tsuga canadensis*	Zone 4	18–23 m 60–75 ft.	• Small dark green needles • Moderate growth rate • Branch tips nodding • Thrives in shade • Cool moist soil • Tolerates heavy pruning when started young

Courtesy of Ontario Ministry of Agriculture and Food

Dwarf Alberta spruce

 **Shrubs**

QUINCES

Q: Can all quinces grown on shrubs purchased from nurseries be safely used in making jam? We have prostrate and upright ornamental quince shrubs that are covered with fruit that I would like to pick and make into jam. When are they considered ripe? *– B.M., Palgrave*

A: The fruit from ornamental quinces may be used for preserves or dried and used as aromatic sachets in your linen cupboards. However, these ornamentals are not as good for preserves as varieties grown for their fruit.

The true quince's botanical name is *Cydonia* and is closely related to apples and pears. Its fruit is useless raw. When cooked, it has a spicy flavour and is highly aromatic. The commonly available species are *oblonga* and *sinensis*. The fruit is ripe when it turns yellow in the fall.

The so-called flowering quince is another genus altogether – *Chaenomeles*. The species *speciosa* which is valued for its flower has fruit that, although tasteless, adds pectin for jelling other fruits.

So if you want to make classical quince preserves, be sure your fruit comes from one of the varieties of *Cydonia*.

ALPINE CURRANT BUSHES

Q: I put in several Alpine currant bushes last spring without knowing anything about this shrub. Are the berries edible? What fertilizer should I use? How should I prune? *– B.A.B., Toronto*

A: The Alpine currant is rated to hardiness zone 2, which means it can thrive on the prairies. It thrives in urban environments and is especially useful for deciduous hedges. It should be clipped in late winter or very early spring before leaves are out, when you can still see the framework of the bushes. Male and female flowers aren't found on the same plant. Only female plants bear fruit which is ornamental and inedible. Female plants should not be planted as they are alternate hosts of blister rust, a disease of white pines. The Alpine currant plant is related to edible currants and gooseberries.

Little if any fertilization is required. Spray only if heavy insect infestation is observed.

LILAC FERTILIZER

Q: Is there a fertilizer that is particularly suited to lilacs? *– L.L.D., Markham*

A: Lilac is not a heavy feeder and does better in alkaline soil. New plants need watering whenever rains fail, but are drought-resistant once established. Bone meal, wood ashes and/or a low nitrogen (first figure) fertilizer such as grade 6:24:24 help bring maturity and blooming. A teaspoon of 6:24:24 is sufficient for a new transplant; a half-cup to a full cup for an established bush.

Lilac

Shrub Guide

COMMON NAME	BOTANICAL NAME	HARDINESS ZONE	HEIGHT	NOTES
ARALIA	*Acanthopanax*	Zone 5	2 m 6 ft.	• Densely branched, spiny shrub with bright green foliage • Can be used as a thorny barrier
BEAUTY BUSH	*Kolkwitzia*	Zone 5	3 m 10 ft.	• A large arching shrub with oval leaves • Turns reddish in fall • Pink flowers in June • Deciduous
BLUEBEARD	*Caryopteris*	Zone 6	1 m 3 ft.	• "Blue Mist Speria" small mound of silvery green leaves • Blossoms in late summer with tight clusters of dark blue flowers • Deciduous
BUCKEYE	*Aesculus*	Zone 4	3 m 10 ft.	• A good lawn specimen but needs room • Spreads by underground suckers • Most plants are wider than they are high • Long white flowers in the summer • Deciduous
BUTTERFLY BUSH	*Buddleia*	Zone 5	2 m 6 ft.	• Large, spikelike clusters of purple flowers in August • Fragrant and attracts butterflies • Deciduous
BUFFALOBERRY	*Shepherdia*	Zone 1	4 m 13 ft.	• Very hardy, with silver foliage • Shrub produces scarlet berries but needs both sexes; so plant several shrubs in a clump • Deciduous
DAPHNE	*Daphne*	Zone 5	1 m 3 ft.	• "Silveredge" low shrub with deep green leaves edged in cream • Has fragrant, pink, star-shaped flowers in late spring • Deciduous
DEUTZIA	*Deutzia*	Zone 5	1 m 3 ft.	• A low, compact shrub with white flowers in early June • Deciduous
DOGWOOD	*Cornus*	Zone 3	2 m 6 ft.	• Many varieties with different leaves, flowers, fruit and bark • Some varieties more tender; check hardiness • Deciduous
ELDER	*Sambucus*	Zone 3	4 m 13 ft.	• Large shrubs with coloured foliage • Some have showy white flowers with edible fruit • Deciduous
FORSYTHIA	*Forsythia*	Zone 6	3 m 10 ft.	• A large vigorous shrub with bright yellow flowers in late spring • Hardy "Ottawa" variety will survive in zone 4 • Deciduous

Shrub Guide
CONTINUED

COMMON NAME	BOTANICAL NAME	HARDINESS ZONE	HEIGHT	NOTES
FOTHERGILLA	*Fothergilla*	Zone 6	2 m 6 ft.	• Large spreading shrub with long spikes of white flowers in late spring • Spectacular autumn leaf colour of red and orange • Prefers acid soil • Deciduous
HAZEL	*Corylus*	Zone 5	3 m 10 ft.	• "Corkscrew Hazel" has twisted and curled branches • "Purple Hazel" has dark purple foliage • Deciduous
HOLLY	*Ilex*	Zone 3	2 m 6 ft.	• Has glossy, oblong, leaves with spines on sides and tip • Bright red berries on the female plant • Evergreen
HONEYSUCKLE	*Lonicera*	Zone 2	3 m 10 ft.	• A large spreading shrub with fragrant bell-shaped blossoms in early summer • Flowers can be white, red, pink or yellow • Fleshy berries attract birds • Deciduous
HYDRANGEA	*Hydrangea*	Zone 3	1 m 3 ft.	• Has large toothed leaves, large flower clusters • White, pink or blue flowers throughout the summer • Deciduous
JUNIPER	*Juniper*	Zone 2	1–2 m 3–6 ft.	• Many sizes and shapes • Foliage varies from bright green to silvery blue • Evergreen
LILAC	*Syringia*	Zone 2	3 m 10 ft.	• Well known for intensely fragrant flowers in late spring • Blooms are small and tubular but appear in large long clusters • Flower can be pale violet, purple, pink and white • Deciduous
PHOTINIA	*Photinia*	Zone 5	4 m 14 ft.	• Shapely shrub with leathery leaves that turn a bright red in the fall • White flower clusters in early summer • Bright red fruit that lasts into the fall • Deciduous
POTENTILLA	*Potentilla*	Zone 2	1 m 3 ft.	• "Cinquefoils" are low-growing shrubs with erect branched stems • Single rose-like yellow flowers in many clusters throughout the summer • Deciduous
QUINCE	*Chaenomeles*	Zone 5	1 m 3 ft.	• Low spreading shrub with slightly angular branches • Bright red flowers grow along the stem almost at the same time as the leaves come out in May • Fruit sometimes used in preserves • Deciduous

Shrub Guide

COMMON NAME	BOTANICAL NAME	HARDINESS ZONE	HEIGHT	NOTES
ROSE-OF-SHARON	*Hibiscus*	Zone 6	3–4 m 10–14 ft.	• Spectacular large flowers from midsummer to fall • Single or double flowers in a wide range of colours • Deciduous
ST. JOHN'S-WORT	*Hypericum*	Zone 3	1 m 3 ft.	• Long-lasting, cup-shaped flowers in clusters of bright yellow • Semi-evergreen leaves turn purplish in autumn • Evergreen
SMOKE TREE	*Cotinus*	Zone 5	3 m 10 ft.	• A massive shrub with large clusters of minute fruit like a cloud of smoke • Foliage and smoke-like flowers both purple • Deciduous
SNOWBERRY	*Symphoricarpos*	Zone 2	1 m 3 ft.	• A graceful branching shrub with clusters of snow-white berries in the fall • Can withstand city smog • Very hardy • Deciduous
SPIREA	*Spirea*	Zone 2	1 m 3 ft.	• Many varieties with flat clusters of flowers • Colours include white, pink, purple, or red • "Anthony Waterer" has mottled red, pink and white leaves • Deciduous
TAMARIX	*Tamarix*	Zone 3	4 m 13 ft.	• Large open shrub with light feathery foliage • Graceful plumes of pink flowers in late summer • Deciduous
VIBURNUM	*Viburnum*	Zones 2–6	2–4 m 6–14 ft.	• Many varieties, some more hardy than others • Flowers usually white • Flowering periods vary • Some fruit lasts well into winter and attracts birds • Deciduous
WEIGELAS	*Weigelas*	Zone 4	2 m 6 ft.	• "Bristol Ruby" has masses of red blossoms in June and then again in summer • Other varieties have white or pink flowers • Deciduous
WILLOW	*Salix*	Zone 4	1–4 m 3–13 ft.	• "Pussy Willow" is the most common • Has fast growing brittle branches with catkins appearing at the same time as the leaves in the spring • All willows do best in moist soil or beside streams • Deciduous
WITCH HAZEL	*Hamamelis*	Zone 6	3–5 m 10–16 ft.	• A tall shrub with leaves that turn yellow or red in the fall • Flowers are shades of red, yellow or orange • Blooms in very early spring • Deciduous

Vine Guide

COMMON NAME	BOTANICAL NAME	HARDINESS ZONE	HEIGHT	NOTES
BITTERSWEET	*Celastrus*	Zone 5	8 m 25 ft.	• Has twining stems with oblong leaves • Masses of orange-red berries in fall
CLEMATIS	*Clematis*	Zone 5	3–5 m 10–16 ft.	• Has large showy cup-shaped flowers June to August • Flower colours range from white to yellow, red, pink, purple and blue • Has twining leaf stalks • Needs partial shade • Roots must be covered and kept cool and moist
CLIMBING HONEYSUCKLE	*Lonicera*	Zone 3	3 m 10 ft.	• Evergreen • "Dropmore Scarlet" is a hardy vine with rosy-orange trumpet-shaped flowers in midsummer • Has twining stems and attractive berries • Can be grown in containers on decks and balconies
CLIMBING HYDRANGEA	*Hydrangea*	Zone 5	7 m 22 ft.	• Slow for first 2 years, then rapidly covers a wall or fence • Flat clusters of white flowers in late June • Clings by rootlets that grow from stems
DUTCHMAN'S PIPE	*Aristolochia*	Zone 6	7 m 22 ft.	• A twining vine used as a dense screen • Yellowish-brown pipe-shaped flowers with long rounded leaves
IVY	*Hedera*	Zone 6	10 m 30 ft.	• Evergreen • Clings by rootlets that grow from stem • Dark green leaves will remain through winter if on protected north or east wall
SILVER-LACE VINE	*Polygonum*	Zone 6	10 m 30 ft.	• A twining vine that requires little care • Has lacy white blossoms in late summer
TRUMPET VINE	*Campsis*	Zone 6	8 m 25 ft.	• Clings by rootlets that grow from stems • Has many scarlet trumpet-shaped flowers in midsummer
WISTERIA	*Wisteria*	Zone 6	5 m 16 ft.	• A strong twining vine with large leaves • Has long chains of white, violet or purple flowers • Flowers are fragrant and develop long seed-pods in fall

Clematis

HEDGES

Formal hedges provide privacy and protection, absorb noise, soften wind, act as a screen to separate parts of the garden and serve as a backdrop to flower borders. But be forewarned: hedges take a long time to grow and require regular maintenance and clipping.

If you need to keep pedestrian traffic off your lawn, a hedge can do the job or mask a chain-link fence by leafing out to cover wire and poles. A very low hedge, such as Arctic blue willow, can establish the boundaries of different activity areas on your property, for example marking off a children's play area. If you require a slightly taller hedge that is particularly adapted to city environments, consider the alpine currant. It is grown not for its fruit, but for its rich green leaves, its pollution tolerance, and its ability to sprout new leaves even in mid-summer.

The choice of hedging is very wide indeed. You can use prickly bushes such as shrub roses, gooseberry and raspberry, though in the case of raspberry, be prepared for suckers to show up in adjoining lawns or flower beds. Hardy forsythia, such as Ottawa or Northern

Gold varieties, will stand very cold winters and still bloom. Lilac, speria, hydrangea and other flowering shrubs are best used as informal hedges, i.e. unclipped and allowed to grow to full height. These and other flowering shrubs are listed in the chart on page 77. If you mix plants within the same hedge, choose those that grow to approximately the same size.

At one time common pines and spruces were recommended for hedging, but the centres of trees used this way eventually die because of the severe clipping of all new growth required for hedge use. As well, full-size trees should not be used as hedging unless you have a full-time gardener on hand to keep them clipped.

In milder areas, hybrid boxwood makes a good broad-leafed evergreen hedge, though the individual

Hardy flowering forsythias make colourful hedge plants capable of withstanding extreme winter temperatures.

bushes are expensive to buy. Box-wood does well in shady spots, as do Japanese and hybrid yews. Boxwood and yew can be frequently clipped without damage and can be kept at any height from 1–2 m (3–6 ft.). Two other attractive but expensive hedge evergreens are the dwarf Serbian spruce, a pretty, upright evergreen with white lines on the underside of its needles, and the nest spruce, which never needs pruning. Some forms of juniper, including the native red juniper, stand up well to clipping and can be maintained in moderately high hedges.

If an existing hedge has become thin at the bottom or too high on top, prune in the spring before the buds come out or spring growth starts. To lower a hedge, cut the main stems back to below the desired height, to allow for new growth and fresh leaves to cover the cuts. In shaping, make the top narrower than the bottom. This prevents top leaves from shading lower ones, and encourages foliage low down on the plant. The result is a thicker hedge. Round the top so that it will shed snow that would otherwise weigh down and bend or break the stems.

Treat hedges to an application of lawn fertilizer from the base of the plants out past their width on each side. If bordered by a lawn, give the grass near the hedge twice as many fertilizer applications as required by the rest of the lawn.

Mock orange blossoms

Hedge Plant Guide

Deciduous Plants				Evergreen Plants			
NAME	LIGHT	HEIGHT	HARDINESS ZONE	NAME	LIGHT	HEIGHT	HARDINESS ZONE
ALPINE CURRANT	○ ●	60–150 cm 2–5 ft.	Zone 2	ARBORVITAE white cedar	○ ◑	2–6 m 6–18 ft.	Zone 3
ARCTIC WILLOW	○	30–100 cm 1–3 ft.	Zone 3	BARBERRY	○ ◐	1–2 m 3–6 ft.	Zone 6
BEECH	○ ◐	2–5 m 6–15 ft.	Zone 6	BOXWOOD	○ ◐	1–2 m 3–6 ft.	Zone 5
BUCKTHORN	○ ◐	1–5 m 3–15 ft.	Zone 2	COTONEASTER	○	2–4 m 6–12 ft.	Zone 4
FORSYTHIA	○ ◐	1–3 m 3–9 ft.	Zone 4	EUONYMUS	○ ◐	1–4 m 3–12 ft.	Zone 5
HAWTHORN	○ ◐	1–3 m 3–9 ft.	Zone 2	FALSE CYPRESS	○	1–5 m 3–15 ft.	Zone 5
MANCHU CHERRY	○ ◐	1–5 m 3–15 ft.	Zone 2	FIRETHORN	○	1–4 m 3–12 ft.	Zone 6
MOCK ORANGE	○	1–2 m 3–6 ft.	Zone 3	HEMLOCK	○ ●	2–5 m 3–15 ft.	Zone 4
PEASHRUB	○	1–5 m 3–15 ft.	Zone 2	HOLLY	○ ◐	1–5 m 3–15 ft.	Zone 6
PRIVET	○	1–4 m 3–12 ft.	Zone 5	JUNIPER	○	1–5 m 3–15 ft.	Zone 4
RUSSIAN OLIVE	○ ◐	1–5 m 3–15 ft.	Zone 2	OREGON GRAPE	◐	1 m 3 ft.	Zone 5
SHRUB ROSES	○	1–2 m 3–6 ft.	Zone 3	SPRUCE	○	1–2 m 3–6 ft.	Zone 2
				WHITE PINE	○ ◐	1–2 m 3–6 ft.	Zone 2
				YEW	○ ●	1–5 m 3–15 ft.	Zone 4

Golden privet

KEY TO LIGHT REQUIREMENTS

○ Full Sun
○ ◑ Full Sun to Partial Shade
◑ Partial Shade
◐ ● Partial Shade to Shade
● Shade

FRUIT TREES

From Planting to Picking

Growing fruit trees in your home garden not only provides fresh fruit for the table, but also gives you beautiful ornamental trees and dense vines that act as protective screens and attract birds and wildlife to the backyard. Each kind of fruit tree, even each variety, has its own climatic adaptations and limitations. For example, the Delicious apple does best in the warmest districts of Ontario, whereas McIntosh excels in the cooler apple-growing regions.

SOIL Fruit trees will grow well on a wide range of soil types if the soil is adequately drained. Tile underdrains improve the natural drainage. Ditching and elevating the fruit-tree area above the lot level improves depth of rooting and water movement in heavy wet soils. Apricots, cherries and peaches are extremely sensitive to imperfectly drained soils and generally perform best on well-drained sandy loam soils. Apples, pears, plums and grapes will produce satisfactorily on either sand or clay loams. If you have a choice, plant on a hill. Cold air falls down slopes. Late spring frosts may kill flower beds or trees at the bottom of a hill without affecting those at the top.

Before planting, the soil should be thoroughly prepared by plowing or digging. Incorporation of organic matter is helpful, and is especially recommended with clay fill or very heavy soils. Well-rotted manure, compost, or peat moss will improve the soil structure and moisture-holding capacity. After planting, other organic materials such as old straw, hay, lawn clippings, sawdust and wood shavings may be applied as a mulch around the tree. The mulch, which should be deep enough to suppress weeds and conserve moisture, should be kept away from tree trunks, but may extend beyond the spread of the tree branches.

In general, fruit trees grown in good garden soil require little or no fertilizer until they are sufficiently mature to bear fruit and benefit

Ripening apricots

from light applications of fertilizers each year in early spring thereafter. Do not apply lime at any time, unless recommended by a soil specialist. Excessive levels or improper balance of nutrients can lead to poor quality fruit and serious winter injury or disease problems.

PLANTING The choice of nursery stock is important. Cheap plants are a poor investment. They may be poorly named, wrongly named, or partly dried out. The best way to obtain good trees is to buy directly from the nurseryman. Order your trees early, and specify the time when they should be delivered, or picked up at the nursery, and plant without delay. Well grown one-year-old trees are preferable to poorly grown two-year-old trees. Peach and cherry should be planted only as one-year trees. One-year trees should have a well grown main stem, while two-year trees should be well branched. Both should have good root systems.

It is usually safer to plant in the spring than in the fall, especially in the colder districts of Ontario. Sweet cherries or peaches usually cannot be grown north of Highway 7. Spring planting should be done as soon as the ground can be worked. Before planting the tree, trim off all damaged or dead root ends. Cut back to healthy root wood and bark. Dig a hole that is not too deep, but is large enough to accommodate the root system. Keep the top soil separate to place over and around the roots. Do not put fertilizer or fresh or strawy manure in the hole. Try to position the tree in your newly dug hole so that ground level relative to the trunk of the tree is no more than 5 cm (2 in.) above that of the nursery. Tamp the soil firmly around the roots. Leave a slight depression to catch rainwater or for watering during the tree's first summer. Water thoroughly after planting.

The transplanted tree should be severely pruned immediately after planting. (See "Pruning at Planting Time" later in this chapter.)

THINNING It is usual for a number of young fruits to drop off during the spring and early summer. This natural thinning is often referred to as the "June drop". With most varieties, too many fruits will likely still remain on the tree. Fruit thinning reduces limb breakage, increases fruit size, improves colour and quality of remaining fruit, and stimulates flower initiation for next year's crop. To be effective, thinning should be completed shortly after the "June drop".

PICKING The home fruit grower can leave fruit on the tree until it reaches peak quality. Fully mature fruit will not keep long. Most pear varieties should be picked when still firm, but somewhat green in colour. Pick apples when the green in their skin colour starts to turn yellow and the flesh texture changes from tough and pulpy to crisp and juicy. Cherries should be left until they reach their prime eating condition. Colour, firmness and flavour are useful indicators to determine when fruits are ready to pick.

INSECT CONTROL It is virtually impossible to grow insect-free fruit without a spray program that starts with a dormant oil spray and continues with a home orchard spray at the first showing of green leaves and every ten days thereafter. Follow package instructions. Wash and wear a mask and don't spray during open flower stages or within the days-to-harvest-time ban listed on the container.

Peach blossoms

Pruning Fruit Trees

Intelligent pruning yields marked improvement in the health, appearance and yield of your fruit trees. By reducing the number of growing points, growth is stimulated at those points that remain. Until a tree matures sufficiently to bear fruit, shape it by pruning lightly each year, removing narrow angles, dead or broken branches, and laterals that point into the centre of the tree or compete with the leader. Excessive pruning at this stage can delay fruiting.

Fruit-bearing trees must be pruned annually, removing weak or dead wood and crowded branches in the interior and top of the tree. Suckers, especially those arising from the rootstock, should be removed. Take your time when pruning, stepping back from the tree to consider each step and to visualize the finished project. Prune with a combination of the following objectives in mind:

1. To reduce the number of fruiting buds, enabling the plant to produce bigger fruit from fewer buds.
2. To shape the plant, opening the centre for full light and easier picking.
3. To remove weak, damaged or diseased wood.
4. To force the formation of fruit-bearing buds.

The effect of pruning is localized. It produces growth in the immediate area in which the cut is made. Strong shoots with large leaves tend to rise just at the back of pruning cuts. Care is required because excessive pruning over-stimulates growth and causes a loss of fruit colour, delayed fruit maturity, and the growth of suckers and watersprouts. The presence of too much succulent growth will increase the hazard of fire blight in apple and pear, canker in peach, and winter injury in all species.

TERMS A fruit tree has a central leader or stem that grows straight up. Topping is the act of cutting this central leader and results in the tree sending out side shoots or laterals. A tree that has been topped tends to become rounder and more bushy. Some of these lateral branches, if left on their own, will tend to act as substitute leaders by bending to grow upward. Trees pruned to discourage the dominance of one central leader are said to be open-centred.

As with ornamental trees (see page 63), pruning to build a strong framework should start when the tree is young. The strongest type of branch is one that grows straight out at a right angle to the central leader. This is called a horizontal branch or limb. The area where a branch meets the stem is called the crotch. A narrow or "Y"-angled crotch is one where the angle of joining is less than 45°. Branches joining the central leader at a narrow crotch should be cut off as soon as possible because they are prone to breakage in storms or when maturing fruit increases the weight of the limb.

At the end of each branch is a terminal bud. These buds grow, adding length to the branch each year. If a terminal bud is cut or nipped off, growth ceases at that part of the plant. The plant energy that would have gone to the terminal bud goes instead to either lateral, side or dormant buds further back on the limb.

WHERE TO CUT To change the direction of a branch's growth, snip it off just above a healthy bud growing in the direction you want the branch to grow. Choose buds that grow away from the tree and other branches. If you are cutting off a whole limb, cut as close as possible

EXCESSIVE PRUNING OVER-STIMULATES GROWTH, CAUSING A LOSS OF FRUIT COLOUR, DELAYED FRUIT MATURITY, AND THE GROWTH OF SUCKERS AND WATERSPROUTS.

Fruit trees add garden colour with both fruit and blossoms. At left, an apricot bough in bloom. Above, ripe sweet cherries.

to the remaining branch or stem. A stub or ragged edges at these points will greatly delay the healing of the wound and increase the probability of drying out and infection.

PRUNING AT PLANTING TIME Fruit trees should be quite heavily pruned at planting time. Pruning at this time reduces water loss, establishes the height of the tree, and commences its training. This initial pruning and those that follow in the next two or three years determine the final strength and symmetry of the tree. A wise selection of branches and the maintenance of a proper balance between them will greatly increase your long-term enjoyment.

Apricot, cherry, peach and plum trees should be pruned to a single whip, and headed at about 1 m (3 ft.). On peaches, if some well developed branches exist, two or three of these may be left as two-bud stubs. Other branches should be removed completely with clean, flush cuts at the trunk. Base your choice of branches to retain by looking for those that are distributed vertically and spirally around the trunk, and are growing out at a wide angle to it.

Pruning to create a strong central leader is recommended for all fruit trees. Some trees, particularly the sour cherry, peach and Japanese plum, do not retain a dominant central leader for long, but this is no cause for concern. A young central-leader tree should have three to five main branches distributed vertically and spirally around the trunk, with the topmost branch or leader well above the lower ones. If the branch angles at the main trunk are greater than 45°, there will be no buildup of bark in the crotches, and a strong tree will result. Keeping the central leader unpruned in the early years encourages wider angles on the framework branches below it. Four or five main branches are usually sufficient to build a good tree.

When to Prune

DORMANT PRUNING Most pruning is done when trees are dormant, between the time when leaves drop in late fall and buds begin to swell in early spring. If you want to stimulate new, vegetative growth, dormant pruning is the approach you should follow. The safest and best time to prune is just before the buds begin to swell. The most risky time is late fall and early winter. Spring pruning must be completed before leaves appear, but pruning followed by low temperatures could produce winter injury, so don't start too early.

EARLY SUMMER PRUNING If you wish to reduce vegetative growth and prevent shoots from developing, prune in June and July. Early-summer pruning has an extreme dwarfing effect, first to the root system and then to the whole tree.

MIDSUMMER PRUNING While pruning at this time of year does not stimulate new growth, it does not have the dwarfing effect of early-summer pruning. Depending on the vigour and age of the tree, this is a good time to reduce height and width by cutting back new growth. A well-grown tree with a good crop of fruit could have its new growth reduced by one-half to two-thirds. This will let in more direct sunlight to colour the fruit and improve its flavour by making more sugars available.

FALL PRUNING Pruning in fall is to be avoided if possible as cuts will not heal at this time of year. If you feel that you must do some fall pruning, prune only the oldest trees and stop well before a severe drop in temperature. Peach trees should not be pruned in fall because of the ever-present threat of canker.

Careful pruning reduces the time a tree needs to heal its wounds. This cross-section of apple-wood shows two pruning cuts that have healed properly because they were made close to the tree's trunk.

Pruning Rules

1. Cut out broken, dead, or diseased branches.
2. Where two branches closely parallel or overhang each other, remove the less desirable, taking into account horizontal and vertical spacing.
3. Prune on the horizontal plane; that is, leave those laterals on the main branches that grow horizontally or nearly so, and remove those that hang down or grow upward. This cannot always be done, but where possible it should be followed.
4. All varieties should be thinned out enough to permit thorough spraying and the entrance of sunlight and air.
5. Where it is desired to reduce the height of tall trees, cut the leader branches back moderately to a well-developed horizontal lateral.
6. Varieties which tend to produce numerous twiggy, lateral growth should have some of this growth removed to prevent overcrowding.
7. Make close, clean cuts. Stubs encourage decay and canker, thus forming a source of injury to the parent branch or trunk.
8. Prune moderately. Very heavy pruning is likely to upset the balance between wood growth and fruitfulness, and generally should be avoided.
9. Prune regularly. Trees which are given some attention each spring are more easily kept in good condition than trees that are pruned irregularly.
10. Prune that part of the tree where more growth is required. This is particularly important with old trees. New growth will be stimulated only in those parts of the tree that were pruned. Reduce pruning to an absolute minimum where growth is already excessive.
11. Do not remove a branch unless there is a very good reason for doing so. It should not be forgotten that the leaves of a tree are the food-manufacturing organs, and if the leaf area is reduced unnecessarily, the tree will be reduced in growth or fruitfulness or both.

 Fruit Trees

PLUM PRODUCTION

Q: How and when do we prune an old plum tree and get it to produce again? Pruning two years ago after a good harvest brought too many shoots.
– *O.B.R., Cobourg*

A: Do your pruning in late winter or early spring. Aim to open up the crown to air and light. Follow the basic rules of pruning: eliminate the weaker of two crossing branches and those branches that join the trunk at a narrow angle. Fertilize sparingly. If the tree is in a lawn which is fertilized it probably gets too much now. Fruit yield may be reduced after pruning. As well, the tree may be a biennial bearer. Use a home orchard spray mix at least twice a season, when first green shows and after blossoms fall. If your plum depended on another neighbourhood tree for cross-pollination and the latter has been removed, you may get little fruit. Most plums varieties require the presence of a second tree for pollination.

Peaches

Stone Fruit Guide

FRUIT	VARIETY	RIPENING DATE*	COLOUR	SUGGESTED USE	CANNING QUALITY	NOTES
APRICOT Hardy to Zone 6b	Harcot	July 25	Red	Fresh	Poor	• Small if not well thinned
	Goldcot	July 30	Clear yellow	Fresh	Fair	• Consistent annual crops
	Alfred	August 1	Pale orange	Fresh	Poor	• Hardy outside Niagara
	Veecot	August 6	Bright orange	Canned	Good	• Consistent annual crops
	Vivagold	August 12	Bright orange	Canned	Excellent	• Colours early before fully mature

FRUIT	VARIETY	RIPENING DATE*	POLLEN COMPATIBILITY†	CRACK RESISTANCE	CANNING QUALITY	NOTES
SWEET CHERRY Hardy to Zone 6b	Viva	July 9	4	Immune	Poor	• Black • Resistant to cracking
	Vega	July 11	0	Fair	Fair	• White • Large, very firm
	Valera	July 13	14	Fair	Fair	• Black
	V69061	July 15	Self-fruitful	Excellent	Good	• White • Resistant to rot and cracking
	Bing	July 15	3	Poor	Good	• Black • Very firm
	V690618	July 17	Self-fruitful	Immune	Good	• Black • Resistant to rot and cracking
	V69068	July 18	Self-fruitful	Immune	Good	• Black • Resistant to rot and cracking
	Stella	July 22	Self-fruitful	Good	Good	• Black • Superior hardiness
	Hedelfingen	July 27	7	Good	Good	• Black

FRUIT	VARIETY	RIPENING DATE*	COLOUR	FREEZING QUALITY	CANNING QUALITY	NOTES
TART CHERRY Hardy to Zone 6	Northstar	July 23	Mahogany-red	Good	Good	• Very hardy • Small tree • Dark flesh
	Montmorency	July 26	Medium red	Good	Good	• Standard pie cherry • Pale yellow flesh
	English Morello	July 30	Dark-reddish skin	Good	Good	• Hardy • Small tree • Dark flesh and juice
	Meteor	July 30	Light, bright red	Good	Fair	• Spur-type growth • Hardy • Very productive

Apricot tree with ripe fruit ready for picking.

FRUIT	VARIETY	RIPENING DATE*	COLOUR	FREEZING QUALITY	CANNING QUALITY	NOTES
PEACH Hardy to Zone 6b	Candor	July 29	75% bright red	Good	Poor	• Requires heavy thinning • Less prone to split pits than other early varieties
	Redhaven	August 18	Medium bright	Good	Good	• Requires adequate thinning for good size • Hardy
	Reliance	August 21	Dull red blush	–	Fair	• Hardy for marginal areas
	Vivid	August 23	Medium dark red	Good	Fair	• Sizes well • Colours early
	Canadian Harmony	September 2	80% medium dark red	–	Fair	• Very productive • Large fruit
NECTARINE Hardy to Zone 6b	Hardired	August 22	Solid red	Poor	Poor	• Hardy • Trees medium sized • Requires adequate thinning
	Fantasia	September 13	Solid red	Poor	Poor	• Large, attractive

FRUIT	VARIETY	RIPENING DATE*	COLOUR	PIT FREEDOM	CANNING QUALITY	NOTES
PLUM (Japanese) Hardy to Zone 7	Early Golden	July 28	Reddish yellow	Semi-free	Poor	• Very vigorous • Requires thinning • Pollinated by Burbank, Vanier
	Burbank	August 24	Dark reddish purple	Cling	Poor	• Pollinated by Early Golden, Vanier
	Ozark Premier	August 26	Bright red	Cling	Poor	• Pollinated by Vanier
	Vanier	August 29	Bright red	Cling	Poor	• Pollinated by Ozark Premier
PLUM (European) Hardy to Zone 5b	Veeblue	September 10	Violet red	Semi-free	Poor	• Pollinated by Stanley, Valor, Verity
	Stanley	September 18	Blue purple	Free	Poor	• Self-fertile • May overbear
	Valor	September 23	Dark purple	Semi-free	Fair	• Pollinated by Stanley, Verity
	Verity	September 27	Dark purple	Semi-free	Fair	• Pollinated by Stanley, Valor
PLUM (Damson) Hardy to Zone 5b	Shropshire	September 20	Dark purple	Cling	Good	• Self-fertile • Very small • Ideal for jam and preserves

Notes: *Harvest dates are correct for Vineland Station, Horticultural Research Institute of Ontario. In other locations, use these dates as a relative indicator of length of growing season.

†Sweet cherry and plum varieties not listed as self-sowing require a minimum of two trees to produce fruit. Sweet cherries must be of differing pollen compatibility groups to produce fruit. Plums must be combined as indicated in "Notes" column.

Apple/Pear Guide

FRUIT	VARIETY	RIPENING DATE*	COLOUR	SUGGESTED USE	NOTES
APPLE	Yellow Transparent	July 28	Light yellow	• Sauces • Pie	• Excellent early-season variety
	McIntosh	September 21	Red, green	• Eating	• Adaptable, hardy • Prefers cool conditions
	Spartan	September 30	Dark red	• Eating	• Firm • Stores well
	Cortland	October 4	Red striped	• Eating • Processing	• Large fruit • Hardy, productive tree
	Red Delicious	October 12	Red	• Eating	• Needs warmer temperatures than McIntosh
	Golden Delicious	October 16	Yellow gold	• Eating • Processing	• Sturdy tree grows moderately
PEAR	Clapp	August 26	Yellow-green, crimson	• Canning	• Creamy-white flesh, tender • Large fruit
	Bartlett	September 9	Yellow with brown dots	• Canning	• Tree fast-growing • Large fruit
	Flemish Beauty	September 23	Yellow, crimson	• Canning • Eating	• Hardiest pear available • Must be fully ripe when picked
	Anjou	October 5	Light green	• Eating	• Long storage life • Mild, fine-textured flesh
	Bosc	October 7	Yellow, cinnamon	• Eating	• Juicy • Aromatic • Large fruit

Note: *Harvest dates are correct for Vineland Station, Horticultural Research Institute of Ontario. In other locations, use these dates as a relative indicator of length of growing season.

Bartlett pears

BERRIES

Growing berries in the home garden can be interesting and rewarding. Berries are delicious when served fresh and can be frozen, canned and made into pies, jams, jellies or juice. In addition to fresh taste, when you grow your own, you know that they are clean and free from chemical pesticides and other additives. The most common berries grown in southern Ontario are blackberries, blueberries, currants, gooseberries, raspberries and strawberries. Strawberries are the most popular and are the easiest berry to grow in a home garden.

STRAWBERRIES Strawberries can be grown anywhere in Ontario. They are the first berries to ripen and, with the new everbearing varieties, can be picked throughout summer and into late fall. Conventional and everbearing strawberries have an ornamental value and can be used as ground cover and as edging plants in a rock garden. They can be grown along the top of retaining walls, and can be grown successfully in containers. You can find wild strawberries growing in open uncultivated fields throughout the countryside and, though the wild berries are small and only ripen once around the end of June, they are usually found in great masses and are fun to pick on a family outing.

A home strawberry bed should be in a sunny spot with well-drained, sandy loam soil. Good drainage is very important as strawberry roots do not grow well in wet soil. Don't plant in an area which has grown strawberries, raspberries, potatoes, tomatoes, peppers or eggplant in the last few years to avoid serious root diseases such as veticullium wilt and black root rot. In new plants, flower clusters emerge in late May and ripen over a four to five week period. When days become long and warm, the plants grow runners which root and produce new plants. (See "Renewing Strawberries", page 99.)

Plant in the spring as soon as the ground can be worked. This allows plants to become established early and start producing runners.

Strawberry

At left, black raspberries. Below, three strawberry plants with root systems exposed. The dark line indicates soil level. The plant in the centre illustrates the correct planting depth, with roots fully buried but just beneath the surface of the soil bed.

Early-formed runner plants produce more berries than plants formed in late summer. Fall planting is not recommended.

Plant the midpoint of the crown level with the surface of the soil. (See photo on page 96.) Strawberry plants have very fine roots which dry out in only a few minutes on sunny, windy days, so be sure to protect them while planting.

After the first frost in late fall, cover plants with straw or some other dry mulch to protect roots from harsh temperatures in winter. Do not mulch too soon, for if plants are not dormant and the ground is wet, they become susceptible to rot. Strawberry roots lie close to the surface, so care must also be taken when hoeing and weeding.

For container gardens, strawberries can be set in holes made in the top and sides of a barrel filled with soil. Most well-stocked garden centres also sell pyramid-shaped containers designed for strawberry plantings. Because berries add so much to the ornamental value of a strawberry plant, everbearing varieties are usually used in container applications.

Conventional varieties suitable for southern Ontario planting include Veestar, Vibrant, Vantage, Sparkle, and Bounty. Recommended everbearing varieties are Ozark Beauty (Autumn Beauty, Cross's Red) and Geneva.

RASPBERRIES AND BLACKBERRIES Raspberries are small shrubs usually grown in narrow rows called "hedgerows". Red, purple and black raspberries are available to the home gardener. Blackberries are very similar, but differ from black raspberries in that the core of each blackberry stays in the fruit when it is picked. Raspberry cores remain attached to the shrub.

The canes of red and purple raspberries grow upright while those of black raspberries and blackberries are long and trailing. Red raspberries are the hardiest varieties and are capable of withstanding southern Ontario winters. Blackberries are the least hardy and should only be grown in protected areas with mild winter conditions. Because their hardiness allows for much wider application, the planting information that follows is for red raspberries.

Choose a well-drained sunny site that has deep, sandy loam soil with plenty of organic matter. Avoid clay soils and low-lying areas which may be poorly drained and prone to frost damage. The root system of raspberries is perennial, but each shoot is biennial, surviving for two years. During the first year, a shoot reaches its maximum height and is called a "cane". In the second year, it produces fruit and dies soon afterward.

Shoots originate from buds that are found either on roots or at the base of old canes. Fruiting canes die when picking is completed and should be cut out and destroyed to remove potential sources of infection and disease. Further pruning should be done in the spring to remove weak canes and dead tips.

Because no crop is obtained the first year, most nurseries sell dormant mature plants that have completed one season of growth. Set plants as deep or slightly deeper than previously planted. Spread the roots out and pack soil carefully around them. Water the plants and add more soil as it settles.

Recommended red raspberry varieties are Boyne, Comet, Festival, Killarney, Lathum, Madawaska, and Newburge.

CURRANTS AND GOOSEBERRIES Blackcurrants are prized for their distinctive flavour in juice, jams and jellies. Red and white currants are also available but are not as popular. Gooseberries are larger and can be eaten fresh or made into jams, pies and other desserts. Both are very low, bushy plants that grow best in cool,

STRAWBERRIES HAVE VERY FINE ROOTS WHICH DRY OUT IN ONLY A FEW MINUTES ON SUNNY, WINDY DAYS. BE SURE TO PROTECT THEM WHEN PLANTING.

moist, rich clay loam. They tolerate shade, but a sunny site with good air movement results in higher yields.

Plant in early spring using strong, well-rooted, year-old plants. Currants and gooseberries bloom early in the spring, though any blossoms which appear in the first year should be removed. This helps plants become established and increases growth. Prune when plants are dormant in late winter.

Blackcurrants produce their best fruit on one-year-old wood. Keep a total of 10 to 12 shoots per mature plant. Remove all shoots more than three years old by pruning close to the ground. Red currants and gooseberries produce most of their fruit on spurs located on two and three-year-old wood. Again, remove all shoots that are older than three years.

Common blackcurrant varieties are Topsy, Baldwin and Consort. Red currants include Red Lake and Cascade. Recommended gooseberry varieties are Clark, Fredonia and Captivator.

BLUEBERRIES Blueberries are delightful whether eaten fresh or made into pies or other desserts. They are attractive ornamental plants, with a profusion of white blossoms in early summer and glossy green leaves that turn red, orange and yellow in the fall. Blueberries grow best in a sunny location and must have an acidic soil. This is why they grow so well up north where years of decaying pine needles have produced a naturally acidic soil.

Because most garden soil is not overly acidic, it is necessary to mix in acid peat when preparing your blueberry bed. An even more effective method of increasing soil acidity is to prepare the bed by mixing sulphur into the topsoil a year in advance of planting.

An early spring planting of healthy two-year-old plants is recommended. Remove blossoms that appear the year the plants are set in the garden. Blueberries have a shallow root system, so mulching to control weeds is also recommended as even light hoeing can cause root damage. No pruning is really needed except to remove dead branches. For better flavour, leave berries on the bush for a few days after they have turned completely blue. Birds love blueberries as much as we do, so you might have to cover or protect fruit as it ripens.

Suggested varieties are Berkeley, Blueray, Bluecrop, and Jersey.

BLUEBERRIES NEED ACIDIC SOIL. MIX IN ACID PEAT WHEN PREPARING A BLUEBERRY BED OR MIX SULPHUR INTO THE TOPSOIL A YEAR IN ADVANCE OF PLANTING.

 **Berries**

TEA AS A BERRY FERTILIZER

Q: Is it true that tea makes a good fertilizer for certain plants? – *L.V., Leaside*

A: Tea is acidic, though the accumulation of old tea bags in one family is not likely to be significant. Tea leaves should go out to the compost heap along with other wet kitchen garbage. If you want to save your tea bags separately, compost them alone and use on acidic soil plants such as gardenia, azalea, blueberry and rose. Do not use on lilacs.

 **Berries** CONTINUED

RENEWING STRAWBERRIES

Q: Our strawberries appear healthy with strong foliage. They are covered with blossoms in spring but don't develop properly. We get only about one fruit to a dozen plants and even these are small and misshapen with a short, mushroom stem that stays white.

I understand that established rooted runners from the previous year are to be rooted in May to start a new bed. What fertilizer should be used and at what time of year should it be applied? — *J.S.B., Islington*

A: Strawberries are not forever. The Ontario Ministry of Agriculture and Food recommends that you keep plants a maximum of four fruiting seasons. Suckers – daughter plants that self-root – should be removed once the hills are full so that rows do not mat together. Let some runners establish themselves on the alley on one side of a row while old plants on the other side are turned under, thus renewing the bed as you go.

Strawberry blossoms are pollinated by bees. Cold, wet weather or urban conditions can reduce bees and their activity; so can spraying at the open blossom stage.

Many insects attack the plants. Plant bugs pierce developing fruit to suck sap causing small, deformed berries; strawberry clipper weevils cut blossom stems, preventing fruit formation while their grubs feed on the stems that remain; strawberry fruitworms eat the berries.

Deformed fruit can be analyzed by the University of Guelph diagnostic clinic, Room B14, Graham Hall, Guelph N1G 2W1. There is a charge for this service.

It is also wise to fertilize an established planting as soon as picking has been completed. Use 1 kg (2.2 lbs.) of grade 8:16:16 or 10:10:10 to every 10 square metres (100 sq. ft.). Use one-third less of farm grade 15:15:15. Broadcast it when foliage is dry.

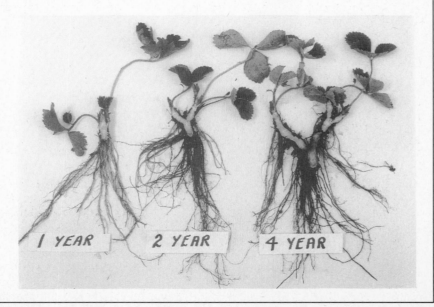

After four years, the roots of strawberry plants become too dense for maximum fruit production and should be replaced.

The Kniffen system of pruning, described on page 103, trains grapevines to produce a strong central trunk and six canes which grow horizontally along three wires. This vine has just been pruned.

GRAPEVINES

The Most Trainable Plant in Your Garden

Grapevines can add a great deal of enjoyment to backyard gardening. With the passage of time, vines can cover an arbour or framework to form a green, shady canopy from which hangs dozens of bunches. While it is unlikely that your home grape vines will yield enough fruit in a season to make very much wine, you can count on an average of 10 kg (22 lbs.) of fruit per vine if properly maintained.

While commercial grape growing is restricted to the warmest areas of Ontario, varieties of dessert and wine grapes can be garden grown in most other areas. If temperatures fall below –26°C (–15°F), winter protection is necessary, but isn't difficult to put in place. Similar protection is also required if you are attempting to grow classic viniferous (wine) grapes like Chardonnay or Riesling anywhere in Ontario outside of Niagara and Essex counties. Note that it is unlikely that these varieties will fully ripen during the growing season anywhere outside of the province's fruit belt. For this reason, they are not listed in the Grapevine Guide found at the end of this section.

PLANTING Grapes do well in a variety of soils, requiring only good drainage and full sunlight. Spring planting is preferred in all but the warmest regions, though the soil where your grapes will be planted should be enriched during the previous fall. This soil enhancement should take the form of a thorough spading of the soil, incorporating organic material like peat moss, compost or rotted manure. If your soil has a clay base, this work in the fall is especially important.

Rooted grapevines ready for transplanting can be purchased at most garden centres. These are usually sold with bare roots and care must be taken to ensure that the root system has not dried out. Before

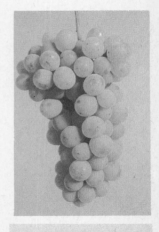

White Seneca grapes

Grapevines can be grown from two and three-bud cuttings. At left, two-bud cuttings shown in three stages of growth: (from left to right) freshly cut and ready to plant; with leaves and roots sprouted; and ready to transplant to permanent bed. Below, two and three-bud cuttings like these should be taken from one-year-old cane in November or December, stored over the winter and planted in spring.

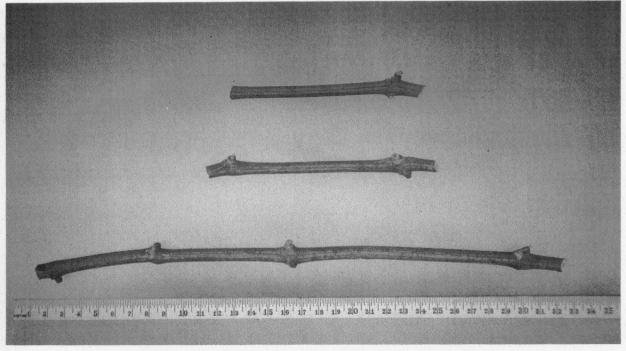

planting, prune back so that all that is left is a strong central cane with two buds and a one bud stub to which a support string can be tied. Dig a hole large enough to accommodate the roots, taking care to keep the topsoil you dig up separate from the subsoil. Place the grapevine in the hole and use the topsoil to cover the root system. Don't use any kind of fertilizer when planting. Mound the soil so that only the top bud is visible. After planting, mulch with grass clippings, sawdust or similar material. Fertilize sparingly, using fruit tree products high in potassium such as grade 5:10:15.

Grapevines can also be grown from cuttings. Take cuttings in late November or December when vines are dormant. Cut 25 cm (10 in.) lengths of one-year-old cane that each contain three buds. In planting cuttings, care must be taken not to plant the cane upside down. The bottom of the cutting is the end of the cane that was closest to the main trunk of the vine. To assist in identifying top from bottom, always cut the bottom of the cane close to the first or basal bud while leaving a little extra cane above the top bud. Cuttings should be stored in a cool damp place until spring. They can be kept in a tightly closed plastic bag in your refrigerator or buried under 10 cm (4 in.) of sand and covered with mulch in the garden.

In spring, dig a trench in the area you prepared last fall. Plant your cuttings with the top bud just above ground level. If several vines are being planted, allow 2 m (6 ft.) between each plant.

PRUNING AND TRAINING Grapevines are remarkably responsive to pruning and training. Two major systems of vine training yield good results in Ontario. Both were developed to meet the needs of professional grape growers, but can be modified to suit your trellis, arbour or framework.

The Kniffen System is the preferred training method if winter temperatures do not fall below –26°C (–15°F) in your area. It makes use of a trellis of three horizontal wires mounted at 75 cm (30 in.), 125 cm (50 in.), and 150 cm (60 in.) above the ground. Galvanized 9-gauge steel wire or vinyl-covered clothesline can be used. As soon as the young grape plant is above ground, tie a string around the stub of the new cane and attach this string to the top wire of the trellis. As the vine grows, pinch back all but the most vigorous single shoot. This main shoot, which will eventually become the trunk of your vine, should be kept loosely twisted around the string until it finally reaches the top wire.

Once the top wire has been reached, tie the trunk to the top and bottom wire and remove the guide string. Cut off all cane above the top wire and all shoots below the bottom. Allow canes to grow along each wire. In each subsequent growing season, select six canes of the previous season's growth, attaching one to each of the three wires on either side of the trunk. Cut back each cane to six to ten buds. Prune all other wood with the exception of one or two two-bud spurs located close to each of the three trellis wires. Over the course of the growing season these spurs will develop into canes ready to bear fruit and be attached to the trellis wires at the beginning of the following season.

Kniffen-trained vines can be continually renewed. Even the trunk can be replaced by training a shoot that originates near the base of the plant. Treat the new shoot as if it were an entirely new vine, running a guide string to the top wire. Once the new trunk has established itself on the trellis, the old trunk can be removed, though this process can take two or three growing seasons to complete.

Red Delaware grapes

The Fan System is preferred if winter protection is required. It also utilizes the same three-wire trellis described above. A fan-trained vine has a short trunk that has been trained to split into two short arms below the bottom trellis wire. Three to five canes are trained to grow vertically from the two arms, forming a fan-like pattern on the trellis. To protect against extreme cold, carefully detach the vines from the trellis and lay them on the ground around the trunk after the growing season. Cover the vines with 7–10 cm (3–4 in.) of soil and mulch with straw or grass clippings.

In spring, uncover the vines and select the three to five canes to be tied to the trellis. Cut these back to 10–12 buds per cane and remove all unnecessary wood. To retain the flexibility necessary to bury the canes each year, renew the arms of the grapevine every few growing seasons by allowing two new canes to grow near the top of the trunk. Train these to be the arms of the fan and, once established, remove the old arms. If necessary, the trunk of a fan-system vine also can be renewed by training a shoot from near the ground to act as a replacement. Tie the replacement trunk to a stake until it has matured sufficiently to grow arms and canes that can be attached to the trellis.

MID-SEASON PRUNING AND HARVESTING

To develop a healthy vine it is best to remove any bunches of grapes that start to form during the first two growing seasons. These bunches should be pinched off in mid-June when individual grapes are no bigger than a match head. In the third year, allow no more than one bunch per strong cane. Yield per vine will gradually increase from 2–5 kg (4–11 lbs.) in the third year to 7–12 kg (12–25 lbs.) in the fifth.

Grapes do not continue to ripen after they have been picked, so it is important to allow them to mature before harvest. Your own taste is the most reliable guide to ripeness. As well, the colour of the grapes begins to change as they approach ripeness. Green varieties turn whitish and blue or red varieties darken. You can hasten ripening by increasing the amount of sunlight that reaches your grapes. Do this by pinching back those side shoots that carry leaves that shade each bunch of grapes. Once you have harvested your crop, discard overripe or damaged grapes and refrigerate.

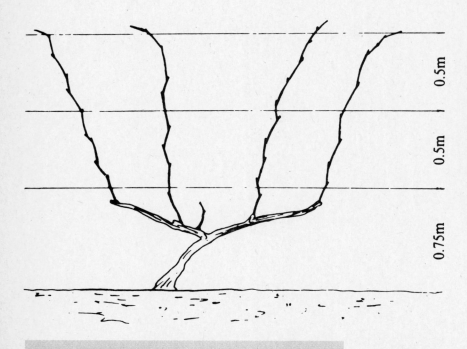

0.5 m

0.5 m

0.75 m

The fan system of vine training

Grapevine Guide

VARIETY	HARVEST DATE *	COLOUR	USE	NOTES
HIMROD	September 2	White	• Dessert	• Seedless, vigorous, winter tender • Protection required outside Niagara
AURORE	September 4	White	• Wine	• Hardy • Subject to powdery mildew
SENECA	September 8	White	• Dessert	• Seeded, firm fleshed • Powdery mildew aggravates winter damage
FOCH	September 11	Blue-Black	• Dessert	• Good sugar content • Very hardy, suffers bird damage
FREDONIA	September 11	Black	• Dessert • Jelly • Juice • Sweet wine	• Very large berries, slipskin • Sweet Concord character • Very hardy, vigorous
VANESSA	September 20	Red	• Dessert	• Seedless, firm fleshed • Hardy
NEW YORK MUSCAT	September 22	Red-Blue	• Dessert • Sweet wine • Juice	• Very sweet, vigorous • Powdery mildew aggravates winter damage
CANADICE	September 23	Red	• Dessert	• Seedless with long attractive clusters • Very hardy
DeCHAUNAC	September 24	Blue-Black	• Wine	• Thin bunches to maintain vigour • Hardy
DELAWARE	September 26	Red	• Wine	• Very sweet, small bunches • Good soil drainage imperative • Powdery mildew aggravates winter damage
NIAGARA	September 29	Yellow-White	• Dessert • Jelly • Juice • Sweet wine	• Large berries, slipskin • Highly perfumed • Very vigorous, hardy
CONCORD	October 4	Blue-Black	• Dessert • Jelly • Juice • Sweet wine	• Typical commercial juice flavour • Hardy, vigorous • Season often too short outside Niagara and Essex

*Note: Harvest dates are correct for Vineland Station, Horticultural Research Institute of Ontario. In other locations, use these dates as a relative indicator of length of growing season.

Rudbeckia

ANNUAL FLOWERS

The Easy Answer to an Instant Garden

Annuals provide a dazzling display of colour in an abundance of shapes and sizes. Most annual flowers bloom in a short time and last almost the whole season. They are easy to plant and need only regular watering to survive. You can mix them in an annual bed or use them to fill in your perennial border. They add colour when planted in front of evergreen shrubs and are perfect container plants for balconies and small spaces. You can pack them into window boxes or let them tumble from hanging baskets. They provide your table with bouquets of cut flowers and, in some cases, even make good houseplants.

A true annual lives for only one season. Most are planted from seed in the spring, mature quickly and produce a great profusion of flowers. Some plants we consider to be annuals are actually tender perennials that will not last through our winters. Others are biennials. Biennials are plants that flower in the year following the planting of seed. They are often planted in late summer or early fall to bloom the next year. Most annuals and biennials are self-seeding if their last bloom is allowed to mature, and are often mistaken for perennials because of this.

Annuals are classified as either tender or hardy. Tender annuals must be started inside or in cold frames and cannot be transplanted to the garden until after the May 24th weekend or until all danger of frost has past. Hardy annuals can tolerate some frost and thus can be sown directly into the garden as soon as the ground can be worked in the spring.

Some annuals love warm weather and bloom best in the heat of the summer, while others are the exact opposite and flourish in cool weather,

Velvet flower

Petunia

though this does not necessarily mean they can withstand frost. Cool weather annuals thrive in breezy open areas with long days and cool nights.

Most annuals require full sun, but some, such as pansies, impatiens, snapdragons, verbena and nicotiana, will tolerate some shade.

GROWING ANNUALS First determine the hardiness of the plant you want to grow. If it cannot survive a cold, wet spring, it is best to buy starter seedlings from a garden centre or start your own seedlings indoors in flats. Most annuals prefer a rich fertile soil with a pH between 5.5 and 7.0. Their bed does not have to be dug as deep as that of perennials because most annuals have fairly shallow roots. Some, such as nasturtiums, cosmos and portulaca, do well in poorer sandy soil, while others, such as pansies, marigolds and zinnias require a richer soil with lots of humus to retain moisture.

If you have to add fertilizer, use only a balanced, slow release mixture. Too much nitrogen will encourage only leaf and stem growth with very few flowers. Do not plant annuals where tree roots are close to the surface and, if soil drainage is poor, build raised beds. Annuals can be planted fairly close together, but need constant thinning. Most varieties will become bushier and bloom longer if spent flower heads are removed before they go to seed.

FLOWERING ANNUAL VINES Annual climbers can produce shoots as long as 3 m (10 ft.) in one season. In tiny, city gardens with good sunlight, their vertical habit expands the garden's possibilities and creates a feeling of space. Vines can also provide a summer screen to cover a porch, shed, fence or ugly wall. They can shade a patio or veranda and can be grown on an apartment balcony.

The morning glory is one such old-fashioned climber. You can get blooms sooner by using starter plants, which are occasionally available at nurseries, but be careful not to disturb their roots when transplanting. You can also grow your own from seed and expect flowers by mid-summer. Nick each seed with a file or knife blade, then soak overnight in lukewarm water for faster germination. Once started, the plants grow quickly. Morning glories climb by stem twisting and need vertical strings, wires or similar sources of support to wrap around.

Other annuals related to the morning glory make attractive garden climbers. Moonflower, as the name suggests, blooms at night. The hearts-and-honey vine is a dwarf suitable for pots. The cardinal climber has bright red flowers while the cup-and-saucer vine has showy violet or greenish-purple flowers and may grow up to 8 m (25 ft.) in a summer.

The nasturtium family offers a climbing annual that is known as the canary-bird flower. It has striped or spotted flowers in orange, red or yellow. The scarlet runner bean is also attractive, but requires a lot of space. Not only does it produce beans that can be eaten before they mature, but also has attractive foliage and bright red flowers.

Another popular climbing annual is the sweet pea. It does poorly in hot weather, but, as its seed is very hardy, can be planted in April to bloom ahead of summer's heat.

Morning glory

Hibiscus

Annual & Biennial Flower Guide

COMMON NAME	BOTANICAL NAME	HEIGHT	NOTES
ACROLINUM	*Acrolinium*	35 cm 14 in.	Small mum-like white or yellow flowers with pungent scent. Compact plant prefers full sun or partial shade.
AFRICAN DAISY	*Arctotis*	25 cm 10 in.	Large daisy-like blooms 7 cm (3 in.) in size. Flowers close at night. Drought resistant. Grey-green leaves. Blooms summer through fall.
ALYSSUM, SWEET	*Alyssum*	8–20 cm 3–8 in.	Popular edging plant. Clusters of tiny flowers bloom throughout the summer if plant is cut back after first flowering. Full sun to partial shade.
ASTER, CHINA	*Callistephus*	15–80 cm 6–30 in.	Varieties range from dwarf to giant and are suitable for everything from edging to cut flowers. Range of colours and flowering times. Grow in new location each year because of soil-borne diseases. Full sun to partial shade.
BABY BLUE EYES	*Nemophila*	15–20 cm 6–8 in.	Five-petaled flowers up to 4 cm (1½ in.) in size. Blue with white centres. Prefer cool summers. Difficult to transplant.
BABY'S BREATH	*Gypsophilia*	45 cm 18 in.	Hardy bushy plants feature masses of tiny flowers. White, rose or red. Sow every two weeks for successive blooming. Prefers full sun and alkaline soil.
BACHELOR'S BUTTON	*Centaurea cyanus*	–	See Cornflower
BEGONIA, WAX	*Begonias*	15–30 cm 6–12 in.	Long-flowering with green or reddish leaves. White, pink or pinkish-red blossoms. Difficult to start indoors. Full sun to partial shade.
BELLS OF IRELAND	*Molucella laevis*	60–90 cm 24–36 in.	Unusual plant with upright spikes covered with bell-like translucent green flowers. Often used in dried flower displays. Full sun.
BLANKET FLOWER	*Gaillardia*	30–60 cm 12–24 in.	Depending on conditions, can also be grown as a perennial. Daisy-like flower in pink, orange, yellow, red. Blooms all summer. Thrives on heat and sun.
BLUE LACE FLOWER	*Didiscus caerulea*	75 cm 30 in.	Tiny, sweet blue flowers in clusters up to 7 cm (3 in.) in size. Prefers full sun, cool weather. Often needs staking.
BROWALLIA	*Browallia*	30–60 cm 12–24 in.	Bell-shaped flowers in white, blue or purple grow up to 5 cm (2 in.) in size. Thrives in partial shade with ample water.
BURNING BUSH	*Kochia*	60–90 cm 24–36 in.	Feathery-green foliage provides superb background for flowers. Turns red in fall. Hedge-like.
BUTTERFLY FLOWER	*Schizanthus*	30–45 cm 12–18 in.	Bushy, compact plant with orchid-like blooms in white, cream, crimson, pink and purple. Often grown indoors in winter. Full sun to partial shade in moist soil.
BUTTERFLY PEA	*Clitoria*	30 cm 12 in.	Purple flowers with yellow and light blue markings. 5 cm (2 in.) in size. Often grown indoors in winter.
CALIFORNIA BLUEBELL	*Phacelia*	20 cm 8 in.	Exquisite bell-shaped blue flowers with white centres. Suitable for mass planting. Difficult to transplant. Prefers full sun and sandy soil.

Annual & Biennial Flower Guide

COMMON NAME	BOTANICAL NAME	HEIGHT	NOTES
CANDYTUFT	*Iberis*	20–40 cm 8–15 in.	Carpet of colour suitable for edgings or rock gardens. Blooms are pink, purple, lilac and red. Prefers cool weather and withstands air pollution.
CANTERBURY BELL	*Campanula medium*	60–75 cm 24–30 in.	Biennial, tending to self-seed. Bell-shaped flowers on large spikes. May require staking. Prefers full sun and soil that drains well.
CHINESE FORGET-ME-NOT	*Cynoglossum*	45–60 cm 18–24 in.	Biennial plant usually grown as an annual. Indigo blue flowers on bushy plant with grey-green foliage. Easy to grow and long-flowering in almost all conditions.
CHRYSANTHEMUM	*Chrysanthemum*	25–75 cm 10–30 in.	Perennial varieties also available. Annuals grow quickly from seed, are hardy and can be easily transplanted. Many varieties and sizes in white, yellow and red.
CLARKIA	*Clarkia*	30–60 cm 12–24 in.	When cut, double flowers open when in water. White, lavender, pink, orange and scarlet flowers. Prefers cool weather and full sun.
COCKSCOMB	*Celosia*	15–90 cm 6–36 in.	Wide variety of forms from stiff rooster-like combs to feathery plumes in red, orange, pink and yellow. Tolerant of poor soil and dry conditions. Full sun to partial shade. Needs heat.
COLEUS	*Coleus blumei*	20–90 cm 8–36 in.	Colourful foliage with a wide range of leaf colours including white with green edges and red with yellow. Pinch to encourage branching. Partial shade results in most vibrant colours.
CORNFLOWER	*Centaurea cyanus*	30–90 cm 12–36 in.	Wide size range with 5 cm (2 in.) flowers in white, blue, pink and red. Grey-green leaves. Prefers cool weather and full sun.
COSMOS	*Cosmos*	45–120 cm 18–48 in.	Fine foliage with brightly coloured daisy-like flowers that can be white, yellow, pink or red. Sandy or poor soil. Full sun.
CUP FLOWER	*Nierembergia*	15–60 cm 6–24 in.	Thick cushion covered with five-petaled 25 mm (1 in.) flowers all summer. White to violet blue. Prefers full sun and moist soil.
DAHLIA	*Dahlia*	30–60 cm 12–24 in.	This tuber will bloom in the first year if grown from seed or transplants. Bushy plant with long-lasting flowers in white, pink, yellow, orange or red.
DUSTY MILLER	*Cineraria*	20–75 cm 8–30 in.	Low hardy plant grown for grey-green to silver-white foliage. Heat and drought resistant. Prefers full sun.
FEVERFEW	*Matricaria*	15–60 cm 6–24 in.	Daisy-like double and semidouble flowers up to 5 cm (2 in.) in size. Make excellent dried flowers. White, cream, pink, yellow, apricot and red. Difficult to transplant.
FLOSS FLOWER	*Ageratum*	12–60 cm 5–24 in.	Fluffy flowers in white, blue, pink and purple. Popular long-blooming edging plant. Wide size range.
FLOWERING FLAX	*Linum*	40 cm 15 in.	Wiry plant covered with a large number of flowers up to 5 cm (2 in.) in size. White, pink, red, purple. Short flowering period, so make repeat sowings. Prefers cool temperatures and full sun.
FLOWERING SAGE	*Salvia*	18–90 cm 7–36 in.	Long-blooming plant with spikes of flowers in white, pink, purple, lavender and red. Dark green leaves. Bushy tender shrub grown as an annual. Full sun or partial shade.

Annual & Biennial Flower Guide

COMMON NAME	BOTANICAL NAME	HEIGHT	NOTES
FORGET-ME-NOT	*Myosotis*	18–30 cm 7–12 in.	Biennial featuring small clusters of blue, pink or white flowers. Blooms early and is often planted with tulips. Full sun to partial shade.
FOUR O'CLOCK	*Mirabilis jalapa*	45–120 cm 18–48 in.	Easy to grow. Trumpet flowers open in late afternoon or earlier in cloudy weather. White, lavender, yellow, pink. Grows quickly. Resists air pollution. Full sun.
GERANIUM	*Pelargonium*	30–60 cm 12–24 in.	Large cluster flowers in all shades of pink, red and bi-colours. Hardy and sun-loving, can be grown in beds, window boxes or containers. Can be grown as a perennial by over-wintering indoors.
GLOBE AMARANTH	*Gomphrena*	25x45 cm 10–18 in.	Ball-shaped flowers in white, pink, purple. Attractive when dried. Prefers hot weather.
GLORIOSA DAISY	*Rudbeckia*	–	See Rudbeckia
HELIOTROPE	*Heliotropium*	40–60 cm 15–24 in.	Fragrant small flowers of dark blue or violet. Sensitive to cold. Prefers full sun and good drainage.
HIBISCUS	*Hibiscus*	150 cm 60 in.	Usually grown as a perennial, but annual varieties have become popular. Huge flowers up to 25 cm (10 in.) in size. White, pink, red and bi-colour combinations.
HOLLYHOCK	*Althaea*	60–180 cm. 24–72 in.	Biennial, but can be grown as an annual. Tall spikes of flowers up to 10 cm (4 in.) in size. White, mauve, pink, red, yellow. Excellent as a screen or background. Subject to rust in some areas. Prefers full sun and well-drained soil.
IMPATIENS	*Impatiens*	15–60 cm 6–24 in.	Adaptable plant that blooms all summer with little care. Can be grown as a houseplant over winter. Flowers of solid colour or flecked in white, pink, purple, orange or red.
LADY'S SLIPPER	*Impatiens balsamina*	30–45 cm 12–18 in.	Waxy flowers up to 4 cm (1½ in.) in size in white, pink, purple or red. Poor tolerance for cold and wet weather. Prefers full sun to partial shade and moist soil.
LARKSPUR	*Delphinium*	35–120 cm 14–48 in.	Early-blooming with large flowers on showy spikes. White, pink or dark blue. Does not transplant well. Prefers full sun to partial shade.
LOBELIA	*Lobelia*	10–30 cm 4–12 in.	Colourful accent plant ideal for edging or rock gardens. Small flowers cover the plant throughout the growing season. Flowers can be white, shades of blue, dark red. Prefers partial shade.
LOVE-IN-A-MIST	*Nigella*	40–45 cm 16–18 in.	Flowers resemble cornflower. Fine leaves. White, pink, purple, dark red. Successive sowings extend short flowering period. Prefers full sun.
MARIGOLD	*Tagetes*	20–120 cm 8–48 in.	Compact plant with numerous varieties features vibrant flowers in white, yellow, orange, red and bi-colours. Hardy with a long flowering season. Prefers full sun.
MIGNONETTE	*Reseda*	30 cm 12 in.	Sprawling plant with small, undistinguished flowers that have a remarkably sweet fragrance. Prefers cool weather and full sun to partial shade.

Pansy

Disco Golden marigold

Annual & Biennial Flower Guide
CONTINUED

COMMON NAME	BOTANICAL NAME	HEIGHT	NOTES
MONEY PLANT	*Lunaria*	90 cm 36 in.	Biennial plant flowers in early summer but is best known for its flat silvery seed pods that look like silver dollars. Very adaptable.
MONKEY FLOWER	*Mimulus*	30 cm 12 in.	Speckled flowers in red or yellow. Tender perennial usually grown as an annual. Blooms in partial shade.
MORNING GLORY	*Ipomoea*	300 cm 120 in.	Easy to grow, climbing annual vine for fence or trellis. Best in full sun and blooms throughout the summer and fall. White, blue, lavender and red. Most varieties close in the afternoon.
MOSS ROSE	*Portulaca*	13–18 cm 5–7 in.	Low to the ground with single or double flowers up to 6 cm (2½ in.) in size. White, lavender, pink, yellow, red. Prefers partial shade and moist soil. Dislikes extreme heat.
NASTURTIUM	*Tropaeolum*	20–60 cm 8–24 in.	Colourful with a spicy fragrance. Requires full sun and well-drained soil. Soil that is overly rich or moist can result in few flowers. Flowers are yellow, orange, pink, red or maroon. Leaves, seed pods (pickled), buds and flowers are edible.
NEMISIA	*Nemisia*	25–30 cm 10–12 in.	Easy to grow border plant with orchid-like blossoms. White, yellow, orange, pink, red. Prefers cool summers, full sun and rich moist soil.
NICOTIANA	*Nicotiana*	25–75 cm 10–30 in.	Strong evening fragrance. Tubular flowers in white, lavender, pink, red. Some varieties close midday; others stay open. Full sun to partial shade. Tolerant of heat.
PANSY	*Viola*	15–25 cm 6–10 in.	Many varieties including biennials. Larger flowered are pansies; smaller are violas. White, yellow, red, purple, blue and combinations. Long blooming. Self-seeds but eventually runs down. Prefers rich soil, moderate sun to partial shade.
PETUNIA	*Petunia*	25–40 cm 10–15 in.	Colourful flowers up to 12 cm (5 in.) in size with a long blooming period. Shear in July for August flowering. Available in most colours. Prefers full sun.
PHLOX	*Drummondi*	20–40 cm 8–15 in.	Star-shaped flowers and long blooming season. White, pink, red, blue and bi-colours. Easy to grow in full sun.
POPPY	*Papaver*	45 cm 18 in.	Early adaptable plant with large flowers. Pink, yellow, apricot, red and combinations. Hardy seeds can be planted early. Difficult to transplant. Prefers full sun.
POT MARIGOLD	*Calendula*	–	See Scotch Marigold
ROSE MALLOW	*Hibiscus*	–	See Hibiscus
RUDBECKIA	*Rudbeckia*	60–90 cm 24–36 in.	Large daisy-like yellow or orange flowers up to 12 cm (5 in.) in size. Easy to grow in most soils, full sun to partial shade.
SATIN FLOWER	*Godetia*	–	See Clarkia
SCOTCH MARIGOLD	*Calendula*	15–50 cm 6–20 in.	Bushy plant with bright flowers in yellow or orange. Adaptable to poor soil in full sun or partial shade. Self-sowing.
SNAPDRAGON	*Antirrhinum*	20–90 cm 8–36 in.	Many varieties and sizes all featuring spikes of distinctive flowers. Great colour range. Self-seeds. Prefers full sun.

Zinnia

Annual & Biennial Flower Guide
CONTINUED

COMMON NAME	BOTANICAL NAME	HEIGHT	NOTES
SNOW-ON-THE-MOUNTAIN	*Euphorbia*	45–90 cm 18–36 in.	Grown for attractive leaves that range from white or red-edged to almost pure white or red. Often self-sows. Sap can cause skin irritation. Prefers full sun and sandy soil.
SPIDER PLANT	*Cleome*	90–120 cm 36–48 in.	Tall plant with fragrant, spidery flowers in white, pink, red, or purple. Flowers close in afternoon. Stems have thorns. Prefers full sun.
STATICE	*Limonium*	60–70 cm 24–28 in.	Straw-like flower tolerant of poor soil. White, yellow, pink, blue. Lasts for months when dried. Prefers full sun.
STOCK	*Mathiola*	30–75 cm 12–30 in.	Spikes of fragrant, colourful flowers on bushy plant. White, yellow, pink, lilac, purple. Prefers full sun.
STRAWFLOWER	*Helichrysum*	30–60 cm 12–24 in.	Bright mum-like flowers in white, yellow or dark red. Superb dried flower. Prefers full sun to partial shade.
SUNFLOWER	*Helianthus*	45–300 cm 18–120 in.	Flowers turn to face sun during day. White, yellow or red-brown. Full sun and no better than average soil.
SWAN RIVER DAISY	*Brachycome*	30 cm 12 in.	Small daisy-like flowers bloom all summer. Sprawling plant may require support. White, pink, violet, blue. Suited for edgings, rock gardens. Prefers full sun.
SWEET PEA	*Lathyrus odoratus*	20–300 cm 8–120 in.	Climbing and non-climbing varieties. White, red, lavender, blue. Wide height range. Tall varieties require support. Prefers cool weather, full sun, rich soil.
SWEET WILLIAM	*Dianthus barbatus*	10–45 cm 4–18 in.	Annual and biennial varieties. Large clusters of flowers in white, pink, red and bi-colours. Self-seeds. Prefers full sun.
TOADFLAX	*Linaria*	60 cm 24 in.	Looks like miniature snapdragon. Foliage covered with long-lasting flowers. Difficult to transplant. Good for edging. Prefers cool summers.
TREE MALLOW	*Lavatera*	30–60 cm 12–24 in.	Bushy, hollyhock-like plant with white, pink, or rose flowers up to 10 cm (4 in.) in size. Prefers cool weather and full sun.
VELVET FLOWER	*Salpiglossis*	35–75 cm 14–30 in.	Also called Painted Tongue. Funnel-like flowers up to 7 cm (2½ in.) in size. Yellow, pink, red, purple. Requires early start and prefers full sun.
VENIDIUM	*Fatuosum*	45 cm 18 in.	Orange and maroon daisy-like flowers with a black centre. Suited to rock gardens. Prefers full sun, heat and sandy soil.
VERBENA	*Verbena*	20–30 cm 8–12 in.	Dwarf spreading plant with small flowers in clusters up to 7 cm (3 in.) in size. White, pink, lavender or blue. Prefers full sun.
WALLFLOWER	*Cheiranthus*	35–40 cm 14–16 in.	Biennial usually grown as an annual. Yellow, orange, red or purple spiked flowers up to 25 mm (1 in.) in size. Prefers full sun.
WISHBONE FLOWER	*Torenia*	20 cm 8 in.	Bi-coloured tube-like flowers in purple or white with yellow centre. Prefers partial shade unless climate is cool.
ZINNIA	*Zinnia*	15–45 cm 6–18 in.	Daisy-like flowers in a wide range of heights, varieties and colours. Easy to grow and long-blooming. Susceptible to mildew in August. Prefers full sun.

Tulips

BULBS

Uses of Bulbs in the Landscape

So great is the variety, and so diverse are the ideal conditions for growth, that bulbous plants can be grown to suit any place where bright colour rather than permanent form is needed in the landscape. Spring crocuses and early tulips give a glorious show of colour soon after the snow disappears; the gladiolus displays its beauty in midsummer, and the dahlia is the most varied of the late-summer flowers.

Often the mention of bulbs conjures up a picture of formal beds crowded with early tulips in blocks of yellow, pink or red. Or we may think of informal groupings of daffodils, and later tulips, along the back of a herbaceous border, with groups of crocuses, squills, and other small bulbs at the front. These smaller bulbs, together with various species of tulips, are also very effective in a rock garden. Another way bulbs can add seasonal colour is to place them in groups among shrubs. The bright colours of the flowers are impressive against the multi-shaded green background.

In addition to the spring-flowering bulbs, there are many hardy examples that flower later in the season (see chart). These bulbs are a very useful addition to the home landscape. Most are hardy throughout our region and provide a contrast when grown among shrubs and lend variety to a perennial border.

Bulbs also add to the attractiveness of other areas. Many wildflowers, such as trilliums and trout-lilies, spring from bulbs that can be left in the same spot in a shaded perennial border or wild garden for several years. Daffodils, when naturalized on a grassy slope or in open woodlands, will grow for several years without attention.

Regina lily

Classification of Bulbs for Garden Use

For gardens in southern Ontario, bulbs are classed as either hardy or tender. Hardy bulbs can be left in the ground over winter; tender bulbs must be lifted in the fall and stored indoors.

There are four types of flowering bulbs. The four types – true bulbs, corms, tubers, and rhizomes – differ in structure and in the way they produce new plants.

TRUE BULBS, such as tulips, are thick, underground stems that have growing points or buds in which the embryos of next year's plants are surrounded by overlapping, fleshy layers of tissue. These scale-like layers make the bulb look very much like an onion. The scales are often wrapped tightly around the growing point, as in the daffodil, or may be loosely joined together at the base plate, as in the lily. The base plate is really the underground stem of the bulb; the bud and scales develop from the upper side of the plate, and roots develop from the edges and lower side.

For new plants, extra buds develop from the top of the base plate and grow between the scales of the bulb. The plants increase by gradual division (one or two new buds), as in the daffodil, or by multiplication (several buds), as in the tulip.

CORMS are solid masses of storage tissue that have one or more growing points on top and a base plate on their underside. Crocuses and gladiolus are corms. During growth, roots spring from the edges of the base plate and the storage tissue shrivels.

After the plant blooms, one or more corms for next year's plants grow on top of the old base plate.

New plants also grow from bulblets or cormels that develop on the roots or edges of the base plate.

TUBERS, like corms, are solid masses of storage tissue but do not have a base plate. Shoots and roots grow from the eyes, or growing points.

Some tubers, like the dahlia, shrivel during growth and increase by growing new tubers, in the same manner as potatoes. Others, like the begonia, increase in size; in these, new plants are obtained by cutting the tubers into pieces, each containing an eye.

RHIZOMES are thick, solid, underground stems made up of storage tissue. Stems and leaves develop from eyes or buds on the top, and roots from the underside. Irises grow from rhizomes.

For new plants the rhizomes are cut into sections, each containing an eye.

Growing, Harvesting and Storing

SOIL In general, if drainage is good, bulbs do well in any average garden soil from light sandy loam to moderately heavy clay. However, they prefer a fairly open, fibrous loam that is neutral or slightly alkaline and contains nitrogen, phosphorus, and potash.

Be sure to provide adequate drainage. Although bulbs need plenty of moisture, it is useless to attempt to grow any bulbs other than daffodils in low spots that are wet in winter or spring. Before planting bulbs on land like this, provide drainage to carry the surplus water away. On clay soil, even with fair drainage, it is also a good idea to put some sand under the bulbs when planting them.

To improve the texture of poor

Lily

Daffodil

TRUE BULBS

soil, lighten heavy clay by adding sand and decaying organic matter. To keep light sand from drying out too quickly, add well-rotted leaf mould or old manure at 12 to 16 litres for each square metre of ground. Do this in the spring to improve the texture of the soil to be used for fall planting, and in the fall for spring planting.

Most soils in southern Ontario are slightly alkaline – up to pH 8 – and benefit from mixing brown sphagnum peat moss into the planting soil.

Add limestone to soil that is too acidic. If the pH of the soil is below 6.5, add limestone at a rate of 250 grams per square metre or 1/2 lb. per 10 square feet of ground for each 0.5 pH value needed to bring it up to 6.5. For example, if the pH is 5.5, add 500 grams per square metre or 1 lb. per 10 square feet.

FERTILIZER Spring-flowering bulbs show little immediate response to fertilizer if the soil contains a reasonable amount of nitrogen, phosphorus, and potash. Since most dormant bulbs already contain their food supply for next year's plants, this is understandable. However, the addition of fertilizer high in phosphorus and potash helps in the formation of better bulbs for the following year. Just before planting bulbs, dig in 5:10:13 fertilizer at about 250 grams per square metre or 1/2 lb. per 10 square feet of ground; and in early spring scatter ammonium sulfate at 50 grams per square metre or 2 oz. per 10 square feet over the same area. New research indicates that tulips need a lawn-type fertilizer with a higher first figure.

LIGHT AND WATER Most bulbs prefer full sunlight if there is a good supply of water. However, it is not necessary to have full light throughout the season.

Watering spring-flowering bulbs

immediately before and after the blooming period helps in the formation of larger bulbs. Light, scattered shade also helps; hardy bulbs do well under deciduous trees, particularly if the branches are high.

Most tender bulbs come from tropical climates, where heat is coupled with humidity. Some prefer full sunshine; others like some shade.

INSECTS AND DISEASES Insects, fungus and virus diseases attack bulbous plants. Protective measures need to be taken against them. For example, thrips, an ever-present pest of gladiolus, are controlled by spraying with an insecticide. Mildew on tuberous begonias is controlled by an application of a fungicide such as sulphur, or consult your local garden centre.

Follow these four general precautions:

1. Practise clean cultivation.
2. Disinfect storage cellars, flats, etc., with fungicide that will not injure the plants.
3. Dust bulbs in storage with a combined insecticide-fungicide.
4. Spray growing plants in the garden with a combination spray to control diseases and insects.

Information on pests of specific plants can be found in the accompanying tables.

HARVESTING AND STORING Bulbs that are not to be left in the ground through the winter should be lifted as soon as their foliage dies. For spring-flowering bulbs, this is usually the end of the September or mid-October.

Except for loosely constructed bulbs like lilies, let the bulbs dry thoroughly to avoid fungus rot. If the tops are green, cut them off short, but allow a bit of green to remain right above the bulb. When the bulbs are dry, clean off tops, roots, and old loose scales.

Discard all bulbs showing signs of

Crocus

Gladiolus

CORMS

Begonia

Dahlia

TUBERS

disease or injury. Save healthy ones of normal size for replanting; and if desired, plant small bulbs in nursery rows for a year to increase in size.

Dust dry, tender bulbs with a fungicide. Store gladiolus bulbs dry, but mix others with very slightly dampened sphagnum moss or vermiculite to prevent desiccation. Store at 5–10°C (40–50°F).

Popular Bulbs

FALL PLANTING

Crocus
- Small, early blooming
- In a sunny, sheltered spot will bloom as soon as snow disappears
- Colours: white, white with blue stripes, blue, purple, yellow

Fritillaria
- Closely related to the lily
- Blooms in spring
- Very tall with many flowers arranged around the top of a stout leafy stem
- Plant at the back of the flower bed because of their height
- Colours: yellow, red-orange, white, dull purple

Glory-of-the-Snow
- Small, star-shaped, upward facing flowers often appear when snow is still on shaded ground
- Seeds freely and will form a thick carpet if grassy foliage not cut
- Colours: blue, rosy pink

Grape-Hyacinth
- Small with flowers shaped like inverted urns or grapes, arranged in a tight spike
- Blooms in May and June
- Leaves grow in fall and should be left undisturbed over winter
- Seed freely
- Tolerant of sun or part shade
- Colours: blue

Iris

RHIZOMES

Iris
- Large
- June flowering
- Grows from rhizomes
- When crowded bloom size decreases
- Divide established clumps or plant new ones in late summer, so they have time to establish new roots before freeze-up
- Colours: hundreds of named varieties in a wide spectrum of colours, except bright red. These include blue, soft brown, violet, orange, yellow, pink and white, blue-black, white with light blue edge, and pure white
- New strains that bloom again in the fall are gradually becoming available. These include Autumn Snowdrift, white; English Cottage, pale blue; Fall Primrose, bright yellow; Lovely Again, blue violet; and September Gleam, yellow tinged with pink

Lily
- Tall
- Flowers from June right through the summer depending on variety
- Some will take shade, but most like sun and well-drained soil
- Buy only the hardiest, disease-resistant varieties
- Colours: cover the whole range except for blue

Narcissus (Daffodil)
- Many different sizes
- The true daffodil has one flower per stem and is yellow with a trumpet cup at least as long as the petals. Other types include large-cupped narcissus, one flower per stem with the cup longer than the petals; small-cupped narcissus, one flower per stem with the cup smaller than the petals; double narcissus, more than one ring of petals; triandrus narcissus, several flowers per stem, and several dwarf varieties
- Colours: yellow, white

Bulb Planting Depth Guide

FALL PLANTING

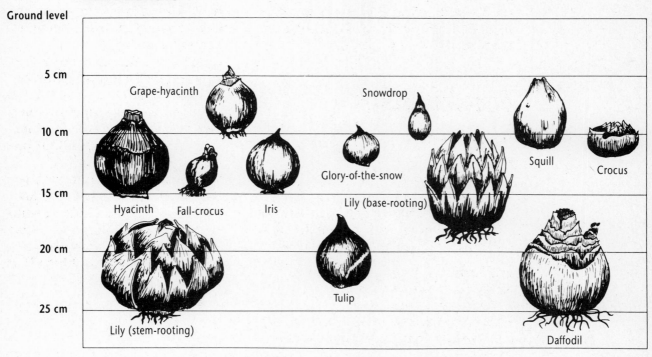

SPRING PLANTING

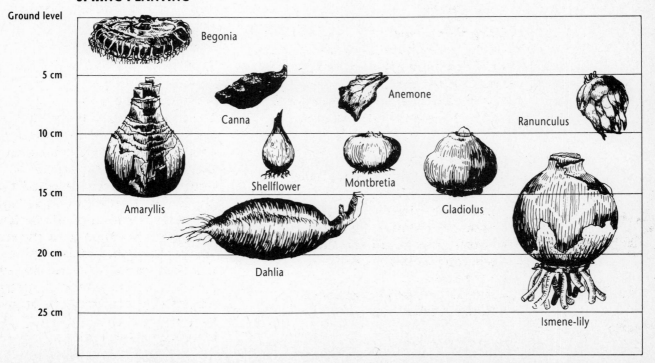

Snowdrop
- Small, early blooming
- Nodding flowers
- Prefers shade
- Colours: white

Squills (Bluebells)
- Small, early blooming
- Bell-like flowers
- Easy to grow in sun or shade
- Several spikes are produced by each bulb
- Will seed freely and form a thick carpet if left alone
- Colours: light blue with dark blue stripes

Star of Bethlehem
- Medium height, early blooming
- Long-lasting with bright green leaves
- Colours: white

Tulip
- Many different sizes
- Classified in four divisions: early-flowering, with both single and double flowers; midseason-flowering, with Mendel, Triumph and Darwin hybrids; late-flowering with lily-flowered, other Darwin, single and double late tulips; and the tulip species division that includes many special hybrids
- Colours: red, yellow, orange, white, pink, purple, black and many bi-colour combinations and shades

SPRING PLANTING

Note: these are tender bulbs that will not survive winter unless they are dug up in fall and stored indoors.

Begonia
- Medium height
- Start inside mid-April and plant outside only after all chance of frost has past
- Large-flowered
- Tuberous
- Blooms from late June to September
- Does well in sun or shade
- Prefers loose sandy soil and plenty of moisture

Dahlia

- Colours: pink, yellow, red, white, orange and bi-colours

Canna
- Tall with many large flowers on each stem
- Start inside mid-April and plant outside only after all chance of frost has past
- Colours: yellow, pink, red, white, orange

Dahlia
- Many different heights and sizes
- Some hybrid flowers are very large and available in both singles and doubles
- Heavy feeders that benefit from lots of well-rotted manure or compost
- Too much nitrogen tends to produce soft growth with few flowers
- Each dahlia tuber must be attached to an old stem on which there is an eye or growing bud
- Tubers rot quickly in cold, wet soil; do not plant them until the soil is warm, in late May or June
- Prune or remove early flower buds to increase size and quality of later blooms and ensure straight stems
- Divide tubers in fall and store indoors
- Colours: yellow, red, pink, orange, maroon, white, purple

Gladiolus
- Tall, various-sized flowers from miniatures to giants
- Corm
- Can be planted early in May and will bloom early (75 days) to late (over 100 days) depending on variety
- Many flowers on tall stalks with lower flowers opening first
- Colours: white, green, yellow, orange, red, pink, purple, blue

 **Bulbs**

TOO MUCH SPRING BULB FOLIAGE

Q: What can I do about spring bulb foliage? My daffodils and tulips do very well, but after blooming time has passed, the remaining foliage threatens to smother the perennials that grow in the same beds. So far my solution has been to tie the bulbs' leaves in knots held in place by rubber bands.

– M.E., Caledon East

A: More gardeners should have your complaint! There is no easy solution. Display garden workers dig out spring bulbs after bloom and replant with annuals. In some cases, tulips are dug up and replanted somewhere out of the way in the garden so that growth can continue until foliage ripens. Both methods are a lot of work each year. I think you have hit on the best solution yourself.

AMARYLLIS

Q: I acquired a clump of strap-like plants with bulbous roots which didn't bloom until I moved them. Then I had an abundance of flowers with very short stems. From their appearance, I would say they are amaryllis. Very healthy foliage appeared last spring, finally dying in late August. Only two flower stems appeared, each with about five pinky-mauve blooms. Does this sound like amaryllis to you? Should I winter the bulbs inside?

– M.D.M., Sunderland

A: Though called hardy amaryllis, this plant is only relatively so. Most local seed houses guarantee them to be hardy to north Toronto, but in your area an early-arriving and reliable snow cover would be necessary for them to survive. Amaryllis also need full sun and a rich diet of minerals. Fertilize every three weeks with diluted 15:15:30 or topdress with dry 6:24:24. Some species require indoor winter storage. Perhaps you could try a division or two of yours indoors next winter.

Amaryllis

Heritage iris

Asters (Michaelmas Daisies)

PERENNIAL FLOWERS

Many of the best known and most attractive garden flowers are herbaceous perennials. The word "herbaceous" means that these plants, like herbs, die down to the ground every year, unlike woody plants that have stems and sometimes foliage that remain above ground. The term "perennial" describes a plant that sends up new shoots each year from its crown, roots or bulb. This description may include some low growing semi-woody plants which are not killed during the winter and also certain biennials which grow from seed, flower the second year and die following seed production. Many perennials such as peonies and irises last for years, requiring only occasional division to prevent overcrowding. Other, short-lived perennials may survive for only a few years and require replanting as they die out.

LOCATION AND SOIL Most perennials grow best in full sunshine though some will succeed in shady locations, provided that the shade is not dense and the soil is not full of tree roots. A half day or more of sunshine is desirable. Strong winds and heavy rains can cause severe damage to tall perennials. A hedge or a planting of shrubs provides protection and a pleasant green background. Make sure that tall trees or other obstructions do not exclude too much sunshine.

Most popular perennials will adapt to a wide range of well-drained soils. Poor drainage encourages root diseases and increases the hazard of winterkill. The subsoil should be open and porous. A hard clay prevents the downward movement of water and restricts root penetration. Soil preparation should be thorough because these plants grow in the same ground for a number of years. Soil should be deeply dug incorporating manure, compost or other organic material.

> THE SUBSOIL IN PERENNIAL BEDS SHOULD BE OPEN AND POROUS. POOR DRAINAGE ENCOURAGES ROOT DISEASES AND INCREASES THE HAZARD OF WINTERKILL.

A most attractive way to group perennials is by co-ordinating colour and blooming time. The size of these groupings, which are known as perennial borders, depends on the interest of the owner and the size of the property. For a small garden, a width of two metres (six feet) is suitable. Where space permits, a curved border is more interesting and allows more natural plant arrangement. Taller plants are generally placed at the back of the border or at the centre of a bed to be viewed from all sides. Groupings should be planned for colour harmony and pleasing contrasts. Striking colours should be used sparingly, with softer colours used in larger masses and repeated frequently. White flowers can be used to separate different colours which are hard to combine satisfactorily, or to achieve appealing contrasts. Having colour from early spring to late fall can be accomplished by selecting plants that flower at various times throughout the growing season.

PROPAGATION AND CARE OF PERENNIALS

Propagation of perennials is accomplished by division, seeding or transplants. For early blooming, seeds may be sown in pots, flats, greenhouses or cold frames. In outdoor beds the soil should be worked up and raked so that the surface is fine. After sowing, the seed bed should be kept moist until germination. For division of existing plants, cut out vigorous young pieces from the outside of the clump. Each division should have roots and top growth or buds from which new growth can start. As a general rule, plants which flower early in the year are best divided in the fall; late flowering kinds in the spring. Large clumps of perennials often become straggly and lacking in vigour. It is wise to divide them.

Care of perennials in the early spring will avoid unnecessary losses. When the soil is fit to work, cultivate the surface lightly, and gently press back into the soil any plants which have been heaved up by the frost. A light dressing of well-rotted manure or compost will improve growth when spread on the soil and dug in lightly. Much work is required if weeds are allowed to grow to a large size. When the soil is dry, plants should be given a thorough soaking. Watering should be done early in the day so that foliage will dry before dark. Tall plants may require support. In late fall cut plants off close to the ground and remove all weeds and debris. After the ground is frozen, a mulch of cedar boughs, bush or straw, may be placed among the plants to hold the snow and prevent freezing and thawing.

PERENNIAL FLOWER GUIDE

KEY TO LIGHT REQUIREMENTS

○ Full Sun

◐ Full Sun to Partial Shade

◑ Partial Shade

◑ ● Partial Shade to Shade

● Shade

ARTEMISIA
Artemisia

○

Propagation:	division, cuttings
Height:	15–150 cm (6–36 in.)
Bloom:	late summer to fall
Varieties:	Silver King
	White Wormwood
	Silver Mound

- Treasured for its white or silvery foliage which provides an excellent transition between other colours.
- Flowers are small and uninteresting, but leaves are soft, aromatic and feathery.
- Divide or layer in cuttings in late summer.

ASTER (Michaelmas Daisy, Perennial Aster)
Aster

○

Propagation:	division
Height:	30–120 cm (1–4 ft.)
Bloom:	mid-summer to fall
Varieties:	Harrington (rose-pink)
	Eventide (violet-blue)
	Frikartii
	(blue with yellow eye)

- Vigorous, fall-blooming clumps of colour.
- Comes in shades of purple, lavender, pink, red, blue and white.
- Divide in early spring and pinch back during summer to induce branching.
- Suffers mildew with August dew.

ASTILBE
Astilbe

◐

Propagation:	division
Height:	40–100 cm (15–36 in.)
Bloom:	early summer to fall
Varieties:	Deutschland (white)
	Fanal (red)
	Peach Blossom (pink)

- Tall plume-like flowers with fern-like leaves.
- Provides graceful, dainty colour for a shade garden.
- Will also grow in sun in damp location.
- Divide plants either in early spring or early fall.
- Heavy feeders needing rich humus soil.

BABY'S BREATH
Gypsophilia

○

Propagation:	seed
Height:	30–100 cm (1–3 ft.)
Bloom:	summer to fall
Varieties:	Bristol Fairy (white)
	Pink Star (pink)

- Airy clusters of tiny white or pink flowers, hundreds in a spray.
- Good for borders, but fairly tall, so give it space or plant toward back of border.
- Plant seeds in spring.
- Tends not to reach full size and bloom until second year.

BALLOON FLOWER
Platycodon

○ ◐

Propagation:	seed
Height:	45–100 cm (18–36 in.)
Bloom:	summer
Varieties:	Album (white)
	Double Blue
	Shell Pink

- Large flowers open from balloon-like buds in mid-summer and last for many weeks.
- Shoots are slow to come up in the spring, so mark them in the fall to prevent trampling.
- Sow seeds in spring in light, slightly acidic, well-drained soil.
- Not long-lived in city gardens.

BELLFLOWER
Campanula

Propagation:	seed, division
Height:	60–100 cm (2–3 ft.)
Bloom:	early summer
Varieties:	Canterbury Bell
	Telham Beauty (light blue)
	Alba (white)

- Large group of plants with bell-shaped flowers that come in various sizes and pastel colours.
- Cut out tall varieties after flowering to encourage them to bloom again.
- Divide or sow seeds in spring and keep soil moist.
- Watch for slugs.

BLEEDING HEART
Dicentra

Propagation:	seeds, division
Height:	30–75 cm (12–30 in.)
Bloom:	late spring to early summer
Varieties:	Dutchman's Breeches
	Alba (white, rare)

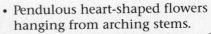

- Pendulous heart-shaped flowers hanging from arching stems.
- Flowers are red-pink but lose colour if they get too much sun.
- Leaves are fern-like, greyish green.
- Divide roots in very early spring.
- Tends to spread by self-sowing if flowers go to seed.

CARNATION (See PINKS)
Dianthus

CHRYSANTHEMUM
Chrysanthemum   ○

Propagation:	division
Height:	30–100 cm (1–3 ft.)
Bloom:	late summer to fall
Varieties:	many and various

- The many varieties of "mum" flower types range from tiny buttons to huge "spider" florets.
- Some varieties are daisy-like. Some have tightly compacted petals and look like pom-poms. Some have spoon-shaped petals. The most familiar, decorative mums, feature large, round flowers with many petals.
- Comes in almost every colour except blue.
- Divide and plant in the spring.
- Even "hardy chrysanthemums" have trouble dealing with freezing and thawing, so mulch heavily in the fall and cover with cedar boughs.

COLUMBINE
Aquilegia   ○ ◑

Propagation:	seed
Height:	30–100 cm (1–3 ft.)
Bloom:	mid-spring to mid-summer
Varieties:	Canadensis (yellow & red)
	Colorado (blue & white)
	Silver Queen (white)

- Columbine comes in almost every colour, including bi-colours in which the inner and outer petals are different.
- A graceful plant with funnel-shaped flowers with long spurs and dainty leaves.
- Seed in spring.
- Remove faded flowers to prevent self-sowing.
- Often short-lived in city gardens.

CONEFLOWER
Rudbeckia   ○

Propagation:	seed, division
Height:	60–175 cm (2–6 ft.)
Bloom:	mid-summer to fall
Varieties:	Black-eyed Susan
	Purple Coneflower

- Daisy-like flowers that provide good fall colour and are easy to grow.
- Most are deep yellow with dark centres except for purple varieties.
- Sow seeds in spring.
- Divide every four years in spring.

CORAL BELLS
Heuchera

Propagation:	seed, division
Height:	30–60 cm (1–2 ft.)
Bloom:	summer
Varieties:	Pluie de Feu (red)
	Rosamundi (coral pink)
	White Cloud (cream white)

- Attractive bell-shaped flowers on wiry stems with dark green mats of leaves at the base close to the ground.
- Sow seeds in spring in fertile rich soil.
- Divide every few years in spring.
- Remove faded flower stems to encourage further blooms.

COREOPSIS
Coreopsis

Propagation:	seed, division
Height:	30–100 cm (1–3 ft.)
Bloom:	summer
Varieties:	Golden Shower

- Flowers are yellow, daisy-like and have a long flowering period.
- Has narrow lance-shaped leaves.
- Will tolerate drought.
- Divide in spring, or sow seed in spring in well-drained, sandy soil.
- Pinch off flower heads to keep in bloom.

DAY LILY
Hemerocallis

Propagation:	seed, rhizome division
Height:	60–125 cm (2–4 ft.)
Bloom:	summer
Varieties:	many and various

- Large, funnel-shaped flowers come in every colour except blue and pure white.
- Most common is the orange day lily found along roadsides, that blooms for a short period in early summer.
- There are many modern hybrids of different colours and blooming periods.
- Divide or sow seeds in early spring or late summer.
- Should be left undisturbed for years.

DELPHINIUM (Larkspur)
Delphinium

○

Propagation:	seed, division
Height:	60–175 cm (2–6 ft.)
Bloom:	summer
Varieties:	Belladonna (light blue)
	King Arthur (purple)
	Connecticut Yankee
	(blue, lavender, white)

- Magnificent tall spikes of closely spaced flowers of many different hues of blue, pink and white.
- Prefers slightly alkaline humus soil.
- Sow seed early indoors for bloom the same season.
- Most will bloom a second time in late summer.
- Overwinters best in cold climates. In milder conditions, cover with a heavy mulch in fall.

EVENING PRIMROSE
Oenothera

○

Propagation:	division
Height:	30–60 cm (1–2 ft.)
Bloom:	summer
Varieties:	Fireworks
	Highlight

- Showy, single yellow flowers up to 5 cm (2 in.) across.
- Leaves are large and tend to spread out at the base.
- Divide plants early in spring and grow in a light, well-drained soil.

FOXGLOVE
Digitalis

◑

Propagation:	seed
Height:	90–150 cm (3–5 ft.)
Bloom:	summer
Varieties:	Excelsior
	Foxy

- Not really a perennial, but rather a hardy biennial that self-sows regularly in cool, damp environment with dappled shade.
- Cut stems of early flowers to encourage rebloom, but leave later flowers to go to seed to ensure healthy plants year after year.
- Tall spikes of tubular flowers in various shades of rose, purple, yellow or white.
- Large leaves at base of plant are poisonous if eaten.
- Sow seeds in late summer for bloom the next spring.

GAS PLANT
Dictamnus

○ ◐

Propagation:	seed
Height:	60–100 cm (2–3 ft.)
Bloom:	mid-spring to mid-summer
Varieties:	Albus (white)
	Purpureus (purple)
	Rubrus (red)

- Flower spikes are usually white on tall stems with rich green leaves to which some people are allergic.
- Name comes from resin found on leaves and upper stem that can be ignited with a match.
- Sow seeds in spring, may take a few years to develop fully.
- Leave plants undisturbed, will not survive division.

GERANIUM (Cranesbill)
Geranium

○ ◐

Propagation:	seed, division
Height:	30–100 cm (1–3 ft.)
Bloom:	mid-spring to late summer
Varieties:	Johnson's Blue
	Wargrave Pink

- Not to be confused with common bedding geraniums *(Pelargonium)*.
- Dainty, 25 mm (1 in.) flowers come in shades of pink, magenta, purple, lavender and blue.
- Easily grown plant that seldom needs division.
- Not entirely hardy in a very cold snowless winter or when many freeze-thaw cycles occur.
- Sow seeds or divide in spring.

GLOBEFLOWER
Trollius

○ ◐

Propagation:	division
Height:	60–100 cm (2–3 ft.)
Bloom:	late spring to early summer
Varieties:	First Lancers (orange)
	Lemon Queen (pale yellow)
	Golden Queen (bright yellow)

- Flowers look like large buttercups.
- Leaves are shiny, dark green.
- Divide plants in early fall.
- Can be planted from seed, but can take over a year to germinate.

HELENIUM (Sneezeweed)
Helenium

○

Propagation:	seed, division
Height:	60–120 cm (2–4 ft.)
Bloom:	late summer
Varieties:	Butterpat (yellow)
	Moerheim Beauty
	(bronze-red)

- Tall daisy-like blooms in shades of yellow, orange and red.
- Sow seeds or divide in spring.

HELIOPSIS (Golden Sunflower)
Heliopsis

○

Propagation:	seed, division
Height:	60–150 cm (2–5 ft.)
Bloom:	summer
Varieties:	Golden Plume
	Summer Sun

- Large yellow sunflower-like flowers at the end of long stems.
- Will do well in any garden soil.
- Sow seeds or divide in spring.

HOSTA (Plantain Lily)
Hosta

●

Propagation:	divison
Height:	30–60 cm (1–2 ft.)
Bloom:	seldom
Varieties:	many and various

- Grown mainly for its unusual leaves which vary in size, shape and markings.
- The leaves are smooth or ribbed and have solid colours of deep blue-greens or are edged in white or yellow.
- Some produce lavender or white bell-shaped flowers on long stems in late summer.
- Divide plants in spring and grow in rich, well-composted soil.
- One of the few hardy perennials that flower in shade.
- Watch for slugs that eat holes in leaves.

IRIS (See section on BULBS)

JACOB'S LADDER
Polemonium

Propagation:	seed, division
Height:	30–100 cm (1–3 ft.)
Bloom:	early summer to fall
Varieties:	Sapphire
	Blue Pearl

◑

- Blue, bell-shaped flowers in bold clusters with fine, divided leaves.
- Will flower all summer long.
- Sow seeds or divide in early fall.

LIATRIS (Gayfeather)
Liatris

Propagation:	seed, division
Height:	60–150 cm (2–5 ft.)
Bloom:	late summer to fall
Varieties:	Blazing Star
	Kansas Gayfeather

○

- Flowers usually rose-purple on a tall spike.
- Buds at the top open first.
- Small lance-shaped leaves.
- Will grow anywhere there is sun and will tolerate infertile soil.
- Sow seeds or divide in spring.

LOOSESTRIFE
Lythrum

○ ◐

Propagation:	division
Height:	60–175 cm (2–6 ft.)
Bloom:	mid-summer to fall
Varieties:	Morden's Pink
	Robert (red)
	Dropmore Purple

- Graceful long spikes of closely set small flowers in shades of pink, red and purple.
- Long lance-shaped leaves.
- Lythrum does well beside a pool or stream.
- Prefers damp soil.
- Divide plants in spring.

LUPINE
Lupinus

○ ◐

Propagation:	seed
Height:	60–120 cm (2–4 ft.)
Bloom:	summer
Varieties:	Freedom (blue)
	George Russell (coral pink)

- Tall spikes of flower clusters in shades of blue, rose, lavender and white.
- Grows in light sandy soil.
- Lupine are not very long-lived, but will often self-seed.
- If self-sowing does not occur, they have to be replanted every 3 years.
- To grow from seed, it is best to nick the seed to hasten germination.
- Start early, indoors.

MONKSHOOD
Aconitum

◐

Propagation:	seed, division
Height:	60–175 cm (2–6 ft.)
Bloom:	mid-summer to fall
Varieties:	Barker's Variety
	Bressingham Spire

- All parts of plant are poisonous if eaten.
- Tall spikes of hooded blue flowers.
- Should be planted in light, well-drained soil that has been deeply cultivated.
- Division is difficult so it is better to leave clumps undisturbed.
- Sow seed in spring.

OBEDIENT PLANT (False dragonhead) ○ ◐
Physostegia

Propagation:	seed, division
Height:	60–100 cm (2–3 ft.)
Bloom:	summer
Varieties:	Bouquet Rose
	Vivid

- Long spikes of many tubular flowers in shades of white, lavender and rose.
- Called "obedient plant" because flowers stay in the position they are placed when turned or twisted.
- Clumps need dividing every 2–3 years.
- Sow seeds or divide in the spring.

ORIENTAL POPPY ○
Papaver orientale

Propagation:	seed, root cuttings
Height:	60–100 cm (2–3 ft.)
Bloom:	late spring to early summer
Varieties:	Barr's White
	Carmine
	(red w/black markings)

- Large showy single and semi-double flowers in shades of white, red, pink, orange and red usually with streaks of other colours.
- Blooms for only short period in early summer, after which the foliage will die back.
- Best planted among later blooming plants for effective colour display.
- Root cuttings, several inches long, are best cut and planted in early fall.
- Sow seed early in spring, though blooming might not occur until the second year.

PEONY, HERBACEOUS ○ ◐
Paeonia

Propagation:	division
Height:	60–125 cm (2–4 ft.)
Bloom:	early summer
Varieties:	many and various

- Large single or double flowers in shades of white, pink, red, maroon and pale yellow.
- Pale flowers are often fragrant.
- Has long arching stems and attractive foliage that lasts all season.
- Before planting, prepare soil by digging deeply and adding lots of compost.
- Likes slightly acidic soil.
- Once planted, roots should be left undisturbed.
- Divide in late summer, 3–5 eyes per division, making sure the eyes are no more than 5 cm (2 in.) below the surface.
- Very long-lasting plants.

Peony

PEONY, TREE
Paeonia

Propagation:	division
Height:	60–125 cm (2–4 ft.)
Bloom:	early summer
Varieties:	many and various

◯ ◑

- A shrub that grows to 150 cm (5 ft.).
- Wide range of colours.
- Does not die back in the winter, but does lose its leaves.
- Varies in hardiness and should have a sheltered location.
- Likes a slightly alkaline soil.
- It is best to buy grafted varieties from the nursery as it is not practical to divide the tree peony.

PHLOX
Phlox

Propagation:	division, cuttings
Height:	30–125 cm (1–4 ft.)
Bloom:	early summer, summer
Varieties:	many, various blooming times

◯ ◑

- Large flower clusters ranging through white, pink, red, salmon, lavender and purple.
- Many different varieties and sizes, some blooming earlier than others.
- Once blooming, most will continue over summer.
- Do not crowd.
- Keeping the plants spaced well apart increases air circulation and helps prevent mildew.
- For best results, thin to about 5 stems per plant.
- Divide plants in spring or take root cuttings in late summer.
- Pinch off dead flowers before they self-seed; self-sown plants produce only pale red flowers.

PINKS (Carnations, Sweet William)
Dianthus

Propagation:	seeds
Height:	30–60 cm (1–2 ft.)
Bloom:	late spring to fall
Varieties:	Grass Pink (tall)
	Carnations (many kinds)

◯

- Pinks range from alpine and rock garden varieties to hardy biennials that self-seed (Sweet William), to border pinks and carnations, to perpetual carnations grown in greenhouses for florists.
- Border pinks and carnations have pink, red or white flowers with pretty bluish-green foliage.
- Some flowers mix the above colours, being white with red edging or visa-versa.
- Pinch off dead flowers to prolong blooming.
- Sow seed in spring, in well-drained slightly alkaline soil (if soil test indicates increased alkaline level is required, do not mulch: add lime).

PRIMROSE
Primula

◑

Propagation:	seed
Height:	20–50 cm (8–18 in.)
Bloom:	spring to early summer
Varieties:	Japonica (white, pink, red)
	Polyahthus (many colours)
	Auricula (yellow)

- Yellow is the most characteristic colour, but many other colours are available.
- Blooms best under cool, moist, spring conditions.
- Sow seed in spring in well-composted, acidic soil.
- If plants become too dense or overcrowded, divide immediately after flowering in early summer.

SALVIA (Meadow Sage)
Salvia

○

Propagation:	seed
Height:	30–125 cm (1–4 ft.)
Bloom:	summer
Varieties:	May Night (deep violet)
	Scarlet Sage

- Related to the herb sage, it has slender spikes of small flowers that bloom over a long period.
- Remove dead flowers to promote further blooming.
- Sow seed in spring.

SCABIOSA (Pincushion Flower)
Scabiosa

○

Propagation:	seed, division
Height:	60–100 cm (2–3 ft.)
Bloom:	summer to fall
Varieties:	House Hybrids
	(various blues)
	Miss Wilmott (white)

- Blue or white flowers with protrudir.g stamens that, when grown in a mass, look like a pincushion.
- Easy to grow with long-lasting flowers.
- Sow seeds in summer or divide plants in spring.

SEA LAVENDER (Statice)
Limonium

Propagation:	seed
Height:	50 cm (18 in.)
Bloom:	summer
Varieties:	Collier's Pink
	Violetta

- Long-blooming plants with sprays of small flowers in pink, purple or white.
- Dark-green, leathery leaves form a rosette at the base.
- Sow seeds in spring in sandy, well-drained soil.
- Has very long roots, so prepare bed by digging deeply.

VERONICA (Speedwell)
Veronica

Propagation:	seed, division
Height:	30–60 cm (1–2 ft.)
Bloom:	summer
Varieties:	Icicle (white)
	Crater Lake Blue
	Minuet (pink)

- Spikes of close-set, small flowers in blue, lavender, pink or white.
- Remove faded blooms to prolong flowering.
- Subject to mildew.
- Sow seed or divide in spring.

YARROW (Milfoil)
Achillea

Propagation:	seed, division
Height:	30–100 cm (1–3 ft.)
Bloom:	summer
Varieties:	Moonshine (pale yellow)
	Coronation Gold (bright yellow)
	Fire King (red)

- Has flat clusters of flowers and attractive fern-like leaves.
- Wild yarrow is white, but garden varieties are yellow, pink or red.
- Can tolerate poor soils and drought.
- Need to be divided every few years.
- Sow seed or divide in fall.

Hybrid tea roses

ROSES

The rose is possibly the oldest flower in cultivation and has always held a special place in the gardens of southern Ontario. New forms of roses are being continually developed, but the main types are hybrid teas, grandifloras, floribundas, climbing roses, shrub roses and miniature roses. Hybrid teas are the most popular because of their low, bushy habit and their continuous, brightly coloured blooms. Hybrid teas have double flowers, usually one to a stem. Floribundas flower in clusters and, though slightly smaller, can have single, semi-double or double flowers. Grandifloras are tall rose bushes with a flower like the hybrid tea, but have several flowers on a stem like the floribunda. Climbers can be ramblers, climbing hybrid teas or everblooming. Shrub roses are hardy, vigorous and have distinctive foliage and wild rose-type flowers with a lovely scent. Miniature roses grow to less than 40 cm (15 in.) high and are especially suited to container growing.

LOCATION Where space permits, a separate garden for roses is desirable. The ideal location is a gentle slope to the south or west that is sunny, well drained and protected from strong winds. Although some light shade may prevent blooms from fading, shade creates conditions suitable for certain fungus diseases. Roses should be planted out in the open where there is good air circulation. Beds wide enough to contain two or three rows of bushes, planted alternately, are generally most convenient. The climbers are suitable for covering fences, trelliswork, and pillars, while shrub roses may be planted as specimen shrubs or with other flowering shrubs in a border.

SOIL Roses thrive in fairly rich clay loam that is neutral or slightly acidic. Clay loams that are well sup-

Peace rose

plied with organic matter retain moisture and plant nutrients much better than lighter soils. In preparing beds for roses, remember that the planting is permanent. The work you put in now will pay off year after year. If there is good drainage, remove the soil to a depth of 50 cm (18 in.); most rose roots will not penetrate any deeper. Loosen the bottom of the excavation with a fork and then refill with successive layers of organic matter and soil. If soil is alkaline, add sphagnum peat moss or slow-release acid fertilizer. If soil is too acidic, apply ground limestone, according to package instructions.

PLANTING The best time to plant is in the spring while roses are still dormant. Fall planting is acceptable in more temperate regions such as the Niagara Peninsula. However, most roses that are planted in the fall do not become sufficiently well established to withstand severe winters even when they are well protected. For best results secure field-grown plants that have three or more stems and buds that are just breaking. As soon as bushes are received they should be unpacked, soaked, and planted.

The hole should be large enough to take the roots without crowding. Make a cone-shaped mound in the centre of the hole and spread the roots down its sides. Make sure that the bud union is at least 5 cm (2 in.) below ground level. Fill in with soil, pack firmly and water generously. When excess water has drained away, mound up around the base of the plant to about 20 cm (8 in.). Cut back branches to 13 cm (5 in.) from ground level after planting. This ensures a compact, well balanced plant.

CARE AND MAINTENANCE Pruning is one of the most important steps in growing roses because it affects the quality and quantity of blooms.

Rambler rose before pruning

Each plant must be considered individually and pruned according to its habit and amount of growth. First, cut back all dead wood and any new shoots or suckers that come from below bud union level.

Hybrid tea roses are pruned after blooms start to wither. Cut back branches to just above the next strong shoot down the stem. With floribundas there are no leaf buds on the flowering stem so cut back to the first leaf bud below it. In spring, after removing dead wood, take out all weak growth and thin canes, leaving about four strong branches. Cut these back to within six buds from the base, making a cut immediately above an outward-pointing bud. Shrub roses are pruned like other flowering shrubs by cutting out the oldest branches as close to ground as possible just after the blooming period.

FUNGI AND INSECTS Injury to rose plants and blooms is often caused by fungi and insect pests. Black spot and powdery mildew are the most troublesome of the fungus diseases. There are also a number of leaf-chewing caterpillars and slugs that can disfigure roses. For those with smaller gardens it is convenient to tackle both problems at once with a insecticide-fungicide mixture. Treatment should begin as leaves develop and continue through the summer. Spray or powder only on a dry, calm day and try to cover both upper and lower leaf surfaces as well as surrounding soil. Avoid spraying water on the leaves in the evening for this encourages mildew. Infected leaves should be removed.

WINTER PROTECTION Most roses require protection during winter. A common method is to mound soil around the base of each bush to a height of 20 to 30 cm (8 to 12 in.). Avoid scooping soil from between your rose plants to build up these mounds. This creates hollows that fill with water and roses are notoriously sensitive to "wet feet". It is better to use soil from another part of the garden. You'll be able to reuse this soil next spring when you gently rake or scoop away the mounds. After the ground is frozen an additional covering of straw, manure, or leaves may be applied and cedar brush or twiggy branches placed on top. The brush helps trap snow which is an excellent insulator. Unless very long canes catch on clothing as you pass by, garden roses do not need to be pruned in the fall. Wait till spring to see how much winterkill there has been.

Large-flowering, repeat-blooming climbing roses are no more winter hardy than non-climbing kinds. To preserve branches – properly known as lengths of cane – unfasten them from their support and lay flat on the ground. Hold in place with pegs or crossed stakes. Cover with a 15 cm (6 in.) mound of earth and add mulch or evergreen boughs after the mounded soil has frozen.

 **Roses**

STARTING ROSE BUSHES

Q: Please advise me how I should start a new rose bush. Do I plant seeds or use branches from an old bush? — *N.A.Z., Toronto*

A: If you are referring to the large-flowered garden hybrids such as floribundas, grandifloras and hybrid teas, they will not come true from seed. And while it is always possible that you will get a plant with valuable characteristics, the chances are more likely that you will get plants far poorer than their parents.

To duplicate a given plant, I recommend a method called layering. Begin by choosing a flexible new branch low on the plant that can be bent to touch the ground. Determine the part of the branch that reaches the ground and nick its underside with a clean sharp knife enabling the branch to form a V-shape with the nicked area at the point of the V. Dust the nicked area with rooting hormone powder purchased at your garden centre. Peg this prepared branch into soft, sandy-humusy soil, burying the nicked area in 5–10 cm (2–4 in.) of soil.

Keep the soil moist but not wet. In a year, roots should be formed and you can sever the plant at the side of the V where the branch is connected to the mother plant. Leave the plant in the same location for a few months or over the winter before transplanting to a new location.

Rambler rose after pruning

Rose Guide

COLOUR	HYBRID TEAS	FLORIBUNDAS	GRANDIFLORAS	MINIATURES	CLIMBERS (c) AND SHRUBS (s)
WHITE	Pascali White Masterpiece	Iceberg Ivory Fashion	Mount Shasta	Cinderella Mary Adair Peachy White	Swan Lake (c) Sea Foam (s)
WHITE WITH PINK EDGE	Garden Party	–	–	–	–
APRICOT BLEND	Seashell	–	Cathedral	Baby Darling Over the Rainbow	Royal Gold (c)
MAUVE	–	Angel Face	–	–	–
MEDIUM YELLOW	–	–	Golden Girl	Yellow Doll	Casino (c) Golden Wings (s)
YELLOW BLEND	Peace	Little Darling Redgold	–	–	Alchymist (s)
DEEP YELLOW	Oregold	Friesia	–	–	–
ORANGE	–	Sensation	–	–	–
ORANGE BLEND	–	Esher O'Farim Traumerei	–	Mary Marshall	–
ORANGE RED	Fragrant Cloud Tropicana	City of Belfast Irish Mist Satchmo	Montezuma Prominent	Hula Girl Scarlet Gem Sheri Anne Starina	Americana (c)
LIGHT PINK	Royal Highness	Bridal Pink	–	–	The Fairy (s)
MEDIUM PINK	Fragrant Hour Miss All-American Beauty Pink Peace	–	Camelot Queen Elizabeth	–	–
PINK BLEND	Chicago Peace Colour Magic First Prize Tiffany	Sea Pearl	Pink Parfait Sonia	Rosemarin	–
DEEP PINK	Electron Peter Frankenfeld	–	–	Pixie Rose	Malaga (c)
MEDIUM RED	Alec's Red Red Lion Toro	–	Carrousel Scarlet Knight	Beauty Secret	Blaze (c)
RED BLEND	Double Delight	Charisma	–	Toy Clown	Handel (c)
DEEP RED	Chrysler John Waterer Mr. Lincoln National Trust	Europeana	–	–	Dublin Bay (c)

ROCK GARDENS

Rock gardens have always been popular and, like so many other aspects of day-to-day life, they are subject to changing fashion. The up-to-date rock garden is designed to create the illusion of a natural mountain outcropping in miniature. Ideally it is placed in the open so that the plants and rocks in it can be observed from many angles. In residential applications, a south or southwest slope set some distance from the house and visible through as many windows as possible is preferred.

SOIL AND SITE PREPARATION Most suitable rock garden plants are native to high altitudes and require full sun and excellent drainage. Unless your site enjoys superb natural drainage, excavate the rock garden area to a depth of 30 cm (12 in.) and build in any slopes and changes in elevation. Then add 10 cm (4 in.) of rubble or coarse stone and a 5 cm (2 in.) layer of crushed stone. The resulting bed is now ready for rocks to be set.

Informality in design contributes to a natural look. Major features like pathways or pools should be located and engineered beforehand, but the exact placement of individual stones is likely to be best achieved through trial and error. To create the illusion of a natural rock formation, all stones used in a garden should be of one kind with uniform colour. Almost any type of stone can be used, but sandstone, which is porous and allows root penetration, is preferred. Weathered limestone of the type seen along the face of the Niagara Escarpment can also be used. Both sandstone and limestone are made up of layers or strata that in nature run in the same direction. Aligning these strata in your rock garden contributes to a natural appearance, as does a combination of large and small stones. Flat stones can be used to create steps or pathways.

Stones of a suitable size for a residential rock garden range from 25 to 125 kg (55 to 275 lbs.). Because of their substantial weight, the cost

TODAY'S ROCK GARDEN IS DESIGNED TO CREATE THE ILLUSION OF A NATURAL MOUNTAIN OUTCROPPING COMPLETE WITH FULL SUN AND EXCELLENT DRAINAGE.

of transporting stones long distances is prohibitive, so it is likely that you will construct your rock garden out of whatever natural stone is found locally. Quarried or artificial stone, broken concrete and paving stones look out of place.

Set each stone into the gravel bed so that it inclines gently backwards into the slope with its broadest face down. To ensure stability, each stone should be at least half buried when the soil mixture is added. Rockery soil can be made from two parts existing garden soil, one part coarse sand, and one part peat moss. Do not use fine sand. Add a layer of soil 15 cm (6 in.) deep. Add acid peat moss to those areas of the rock garden where broad-leaved evergreens are going to be planted. Take care to pack soil firmly around each stone so that air pockets are avoided as these are fatal to plant roots. Your rock garden is now ready for planting.

ROCK GARDEN PLANTS A surprisingly broad range of plants can flourish in a rock garden environment. Traditional rockery plants are dwarf herbaceous perennials that originated in the Andes, Alps, Himalayas, Rockies or Atlas Mountains. They are hardy, low-growing and sun-loving and thrive on gritty well-drained soil. Edelweiss and rock cress are typical examples. In addition, dwarf coniferous and broad-leaved evergreens, low-growing shrubs and dwarf bulbs each can be employed in your rock garden. Lists of each of these plant types can be found at the end of this chapter. Because most rock gardens will have at least a small shaded area near the rocks themselves, several perennials that thrive in partial shade are included.

ROCKERY MAINTENANCE Like other garden areas, a rock garden benefits from a general cleanup in spring. Dead leaves and accumulated debris must be removed and any plants that have been partially uprooted by frost heaves must be carefully pushed back into the soil. Spring is also the time to topdress individual plants that require acid or alkaline-rich soil environments. Keep top dressing to no more than 1 cm (½ in.) in depth.

In summer, keep your rock garden weeded and remove dead flowers and foliage. Water thoroughly when dry. Frequent light sprinklings are to be avoided. The hardiness of rock garden plants and the excellent drainage of the rockery tend to reduce insect and disease problems. In a particularly wet summer, watch for slugs and snails.

Because the growth rate of individual rock garden plants varies, you must make sure that invasive varieties don't take over the garden. Cut back as necessary.

The fall is the best time to transplant or divide many rock garden plants. Just before winter a light covering of straw or evergreen boughs will provide protection from freezing and thawing. In their natural environments, many rockery perennials depend on a thick blanket of snow to protect them through the winter.

Rock Garden Plant Guide

SPRING FLOWERING PERENNIALS
Basket-of-Gold
Candytuft
Moss Pink
Mossy Saxifrage
Persian Candytuft
Prairie Crocus
Rock Cress
Sea Thrift
Soapwort
Spring Gentian

SUMMER AND FALL FLOWERING PERENNIALS

Sunny Locations
Asiatic Gentian
Baby's Breath
Bellflower
Cinquefoil
Globeflower
Houseleek
Maiden Pink
Mother-of-Thyme
Stone Crop
Sun Rose

Semi-shaded Locations
Bugle Flower
Primrose
Rock Jasmine
Violet

BULBS AND TUBEROUS PLANTS

Sunny Locations
Allium
Crocus
Dwarf Iris
Dwarf Tulips
Grape Hyacinth
Narcissus
Winter Aconite

Semi-shaded Locations
Squills
Snow Drops
Trillium (nursery grown)

DECIDUOUS SHRUBS
Note: Because of space limitations in rock gardens, it is crucial to obtain true dwarf varieties. Consult the staff at your garden centre.

Cutleaf Japanese Maple
Dwarf Birch
Dwarf Highbush Cranberry
Kelsey Dogwood
Little Princess Spirea
Low Grow Fragrant Sumac

CONIFEROUS EVERGREENS
Note: Because of space limitations in rock gardens, it is crucial to obtain the smallest dwarf varieties. Consult the staff at your garden centre.

Bristlecone Pine
Creeping Juniper
Dwarf Alberta Spruce
Dwarf Blue Spruce
Dwarf Serbian Spruce
Eastern Hemlock
Eastern White Cedar
Hinoki False Cypress
Japanese Garden Juniper
Mugo Pine
Nest Spruce
Norway Spruce
Sawara False Cypress
Scots Pine
Shore Juniper
Single Seed Juniper
White Pine

BROAD-LEAVED EVERGREENS
Alpine Heath
Bearberry Cotoneaster
Hybrid Boxwood
Korean Boxwood
Pachistima
Rose Daphne
Winter Creeper
Wintergreen

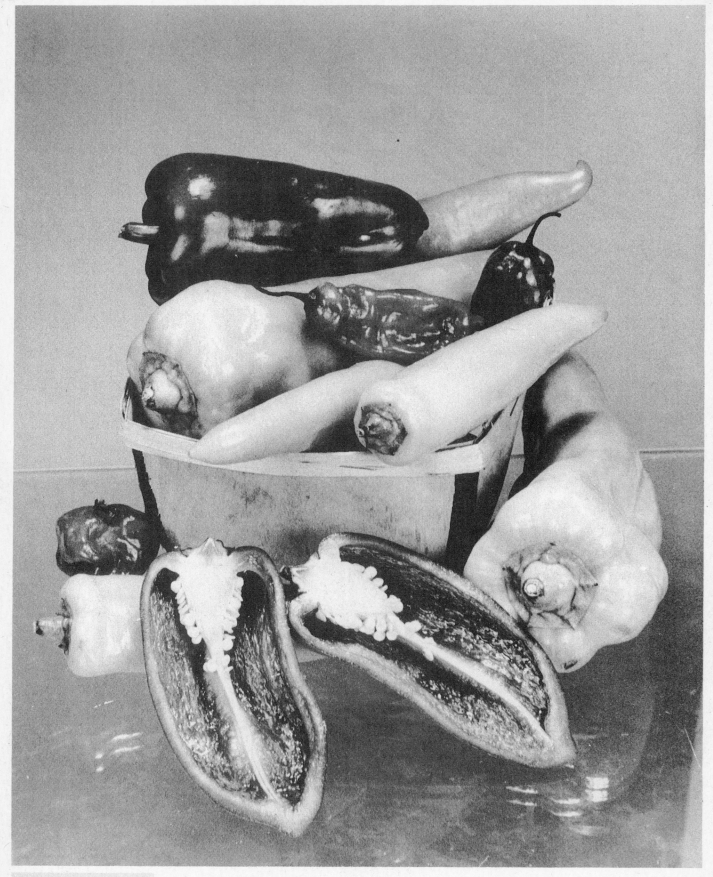

Peppers

GROWING VEGETABLES

To start a new vegetable garden, choose the location with care. Few vegetables thrive without full sun and the site should be near an outdoor water supply. Ideally, the garden should slope to the southwest. Such a location will warm up faster in spring, actually receives more light than a level piece of ground, and stays warmer in the autumn. Do not locate it at the bottom of a rise, where cold air settles and where it will be more susceptible to late spring and early fall frosts.

Too large a vegetable plot is the biggest mistake made by first time growers. It is better to err on the small side: start out small and work on plans to enlarge it. Weeding and maintenance are time consuming and don't get easier as your garden gets bigger. As a rough guide to the amount of food you can raise, consider that a family of six can be fed over the summer on the following: (based on rows 6 m [20 ft.] long)

- three rows of green or yellow wax bush beans
- four rows of beets
- four rows of carrots
- one row each of three different varieties of lettuce
- three hills of cucumbers (in a band eight feet wide)
- 15 tomato plants (one row 120 cm [4 ft.] wide with plants staggered)
- radishes and green onions grown among other plants

In addition, green peas can be seeded in late April to early May for an early crop – they do not do well in hot weather; their space may later be used for more rows of other vegetables like late lettuce and spinach. Trailing plants like melons, squash and pumpkin can be planted in hills at edge of garden. Let their vines run out of the garden or under taller plants. Some vegetables can be planted very effectively in containers. These include eggplant, tomatoes, peppers, climbing squashes,

THE BIGGEST MISTAKE MADE BY GARDENERS IS TO ATTEMPT TO GROW TOO LARGE A VEGETABLE PLOT. START SMALL. LOOK FOR FULL SUN AND SOUTH-WEST EXPOSURE.

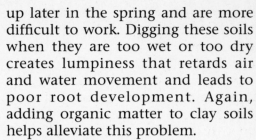

cucumbers, and melons. Many vegetables need support and are ideal for growing against a fence or trellis. These include pole beans, peas, vine tomatoes and any other climbers.

Unless you are a devoted fan, do not waste space on potatoes and corn. They take a lot of room and are cheap to buy in season. Corn must be planted in a series of rows so that the wind can distribute the pollen effectively. A small group of plants will not be sufficient. Cabbage, cauliflower and celery are hard to grow and often attacked by pests. Broccoli and Brussels sprouts are a bit more hardy, but the results often don't match the effort you have to put in. Another vegetable that takes extra effort is asparagus. This perennial, which is a member of the lily family, takes two to three years before it starts producing and needs its own bed. Along with potatoes, there are other root crops that take up a lot of space, such as parsnip, turnips and rutabagas. The choice, though, is up to you. If you have lots of time, space, sun, water, and good soil, you can grow anything you want.

Preparing the Vegetable Garden

Plant roots require nutrients, air and water; if any of these are lacking, growth will suffer. Vegetable plants are easier to manage and require less frequent attention in a soil that is well drained and loose, and contains adequate organic matter. Gravelly loam, sandy loam and sandy soils are classified as early soils because they warm up quickly in the spring. However, they lose moisture rapidly during dry weather; organic matter such as brown peat moss or compost incorporated into the soil reduces the rate of moisture loss. Clay loam or clay soils warm

up later in the spring and are more difficult to work. Digging these soils when they are too wet or too dry creates lumpiness that retards air and water movement and leads to poor root development. Again, adding organic matter to clay soils helps alleviate this problem.

Soil that has living tree roots growing in it is undesirable for vegetable production because the roots compete with the vegetables for nutrients and moisture; and the trees will win.

Dig or roughly plow clay soil in the fall if possible. This rough digging allows freezing and thawing to penetrate the soil clumps, improves the soil structure and helps kill overwintering pests. If it is available, spread rotted manure over the surface before digging. In the spring, work the garden to a depth of 25 cm (10 in.) and cover all manure or compost after thoroughly mixing it into the soil. Turn existing sod over and cover it completely. If couch grass is present, use a digging fork to shake out the roots and discard them. Thoroughly pulverize and level the surface of the soil to obtain a uniform stand of plants from seeds or transplants.

If your garden is in a low, depressed area, you might consider raised beds. They are not difficult to build. Determine how the rows are going to run in your garden and then scrape the soil from between them. Add this soil to the rows, building them up still further. This method is especially beneficial in gardens where there is water lying on the surface of the soil.

Planting Vegetables

If possible plan your garden so that tall plants are located on the north side where they will not cast a shadow over smaller ones. If there is a slope to your garden make sure that

Staked tomato plant

the rows run across and not down the slope. This will prevent erosion caused by water runoff. Any perennial vegetables or fruits such as asparagus, rhubarb, strawberries and many herbs should planted to one side in their own space so as not to be disturbed from year to year.

Cool season crops sown outdoors in early spring when the weather is still cool include: beets, chard, cabbage, collards, broccoli, Brussels sprouts, lettuce, onions, parsley, peas, potatoes, radishes, spinach, turnips, and carrots.

Warm season crops sown in warm weather include: beans, eggplant, sweet corn, cucumbers, okra, squash, and melons.

Long-season crops (requiring two to four months) include: sweet corn, eggplants, tomatoes, peppers, melons, leeks, onions, squash, and potatoes.

Short-season crops (requiring less than two months) include: beans, beets, carrots, lettuce, radishes, spinach, and turnips.

A succession of seedings at regular intervals of some of these vegetables is desirable to assure a constant supply of produce throughout the growing season. In fact, you should plant half rows of lettuce, beets, carrots, spinach, and radishes every two weeks. Cabbages and beans can be planted twice during the season. Your planting schedule depends on how much food your family consumes, but there is nothing worse than seeing unpicked lettuce or spinach going to seed and being wasted.

A square or almost square garden is usually easier to handle than a long narrow one. If possible, rotate your crops so the same kinds of plant do not occupy the same portion of your garden year after year. Rotation is done to reduce the buildup of disease or pest organisms that occurs if the same soil is planted with the same vegetables every year. Note that root crops should not be planted in soil that has had sod on it in the previous year.

When planting seed, consult the package for dates of sowing, depth of planting and spacing of rows. Sow only enough seed to ensure a good stand of plants. Thick sowing wastes seed and increases the labour of thinning. Stretch a line of string tightly to mark the rows and open a furrow by drawing the corner of a hoe along the line to the required depth. If the seed is very tiny and does not need a lot of soil on top of it, you can make a small indentation with the handle of a hoe or rake. This is another way to get straight lines which make it easier to weed when the plants are very small. Make the furrow an even depth so that the seed will germinate uniformly. Place large seeds such as beans and peas individually at the specified distances apart. For these it is best to use an old pencil stub with an elastic around it to indicate the proper depth. Then cover the seed with soil and press firmly over the furrow.

After planting you should water the soil by sprinkling. Many seed packets state the average time required for that particular seed to germinate. Until germination the soil should be kept moist, but not soaking wet or the seed will rot. In windy areas the first couple of inches of soil will dry out very quickly, so keep a eye on the garden until the plants are well established. Another problem can be a severe, hard rainfall that pounds the ground exposing the seed and hardening the surface of the soil. When the sun later comes out it can bake the soil and roast the seed. A fine mulch can prevent this from happening by protecting the seeds and retaining moisture.

When the seedlings are well up, thin the plants to distances recommended on the package. Do this on

Vinedale red pepper plant

a dull day when the ground is moist. Water afterwards to settle the soil around the remaining plants.

COMPANION PLANTING There is no rule that says that plants have to be grown in their own rows or plots exclusively dedicated to just one vegetable. It is sometimes more convenient and beneficial to grow different plants together. This is called "companion planting." For example, strawberry plants make a first rate ground cover between the thorny stems of roses. The strawberry leaves are a nice bright green; the flowers an attractive white; the berries both bright and tasty; and the runners quickly fill the space between the rose bushes with dense growth that shades out most weeds. Blueberries can be planted between or to edge rhododendrons and azaleas, since both require an acid soil. Radishes come up and mature fast and could be grown among slower growing transplants such as carrots or parsley. While their foliage is not that attractive they are likely to be eaten before the other plants need the space. Many herbs can be planted in patches anywhere.

Growing edible plants with decorative ones may in fact help the plants. Garlic grown among roses is supposed to reduce blackspot; marigolds repel insects, animals and nematodes (slender worms). Certain plants add nutrients to the soil that other plants need and *vice versa*. Examples of good partners are squash with dill, tomatoes with basil, and corn with beans.

Vegetable Profiles

ASPARAGUS Asparagus is a perennial vegetable that is difficult to grow, but rewards the gardener by producing tender spears for many years. It requires a permanent site of its own where it can be left undisturbed.

Year-old asparagus

Start seedlings in the second half of May and then transplant to a permanent bed in the following spring. In this permanent bed, seedling roots are planted in an open trench which has been deeply dug and heavily improved with well-rotted manure or compost and bonemeal below the planting level. Carefully add topsoil from the side of the trench to just cover the crowns of the seedlings. (The crown is the junction of root and stem.) As the new shoots grow, gradually fill the trench, until you finish with a wide mounded row. A grass killer is necessary to keep down competition.

You won't be able to harvest until the third year after planting, so this crop needs a long-term commitment. Note that two-year-old roots can be obtained from your nursery. These allow you to harvest in the second year after planting. When the plant is well established it will send up spears early in the spring. When the spears are 20 cm (8 in.) tall, cut them off just below soil level. Be prepared to harvest every other day for four weeks. When you notice that harvest-length spears are less than 6 mm (¼ in.) thick, stop picking and let the rest develop into foliage.

BEANS The most common varieties grown in the garden are green beans and yellow wax beans though you can also grow purple beans, lima beans and soybeans. Beans thrive most of the season and ripen swiftly and continuously over three to four weeks in mid-summer. Beans need full light and good drainage, but are otherwise easy to grow. Plant six to eight weeks after the last frost. Lima and soybeans need a long growing season, so make sure you get early varieties and plant as soon as possible. Bush beans can be planted in rows while pole beans should be planted against a fence, trellis or around a sturdy pole sunk in the ground. Pick snap beans when the pods are pencil size and before the beans inside get too lumpy. The more you pick the more you get, for if bean pods are left to hang, the plant will stop producing. Beans are true legumes, and like peas, their root nodules fix nitrogen in the soil around them.

BEETS Beets are easy to grow, take up little space, can tolerate some shade. Both leaves and roots are delicious to eat. Beet greens have large amounts of vitamins and iron. Beets can be sown directly into the ground as soon as it can be worked. Keep the plants thinned so that there is 8 cm (3 in.) between them. To prevent beets from becoming hard and woody, make sure they get a steady supply of water, well-worked loose soil and proper thinning. While beets are growing, you can pick up to a third of the leaves off each plant to use as cooking greens. When the beet roots are 5–8 cm (2–3 in.) in diameter, it is time to harvest the whole plant.

BROCCOLI and BRUSSELS SPROUTS Both these vegetables need a long season to mature, but do quite well in our southern Ontario climate. Plant seeds directly into the ground after last frost in the spring. Sow seeds in rows 5 cm (2 in.) apart, but gradually thin so the sturdiest plants are about 50 cm (18 in.) apart. A deep mulch around the plants will aid the retention of moisture and save labour in weeding.

Harvest broccoli when the first bunch is formed in the center of the plant. Cut it off 10–15 cm (4–6 in.) down with a knife. New bunches will form in the leaf axles around the stalk. Keep picking them or they will send out flowers and stop producing.

Brussels sprouts can take a touch of frost, which actually adds to their flavour. Picking takes place in late summer and all through the fall. Start picking the sprouts from the bottom of the plant when they are about 25 mm (1 in.) across in size.

CABBAGES and CAULIFLOWER These vegetables are grown less and less in home gardens because they are cheap to buy, take up a lot of space, are fussy to grow, need a very long and warm growing season and are susceptible to pests and disease.

Even the earliest varieties of cabbage will take 80 to 120 days to mature if planted from seed. Cabbages need steady growth or they tend to crack down the middle. This is caused by rapid inside growth due to heavy rain or watering. To prevent cracking twist the plant a half turn or cut the roots on one side with a spade. Harvest when heads look completely formed, but are still firm to the touch.

Cauliflowers grow to about 30–40 cm (12–15 in.) in height and have a flower head, which is the edible part, that is 10–20 cm (4–8 in.) across when mature. They prefer cool damp weather and don't do well in extremes of hot, cold, or dry spells. As soon as the heads are the size of tennis balls, they should be blanched by tying up their leaves so that the head is covered. Unblanched heads turn green and don't taste as good as white ones. Harvest when the heads are large, but still tight and the buds have not opened.

CARROTS Another cool weather crop, carrots do well anywhere in Ontario, but are subject to carrot rust fly larvae. Delay planting to July 1 if this is a problem in your area. Like all root crops, carrots like a deep, loose, sandy loam soil. If the soil is not well-drained, aerated, and free from clumps, stones and rocks, the tuber will grow stunted and misshapen. Sow the seeds directly into the ground about the time of the last frost. Plant in single straight rows to make it easier to weed or mulch. Keep the seeds moist until they

Cauliflower

germinate and be patient, for they take up to 21 days to sprout. When their shoots are about 8 cm (2 in.) high, start to thin and continue to do so until the remaining carrots are 8 cm (2 in.) apart. Harvest carrots when they are very small and tender or let them grow to full size. Harvesting can occur over a period from one to two months long, but carrots begin to get tough and woody if the weather gets too hot or they are left in the ground too long.

Give carrots a good twist when you pull them up. This ensures that the leaves don't break off in your hand. Once harvested, cut off the leaves right away.

CORN If you live in the city or have a small garden, you will not likely be successful growing corn. Each plant requires a lot of space and a large number of plants are required to ensure adequate pollination. Corn grows 150–240 cm (5–8 ft.) tall and you can only expect to harvest two ears per stock. It is wind pollinated from the tassels that form at the top of the plants, each female tassel representing one kernel of corn.

If you do plant corn, make sure it is on the north side of the garden so it does not shade the rest of your plants. Corn needs lots of nitrogen to do well, so work a lawn-type fertilizer or compost into the soil before planting. After the last frost date, sow seed in rows 60 cm (2 ft.) apart and thin plants to 15 cm (6 in.) from each other. Plant four rows of each variety. Corn is ripe when its silk tassels are dry and its top kernels are full. Sweet corn starts losing its sugar content as soon as it is picked, so have the water boiling before you go out to the garden to pick it.

CUCUMBERS The cucumber family includes squash, pumpkins, melons and gourds. They all are warm-weather plants that produce vigorous fast-growing vines with an abundance of fruit. They do best if they have plenty of humus, water and warmth. Some gardeners just throw the seeds on the edge of a compost pile and let the vines trail out from there. The best way to plant them in the garden is to scoop out the soil for a hill, plant four seeds in a circle and one in the middle, and then fill in the hole with well-decayed humus material. Bank up the hill with soil once the plants have started and water regularly. The most common pest is the cucumber beetle, a striped insect that resembles the potato beetle. Keep a close eye on the leaves. If something is eating them look for these beetles and pick them off by hand. Do not let cucumbers get overripe or their taste becomes bitter. Pick small and often.

LETTUCE There is head lettuce and leaf lettuce. Head lettuce, such as iceberg lettuce, is what you see most commonly in the supermarket because it is big, firm, and clean and will keep for weeks if refrigerated. It is more demanding to grow than leaf lettuce for it needs more space and will not survive heat. All lettuce are cool weather plants. Hot summer weather causes them to bolt to flower and seed prematurely. For this reason you should stagger the planting of leaf lettuces and pick them continuously so they don't flower. It is also a good idea to plant them near taller plants so that they get some shade during the day. Stagger your planting of several small patches rather than putting in a large amount at one time. Crisp head lettuce takes up to 90 days to mature and will bolt in temperatures over 21°C (70°F), while leaf lettuce will mature in 45–60 days and takes the heat a bit better. Buttercrunch types are slower to bolt than iceberg types. Lettuce must be kept moist but, if too wet, will attract

Cucumbers

slugs and encourage mildew. Try growing more than one variety and crop often.

MELONS need a long season and really don't perform well in Ontario. On the other hand, **SQUASH** and **PUMPKINS** do extremely well and are relatively easy to grow. Harvest everything before the first major fall frost, with the exception of pumpkins which can survive first frosts though their vines will die.

ONIONS Every garden should have onions. They are fast growing, take up little space, repel animals and are one of the most prolific garden plants. There are many different kinds: globe onions such as Spanish, scallion or bunch onions, pickling onions, leeks, and garlic. All require sunny, sweet, well-drained soil with lots of humus. Most pickling or storage onions are started with sets, which are little bulbs, and should be planted so that just the pointy tips are showing above the ground. Globe onions can be started from seed, but take a long time to mature. It is recommended that you buy transplants started by the nursery. Bunch onions, sometimes called spring or salad onions, can be planted in the garden from seed. **LEEKS** are tall, cylindrical, thick onions that are also best grown from starters. To grow **GARLIC**, buy one head, separate the cloves and plant, pointed end up about 5–8 cm (2–3 in.) deep, preferably in fall for harvest the following season.

Onions can be grown between other plants, in patches, or in rows. Close planting in wide rows followed by thinning every second plant loosens the soil throughout the season. It is important to pinch out any flowering stock that emerges from the top. When mature, the tops will yellow and start to fall over. At this time pull the whole plant out of the ground, braid the dried tops and hang to dry.

Scallions can be picked any time and used immediately in salads. **CHIVES** are another member of the onion family, covered in the chapter devoted to herbs.

PEAS Garden and edible pod peas are strictly a spring crop. Plant peas as early as you can work the ground as long as it isn't soaking wet. Ground that is too wet creates seed rot. Don't worry about a late spring frost, for peas thrive on cooling temperatures. Plant directly into the ground according to instuctions on package. All varieties of peas need some sort of support to keep their vines off the ground and prevent mildew except new "leafless" kinds such as Curly, Lacy Lady and Novella. Plant them beside a fence, a trellis or commercial wire cages. If you have a large open garden, you can stick dead branches or brush into the ground and allow the vines to grow up around them. For row planting, place 120 cm (4 ft.) stakes at either end of the row. Broken hockey sticks are perfect. Stretch string that won't rot between the stakes to form a lattice.

Pick peas as soon as they are firmly formed, starting from the bottom of the plant and working up. Most edible-pod peas are picked before the peas form, when the pod is still flat. Sugar Ann and Sugar Daddy varieties can be picked young or when pods are full. As soon as peas are picked, the sugar in them starts turning to starch, so for maximum sweetness pick just before eating. Peas cannot tolerate heat, so your whole crop will disappear by the end of June. Remove all the dried pods, leaves, and vines, but leave the roots as they add nitrogen to the soil.

PEPPERS There are many kinds of peppers, ranging from sweet bell peppers to large cherry peppers to the long hot red peppers. With pep-

Sweet red peppers

pers, "hot" means firey hot to the tastebuds, so ask your stomach lining how hot you want to go. Store-bought green peppers are picked before they fully ripen, but you will have sweeter peppers from your garden if you leave them till they turn yellow or red.

Like tomatoes, peppers demand warmth, sun, and water. Start seeds indoors eight weeks before planting or buy starters from your nursery. Set out the transplants only when the air and soil have warmed up. Night temperatures should be over 13°C (55°F). Unlike tomatoes, most peppers don't have to be staked. Don't worry if you see flowers drop off, as the plant will form new flowers that set fruit. Picking fruit may be done at any time by using a sharp knife or clippers. Do not pull off by hand as this damages the stem. The more you pick, the more peppers the plant will produce, but they are a temperamental vegetable to grow in our climate.

POTATOES The potato comes from the same family of plants as the tomato, pepper and eggplant. Ideal potato soil is usually described as "a deep, crumbly, well-drained, sandy loam, free from stones, moderately acid (pH 5.5–6.0), and containing adequate organic matter". Such soil warms up quickly in the spring, holds water well and provides good aeration for development of tubers. If the soil is too acidic, dolomitic limestone should be added before planting. Lack of moisture in July and early August can seriously limit the crop results. Potatoes are susceptible to pests, the most prevalent being the Colorado potato beetle which is yellow with black stripes. Their larvae look like bloated pink ladybugs. Sooner or later, every potato patch will get them, but they are not difficult to pick off by hand.

Only buy certified disease-free seed potatoes each year. Many supermarket potatoes have been treated with an anti-sprouting chemical and will not grow. Cut potatoes into pieces that have one or two good eyes and let them air dry in a cool spot for a day before planting. Plant the pieces in a shallow trench 15 cm (6 in.) deep that is partly filled with soil. Place the eyes facing up. You can also plant small, whole potatoes. These are less subject to rot in cold, wet soils.

As the plants grow, gradually mound the soil around them to provide more and more underground space for the tubers to grow under cover and away from light. Light turns potatoes green and poisonous. If the ground is too wet, the potatoes become susceptible to fungi and rot.

A few weeks after planting you will see green foliage. Start hilling when plants are 10–15 cm (4–6 in.) tall, bringing the soil almost up to the top of the leaves. Hilling is a form of cultivation that smothers small weeds and provides a suitable volume of well-aerated soil in which the potatoes can grow. After the foliage dies you can leave potatoes in the ground for a few weeks, but be sure to dig them out before a heavy frost. New potatoes can be harvested any time for immediate use, but for storage potatoes, wait till the skins are mature enough that they do not peel easily. Dig carefully, from underneath and outside the hill when the soil is dry.

RADISHES Radishes are the perfect vegetable for children to plant. The seeds are just big enough to plant one at a time, they only take three to four days to germinate and are ready to eat in about three weeks. Radishes are cool weather plants and should have some shade in the heat of the summer. Don't let them go to seed; pick the common Cherry Belle radish as soon as it takes on a rosy colour. Pick radishes when they

MANY SUPERMAR-KET POTATOES HAVE BEEN CHEMICALLY TREATED AND WILL NOT SPROUT. BUY ONLY CERTIFIED DISEASE-FREE SEED POTATOES EACH YEAR.

are less than 3 cm (1 in.) in diameter as bigger radishes acquire a pithy texture. Radishes act as a deterrent against cucumber beetles and will attract root maggots away from cabbage and cole crops.

SPINACH Like lettuce, spinach is a cool weather leaf crop. Plant as soon as possible in the spring and you will be able to harvest 40–50 days later. Spinach will bolt (go to seed) quickly in the heat. Plant seed 15 mm (half an inch) deep in close rows or in blocks. Constant thinning is required so that the final plants will be 30 cm (1 ft.) apart. You can pick the outside leaves as you need them for use in salad, but as soon as you see buds starting to form at the centre, harvest the whole plant. Stagger spring plantings, don't plant in summer and try a fall planting by starting in mid-August.

TOMATOES Everyone from producers to box plant sellers agrees that the tomato is the favourite home garden vegetable/fruit. Literally hundreds of varieties are available, as are numerous products to help you grow them, from special grades of fertilizer to cages, tents and sunhats. Tomatoes have been grown in bales of straw, in perilite with nutrient solutions, in pure compost, in pots of every description and in soils as varied as sands, clays, and mucks, which all goes to show you just how versatile the tomato plant is. The reason for their popularity is simple: nothing tastes as good as a fresh, garden-grown tomato.

The huge selection of tomatoes offered can be confusing. Maturity dates (time it takes from when transplants are planted to first harvest) vary from 45 days to almost three months. Fruit sizes range from as small as a cherry to as large as a grapefruit; texture from heavy pulp suitable for paste to others rich in juice; and shape from cherry, plum and pear to spherical, ovoid and even the infamous square tomato. For these reasons it is recommended that you go to a local reputable nursery and tell the people what you plan to do with your tomatoes. Chances are that the transplants they started have been selected with your area in mind. You can choose early and main season varieties as well as sweet tasting and firm kinds for the table, or pulpy heavy tomatoes for canning or making into paste. It is best to try a couple of varieties with different maturity dates until you establish which are your own favourites.

Although certain varieties of processing tomatoes are grown directly from seed in milder areas of south-western Ontario, direct seeding is not recommended for home gardens. It is usually more practical and less costly to purchase greenhouse-grown tomato seedlings than to grow plants from seed. For best results, select stocky, medium-green, vigorous plants which are about 18–23 cm (8 in.) tall.

If you want to grow your own, start seeds in a shallow, well-drained container six to seven weeks before planned garden planting. Although exposure to light is not necessary for germination, as soon as the seeds come up give them as much light as possible. Keep the soil moist (but not wet) to maintain steady growth. The kitchen window sill, a favourite spot, may give adequate sunlight to seedlings if it faces south, but remember that high temperatures of 27°C (80°F) or more may promote "leggy" growth. Pinch back the growing tips if your plants show signs of becoming spindly. If you are using fluorescent lamps, use an off/on timer, for seedlings should not get less than 16 hours of light a day.

One week before plants are to be set in the garden, begin the process of hardening off or gradually checking their growth by reducing temperature to about 16°C (60°F). Gradual exposure to outdoor condi-

Above and on the following two pages, three pruning techniques for tomato plants.

tions is very good practice. Set tomato plants in the garden, when there is no risk of frost, towards the end of May or beginning of June. Little is gained by planting earlier because air and soil temperatures are generally too cold for good growth.

Set plants that are in peat pots directly into soil without removing pots. To allow roots to spread, punch holes in the sides or bottom of the pot or simply remove the bottom before planting. With bare-rooted plants pulled from flats, be careful not to disturb their roots. Plant so that the main stem is at least 5 cm (2 in.) deeper than it was originally. Set leggy, tall plants even deeper or bury the stems in a sloping position, leaving only the top 15 cm (6 in.) above ground. Press firmly around each plant. Dry soils or hot weather could cause seedlings to wilt. If it is hot or sunny, it is best to plant in late afternoon or evening. Water well with a transplanter solution.

Spacing of tomato plants depends on the variety, soil fertility, and whether or not plants need to be staked. If tomatoes are to be staked, the stakes should be put into the ground before transplanting so as to not disturb roots later on.

To obtain maximum tomato production in a small garden space, it is better to stake and grow a number of plants close together than a few plants at wider spacings. For table use, it is suggested that you grow three plants per person in your household. Grow twice as many plants for canning.

Tomatoes need an abundant supply of water for vigorous, uniform growth. If there is no rainfall for a week, water plants thoroughly. Heavy soakings at weekly intervals are better than several light sprinklings. Do not wet foliage any more than is necessary. Prune tomatoes by snapping off the small side shoots where the leaf stem joins the main stem. Flower clusters arise directly from the stem, so start removing new flower clusters after the end of July. This conserves food for the fruits already set.

Pick tomatoes when fully ripe for best flavour, colour and texture. In the fall, harvest all ripe and mature green tomatoes before a predicted heavy frost. Fruit ripening and quality is strongly influenced by temperature. If mature, green or turning tomatoes can be ripened satisfactorily indoors. Fruits exposed to cool or chilling temperatures do not keep well and are susceptible to rotting.

TURNIPS AND RUTABAGAS Turnips are a strong-flavoured root vegetable with leaves that sprout right from the root itself. Like radishes, turnips do better in cool weather, so it is important to plant early varieties. The rutabaga is bigger, but also takes longer to mature (90 days rather than 45–60 days for turnips). A sunny bed of 1 square metre (1 square yard) will yield up to 30 turnips. Seeds can be sown directly into the garden as soon as the soil can be worked. Turnips and rutabagas need frequent weeding and a good, deep soaking once a week if the weather is dry. Their leaves make delicious and nutritious salad. Dig up turnips when they are 5–8 cm (2–3 in.) in diameter. Rutabagas will grow twice as big. Both vegetables can tolerate a light fall frost and some say that a frost improves their flavour. Dipping them in paraffin wax will keep moisture from escaping and prolong their storage life. Both turnips and rutabagas are very cheap to buy, so plant them only if you have lots of sunny garden space.

Tomato plant respond to various pruning techniques.

Q&A Vegetables

BEEFSTEAK TOMATOES

Q: What happened to beefsteak tomatoes? I have grown them successfully for over 45 years. In 1986 I planted Bonny Best and Beefsteak plants in the same location as usual and fertilized a few times with grade 4:10:12. The crop of Bonny Best was fine, but the Beefsteaks grew into 2 m (6 ft.) plants with luxurious foliage, but no fruit.

This year, I planted Early Girl and Beefsteak. The Beefsteaks were planted where Bonny Best was located in 1986 and vice versa. I used the same fertilizer. The Early Girls are doing well on average-sized plants. The Beefsteaks are again large plants with lush foliage, but no fruit.

How can I correct this situation next year?   – *R.S.S., Willowdale*

A: I must again express a sense of wonder at gardeners using such inferior old selections as Beefsteak or Bonny Best. Far, far better new hybrids are available. One seed firm says that Bonny Best, which dates to before 1934, is listed for sentimental reasons only. The Beefsteak cultivar is an 80-day type that tends to blemish from cracked or split shoulders and uneven ripening. Few catalogues now list it.

Seed strains can run down.

Instead, try Beefsteak VFN at 60 days; Bush Beefsteak (62 days) or better, some modern hybrids such as Ultra Girl (62 days), a staking hybrid; Better Boy (72 days); or for a long-season crop, Burpee's Big Boy (78 days); Glamour (75 days); or Floramerica (73 days) which is resistant to or tolerant of more than 15 diseases.

In the situation described above, you may be using too much fertilizer or watering too much. Instead, try using moderate quantities of wood ashes and bone meal. Dig lots of compost into the soil to help it retain moisture while, at the same time, draining efficiently. Try to rotate crops so your tomatoes don't grow in the same place more often than every four years.

Your biggest problem, however, could well be too much shade. If you have been gardening on the same lot for 45 years, it is likely that nearby trees and, perhaps, buildings have increased in size. Full sun is crucial for a successful crop of tomatoes.

"Square" tomatoes

Pruned tomato plant

Vegetables CONTINUED

GREEN PEPPER SEEDS

Q: I am unable to find sweet green pepper seeds at my garden centre. Are they particularly difficult to grow?
– V.C., Cannington

A: There seems to be a general misunderstanding of what green bell peppers are. These popular salad and cooking ingredients are, in fact, unripe fruit of the pepper plant, which is native to much warmer climates than our own. Ripe peppers can be red, yellow, orange, purple or brown. But only unripe peppers are green.

It is true that certain cultivars produce big, fleshy peppers that may be picked green for table use. But they are also picked green and unripe because they are firmer and last longer on counter shelves. They also bruise less easily than ripe peppers.

One cynical comment I heard was that producers and food retailers promote the use of unripe peppers because they have a longer shelf life and travel better. Certainly they are cheaper to buy. But ripe red sweet peppers are as easy for the home gardener to grow as the kinds that usually are sold unripe.

The other side of the coin is that neither does as well here as in climates that are more reliably warm. Our climate provides a roller coaster ride of heat and cold waves. Despite the search for new cultivars more suitable to our climate, there is a net deficit of sweet peppers in Ontario – we buy more than we grow. According to the Ontario Ministry of Agriculture and Food, "The north shore of Lake Ontario and Lake Erie are the northern limit for the species, failure is easy and extra skill is needed to produce profitable crops." Commercial growers have more failures with peppers than with any other crop.

Peppers need warm soils and are sensitive to varying weather. They like hot, humid weather but won't set fruit in high temperatures. They drop blossoms at temperatures higher than 32°C (90°F). Their red colour develops best between 18–24°C (65–75°F). As temperature falls, colour development decreases and stops completely at 13°C (55°F).

Peppers will succeed on a range of soils, but do best on sandy loams that warm up in early spring.

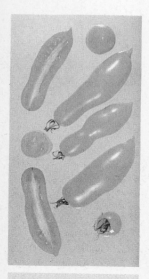

Peppers

 **Vegetables** CONTINUED

DIVIDING RHUBARB

Q: The rhubarb in my yard is 25 years old. Last year we divided it in three and transplanted it from a shady flower garden to a sunny vegetable plot. It grew spindly. Why? Does it need fertilizer? Should it be picked next spring?

– B.L., Rexdale

A: The spindly stalks are due to the plant being divided and moved. Like any other plant, it needs time to grow new feeder roots and new leaves to make food to store in the tuberous roots.

Decayed leaves or worked compost plus a leaf-stimulating product (20:5:10 fertilizer) should be piled around the plants in fall. Do not cut leaves from plants next spring. Wait a year. It is also unwise to cut stalks in August. The plant needs its leaves to make food at this time.

RHUBARB WORM

Q: What can I do about rhubarb worm? This year has been worse than ever before. Stalks were very tender and red early in the season, but have been almost useless after June 1. Since then they have grown only to the thickness of a pencil with a row of eruptions the whole length of the stalks.

– M.L., Grimsby

A: Rhubarb is subject to a pest called the rhubarb Curculio or weevil. This is a form of snout beetle up to 12 mm (½ in.) long. The female punctures the stalks and lays eggs in them. The hatchlings eat their way out.

But the larvae do not develop on the rhubarb itself. Instead they feed on a common perennial weed called curled dock. Dock plants are often found near rhubarb plantings. Their lower leaves are long and narrow with a wavy margin. The stems are sturdy with flowers appearing in dense clusters at the top in early summer. The root is a large taproot.

Treatment includes hand picking and destroying all beetles and all dock plants nearby. This means digging out the taproots, preventing seed formation and carefully spraying all dock leaves and stems with glyphosate which is sold ready-mixed in spray bottles. This herbicide penetrates to the root and usually kills the whole plant in ten days. It is not selective, so use it carefully. It will not harm the soil or the brown bark of mature shrubs or trees.

The European corn and stalk borer have been known to tunnel in rhubarb stalks. The eggs from these late summer moths overwinter on nearby grass and weeds, hatch in spring, and then enter rhubarb stalks and burrow up. It is usually too late to stop damage once it has been noticed. Sanitation is the best control. Discard leaves and tips in a compost pile. Keep grass edged well back of the cultivated area around rhubarb crowns and keep the area of the bed weed-free.

Rhubarb

Vegetable Guide

NAME	WHEN TO PLANT	SEED OR TRANS- PLANT	PLANTING DEPTH	DISTANCE BETWEEN PLANTS	DAYS TO YIELD	POSSIBLE SOWINGS	NOTE
ASPARAGUS	May 15–30	Transplant	4 cm 1½ in.	30 cm 1 ft.	3 yrs.		Transplant seedlings to permanent bed in second spring, before the buds on the crown break dormancy.
BEAN, BUSH	May 5–25	Seed	5 cm 2 in.	8 cm 3 in.	50–70	4	Best on warm loam where nights are dry. Bears more pods if picked young.
BEAN, LIMA	May 20–30	Seed	5 cm 2 in.	5 cm 2 in.	70–80	1	Warm climate preferred.
BEAN, POLE	May 5–25	Seed	5 cm 2 in.	25 cm 10 in.	60–70	1	Grows best when trained on fences or poles.
BEET	April 20–May 10	Seed	1 cm ½ in.	5 cm 2 in.	55–70	many	Use thinned plants for greens.
BROCCOLI (early)	April 25–May 5	Transplant	1 cm ½ in.	60 cm 2 ft.	60–70	1	In spring, transplant as early as possible to miss summer heat. Always harvest when the individual buds on the cluster are still tight. After the central head is harvested, small side branches develop and may be picked every few days.
BROCCOLI (late)	May 5–July 10	Seed	1 cm ½ in.	60 cm 2 ft.	60–70	1	Late sowing helps plants escape summer heat at heading time.
BRUSSELS SPROUTS	April 5–25	Transplant	6 mm ¼ in.	60 cm 2 ft.	70+	2	Nip out growing point of plant once sprouts start to form.
CABBAGE (early)	April 5–25	Transplant	1 cm ½ in.	45 cm 18 in.	70–105	2	Heavy feeders. Grow on rich soil. Bolts more easily when exposed to prolonged cool weather, so do not plant earlier than recommended.
CABBAGE (late)	May 10–June 1	Seed	1 cm ½ in.	45 cm 18 in.	70+	1	Do not attempt late sowing in districts with short growing seasons.
CARROT	April 15–May 5	Seed	15 mm ¾ in.	5 cm 2 in.	65–75	many	Thin at bunching stage. In heavy soils use short varieties.
CAULIFLOWER (early)	May 5–10	Transplant	1 cm ½ in.	45 cm 18 in.	60–75	1	Tie leaves over heads when nearing maturity. Purple type does not need tying. Harvest before heads become coarse and "ricey".
CAULIFLOWER (late)	June 25–July 25	Transplant	1 cm ½ in.	45 cm 18 in.	60–75	1	Can be transplanted well into June for fall maturing.
CELERY (early)	May 5–15	Transplant	3 mm ⅛ in.	15 cm 6 in.	120–150	1	Seed heavily as germination is often poor. Do not sow late in districts with short growing seasons.
CELERY (late)	April 10–20	Seed	3 mm ⅛ in.	15 cm 6 in.	120–150	1	Both early and late varieties very sensitive to high and low temperatures.
CHARD, SWISS	April 10–June 1	Seed	15 mm ¾ in.	25 cm 10 in.	55+	many	Harvest outside stalks only.

NAME	WHEN TO PLANT	SEED OR TRANS-PLANT	PLANTING DEPTH	DISTANCE BETWEEN PLANTS	DAYS TO YIELD	POSSIBLE SOWINGS	NOTE
CHINESE CABBAGE	April 10–June 1	Seed	6 mm 1/4 in.	25 cm 10 in.	75+	1	Grows best in fall. Sow late.
CORN (early)	April 25–July 1	Seed	25 mm 1 in.	45 cm 18 in.	70–80	2	Plant three or four rows of each variety to ensure pollination. Don't mix ordinary with super-sweet cultivars. Use dwarf varieties in small gardens. If only one variety is being replanted, do so one week after first planting.
CORN (late)	April 25–June 15	Seed	25 mm 1 in.	45 cm 18 in.	85–95	2	Make successive plantings of late varieties every 15 to 20 days.
CUCUMBER	June 10–15	Seed	25 mm 1 in.	45 cm 18 in.	60–70	2	If started indoors, plant in pots or bands. Harvest before fruits yellow.
EGGPLANT	June 1–14	Transplant	15 mm 3/4 in.	60 cm 2 ft.	70–80	1	Grow in a protected site in rich, warm soil. Harvest before the glossy stem colour becomes dull and the flesh becomes tough.
ENDIVE (early)	April 20–May 10	Seed	1 cm 1/2 in.	25 cm 10 in.	90+	2	Sow in early spring as early as possible.
ENDIVE (late)	June 1–20	Seed	1 cm 1/2 in.	25 cm 10 in.	90+	2	Grows best in fall.
KALE	April 1–June 1	Seed	6 mm 1/4 in.	60 cm 2 ft.	55–60	1	Light autumn frost improves the quality.
KOHLRABI	April 30–June 1	Seed	25 mm 1 in.	10 cm 4 in.	60+	3	Use when stems are slightly smaller than tennis balls.
LEEK	May 10–30	Seed	1 cm 1/2 in.	15 cm 6 in.	150	1	Bleach stems by banking with earth, though this may not be necessary with newer varieties.
LETTUCE, HEAD (early)	April 1–10	Seed	1 cm 1/2 in.	30 cm 1 ft.	75–86	many	Sow either early or late, as it grows best if heading does not occur in summer heat.
LETTUCE, HEAD (late)	June 25–July 5	Seed	1 cm 1/2 in.	30 cm 1 ft.	75–86	many	As above.
LETTUCE, LEAF	April 1–August 1	Seed	1 cm 1/2 in.	25 cm 10 in.	40–45	many	Extra tender if not thinned.
MUSKMELON	May 20–June 10	Transplant	15 mm 3/4 in.	45 cm 18 in.	80–120	2	Guard against cucumber beetle but do not use malathion insecticide.
OKRA	May 25–June 1	Transplant	25 mm 1 in.	30 cm 1 ft.	50–60	2	Requires heat and a lot of attention. Used to flavour soup. Pick young tender pods every other day.
ONION (seed or set)	April 5–25	Seed	25 mm 1 in.	8 cm 3 in.	145–165	2	Sets favoured for early bulbs and green onions.
ONION (transplants)	April 10–20	Transplant	– –	10 cm 4 in.	115–135	1	A healthy plant that is easy to grow.

Vegetable Guide
CONTINUED

NAME	WHEN TO PLANT	SEED OR TRANS-PLANT	PLANTING DEPTH	DISTANCE BETWEEN PLANTS	DAYS TO YIELD	POSSIBLE SOWINGS	NOTE
PARSLEY	May 10–15	Seed	1 cm 1/2 in.	10 cm 4 in.	80+	3	When potted, also use during winter to garnish food.
PARSNIP	April 10–May 30	Seed	15 mm 3/4 in.	10 cm 4 in.	110	1	Must use fresh seeds every year. Very slow to germinate.
PEAS	April 10–May 25	Seed	5 cm 2 in.	5 cm 2 in.	60–75	3	Sow early. Will not grow successfully in summer heat.
PEPPER	May 25–June 20	Transplant	15 mm 3/4 in.	60 cm 2 ft.	65–75	1	Needs a protected site with rich warm soil. Green peppers are red peppers that have not fully ripened.
POTATO (early)	April 5–May 5	Seed	10 cm 4 in.	30 cm 1 ft.	80–100	1	Fertilize according to soil test. If a test is not available, work in 8:16:16 fertilizer before planting. When crop is 15–30 cm (6–12 in.) high, broadcast 34:0:0 and hill the crop immediately. Control insects. Keep harvested potatoes from light or skins will turn green.
POTATO (late)	May 1–June 1	Seed	10 cm 4 in.	30 cm 1 ft.	110–130	1	As above. Later varieties are best for storage. Yukon Gold is an excellent keeper.
PUMPKIN	May 25–June 10	Seed	25 mm 1 in.	120 cm 4 ft.	100–110	2	Place plenty of compost under trench in which seed is sown.
RADISH	April 1–15	Seed	1 cm 1/2 in.	25 mm 1 in.	28–35	4	Will grow right up to first snow flurries. Lack of water causes no flavour and woody texture.
RHUBARB	April 14–May 1	Transplant	– –	90 cm 3 ft.	–	–	Requires rich topsoil.
SPINACH (early)	April 1–20	Seed	25 mm 1 in.	15 cm 6 in.	40–45	2	Does not grow on hot, sandy soil. Does best under cool conditions on rich loam.
SPINACH (late)	July 15–August 1	Seed	25 mm 1 in.	15 cm 6 in.	40–45	2	As above.
SQUASH	May 25–June 10	Seed	25 mm 1 in.	90 cm 3 ft.	95–110	2	Dust vines for cucumber beetle.
TOMATO (unstaked)	May 15–June 1	Transplant	1 cm 1/2 in.	90 cm 3 ft.	62–66	2	Use a 1:2:3 fertilizer ratio as a side dressing after first flower cluster has set fruit. Leaves are poisonous if eaten.
TOMATO (staked)	May 15–June 1	Transplant	1 cm 1/2 in.	60 cm 2 ft.	75–82	1	As above.
TURNIP	July 15–August 1	Seed	1 cm 1/2 in.	10 cm 4 in.	50–55	1	Best as a fall crop.
WATERMELON	May 20–June 10	Transplant	25 mm 1 in.	45 cm 18 in.	80–95	2	Use a 1:2:3 fertilizer ratio at planting time.

HERBS

The term "herb" can be applied to a great many plants, but the ones discussed here are mainly used as food seasonings or flavourings. Many of these are fragrant and colourful as well. Because of their versatility, the four most widely used herbs are savory, marjoram, basil and thyme.

LOCATION AND CULTURE Generally speaking, herbs do best in full sunlight and in a protected location on well-drained sandy-loam soil away from competing plants. The plot need not be large as only a few plants of each type are needed for most home requirements. In olden days, gardeners would place a wagon wheel flat on the ground and in the area between each spoke, plant a different herb.

Herbs are remarkably easy to take care of and do not need high soil fertility to do well. Indeed, the reason many herb gardens are not as successful as they otherwise might be is that they have been treated too well. Once planted, herbs require no fertilization, very little water, no spraying and only occasional weeding.

Herbs can be annuals, biennials or perennials, though those left to overwinter should be mulched with straw to protect their roots. Some tender perennials, such as rosemary, must be dug up in the fall, potted, and grown inside in a sunny window for the winter.

Seeds may be sown directly into the garden after the ground warms up in the spring. Prepare a deep, fine seedbed and plant to a depth of at least twice the diameter of the seed. Thin the seedlings to a proper spacing as they grow. Annuals need to be sown every year, perennials may be sown from seed or obtained from cuttings or division. For cuttings, take an 8–10 cm (3–4 in.) tip or stem cutting and root it in moist sand or vermiculite. Remove the leaves or buds from the bottom half of the cutting, then stick it in the rooting medium and cover with

MANY HERB GARDENS FAIL BECAUSE PLANTS HAVE BEEN TREATED TOO WELL. ONCE PLANTED, THEY REQUIRE LITTLE WATER AND ONLY OCCASIONAL WEEDING.

plastic to keep the humidity high. For division, divide the clumps at the crown (junction of roots and stem) into separate pieces in the spring, and replant the pieces.

HARVESTING Herbs can be eaten fresh, or preserved by drying or freezing. The most commonly used plant parts are the leaves and seeds which contain the flavouring oils. Drying concentrates and preserves these oils, but must be timed properly to preserve maximum flavour for the longest period of time. Leaves should be harvested just before or as the flower buds open. Harvest seeds when they are just ripe. Always keep at least two sets of leaves at the base of the stem so the plant will continue growing. Harvesting is best done early in the morning, after the dew has evaporated and before the heat of the sun dissipates the fragrance.

Chives can be harvested weekly over the outdoor season and grown indoors under lights.

Dry leaves by hanging the cut stalks upside down, tied together in bunches, in a warm, dry, well-ventilated and preferably dark room. When they begin to shrivel, put a brown paper bag around them to catch the falling leaves. Store away from direct light in a cool dry place. Seeds can be dried on screens, only one layer deep, and then stored in sealed containers.

Herbs can also be preserved by freezing them in plastic bags. Wash, drain and quick-freeze entire stalks with leaves. While blanching is not necessary for all herbs, dill, chives, tarragon and basil are blanched by dipping the stalks in unsalted, boiling water for 50 seconds.

Basil

Herb Guide

NAME	USES	CHARACTERISTICS	PROPAGATION	CULTURE	HARVEST
ANISE *Pimpinella anisum*	• Green leaves and seeds in salads, meats, bakery goods • Tastes somewhat like licorice	• Annual • Slow-growing • Whitish flowers in flat clusters • Finely cut lobed leaves	• Seed • Use fresh seed stock	• Likes sun • Space 15–20 cm (6–8 in.) apart	• Use leaves fresh • Harvest seeds when ripe • Dry seeds, remove from stems and store
BORAGE *Borago officinalis*	• Young leaves have cucumber flavour. Use in salads and pickles • Use fresh leaves in eggs and with fresh flower sprays in fruit drinks	• Annual • Bushy plant • Coarse velvety leaves • Grows 1 m (3 ft.) high • Blue flowers	• Seed • Sow early spring • Self sows	• Needs dry, sunny location	• Pick blossoms as they open • Pick leaves fresh
CARAWAY *Carum carvi*	• Seeds used to flavour bread, pastry, meat, soups, sauces, confections	• Biennial • Feathery foliage • Creamy flowers • Resembles carrot	• Seed • Sow fall or spring	• Full sun, light soil • Seeds produced second year	• Dry seed heads • Harvest seeds in autumn of second year
CHEVRIL *Anthriscus cerefolium*	• Leaves fresh or dried used as a garnish for fish, in soups, in omelettes or mixed with salad greens	• Annual • Goes to seed in June • Leaves are parsley-like, ferny	• Seed • Sow in fall and spring for succession of greens	• Partial shade • Rich organic soil	• Leaves best used fresh • Freezing is the best way to preserve
CHIVES *Allium schoeno-prasum*	• Clumps and blooms decorative in gardens • Leaves used fresh or dried in salads and as seasonings • Has onion flavour	• Perennial bulb • Can be used the first season • Resembles fine-leaved onions • Grows in clumps • Violet flowers	• Division of bulbs or seed	• Rich moist soil • Plant same as onions • Divide clumps and pot for indoor use during winter	• Leaves best used fresh • Holds flavour better frozen than dried • To dry, cut into small pieces and dry 7 days
CORIANDER *Coriandrum sativum*	• Seeds used for spices in baking, dressings • Tastes and smells like orange leaves in stuffings, curries	• Annual • 60 cm (2 ft.) tall, rampant • Pinkish flowers • Disagreeable odour	• Seed • Start early inside in cold frame	• Needs space, full sun, light soil	• Harvest seeds as soon as ripe before shattering occurs • Seed flavour develops upon drying • Dry leaves for use
DILL *Anethum graveolens*	• Leaves used for salads • Fresh leaves and seed stalks for dill pickles • After drying, use to season meats, fish, vegetables	• Annual • 1 m (3 ft.) tall, rampant • Feathery foliage	• Seed • Sow early • Repeat sowings for summer-long supply	• Needs space, rich soil	• Leaves are best just as flowers open • Harvest seeds as soon as ripe • Cut off whole plant and hang to dry
FENNEL *Foeniculum vulgare*	• All parts of leaves, stems, and seeds aromatic • Used for fish seasonings and sauces • Ornamental background plants for garden	• Annual • Tall, rampant, branching • Thread-like foliage to 1 m (3 ft.)	• Seed • Best sown directly in garden	• Hot, sandy locations • Needs space, rich soil	• Flower stalks harvested just before bloom • Can be eaten like celery • Leaves best fresh

Herb Guide
CONTINUED

NAME	USES	CHARACTERISTICS	PROPAGATION	CULTURE	HARVEST
GARLIC *Allium sativum*	• Chopped cloves season meats, vegetables, sauces • Garlic salt obtained from pulverized dry cloves	• Annual bulb • Flat, onion-like leaves • Grows to 60 cm (2 ft.)	• Sets • Planted annually as onions	• Grows in any good garden soil	• Dig bulbs, break into cloves, and dry
LAVENDER *Lavendula officinalis*	• Fresh and dried flowers and seeds used as fragrance sachets • Scented oil distilled from flowers and seeds • Good border or hedge plant	• Perennial • Somewhat woody • Grows to 1 m (3 ft.) • Not very hardy • Green-grey leaves	• Seeds or cuttings	• Sun and poor soil yield most fragrance • Needs protection or take indoors in severe winters	• Cut and dry whole flower spikes when flower begins to open • Do not use excessive or prolonged heat when drying flowers or seeds (oils are very volatile)
LEMON VERBENA *Lippa citriodora*	• Leaves used for fragrance and to give lemony taste to beverages	• Non-hardy perennial • Tender woody shrub • Narrow, shiny leaves are lemon-scented	• Cuttings	• Take indoors in winter	• Strip leaves individually from plant before blooms come out • Dry on screens
MINT Spearmint *Mentha spicata* Peppermint *Mentha peperita* Lemon mint *Mentha citrata*	• Fragrance used for scent • Crushed leaves flavour tea, candies, mint sauce • Oil from plant is source of menthol	• Perennial • Purple flowers • Refreshing odour • Large leaves • Spreads by surface runners • Plant in tubs to keep roots restricted	• Surface or underground rhizomes	• Thin beds and renew every 3–4 years • Will grow in semi-shade • Needs rich, moist soil	• Pick leaves individually from plants • Can be used fresh or dried • Pick just as flowering begins
OREGANO *Origanum vulgare*	• Fresh and dried leaves used as meat and vegetable seasoning • Used on pizza • Flowers are fragrant	• Perennial • Soft, rounded leaves • Grows in 60 cm (2 ft.) high clump	• Seeds or division	• Grows well in poor soil • Does well in containers and as ground cover for banks	• Cut stalks when plant starts to flower • Hang to dry 2 weeks • Remove leaves, crumble, and store
PARSLEY *Petroselinum crispum*	• Decorative as an edging plant • Rich in vitamins A and C • Leaves best used fresh • Seasoning for soup, meats, salads	• Biennial • Finely curled leaves • Flowers second year • 20 cm (8 in.) compact plant	• Seed • Sow early inside • Self sows	• Sun or part shade • Needs medium-rich soil • Best started in cold frames • Space 15–20 cm (6–8 in.) • Start new plants every year	• Both leaves and roots keep flavour when dried or frozen • First season of growth is best for use
ROSEMARY *Rosemarinus officinalis*	• Used ornamentally as a specimen pot plant • Use fresh or dried leaves as food seasoning, especially on poultry	• Evergreen • Narrow leaves • Shrubby • Not reliably hardy • Leathery leaves have spicy odour	• Stem cuttings • Seed germinates slowly	• Needs full sun and wind shelter • Avoid acidic soil • Keep foliage misted • Space 1 m (3 ft.) apart • Overwinter in cool, sunny spot in house	• Cut leaves when flowers are beginning • Do not use excessive or prolonged heat when drying (oils are very volatile) • Freezing not recommended

Herb Guide
CONTINUED

NAME	USES	CHARACTERISTICS	PROPAGATION	CULTURE	HARVEST
SAGE *Salvia officinalis*	• Leaves used fresh or dried as poultry dressing or stuffing, or as meat seasoning	• Perennial • Grey, shrubby, woody • Blue flowers • Sprawly habit • Leaves are woolly and grey	• Seed, stem cuttings or crown division	• Needs well-drained soil • Space 75 cm (30 in.) apart in sun • Cut back in spring for new foliage	• Cut leaves or tops of stalks when starting to flower • Freezing not recommended
SWEET BASIL *Ocimum basilicum*	• Border plant for garden or in pots for patios • Chopped leaves fresh or dried have clove-pepper odour and taste • Seasoning for vegetables and meat	• Annual • Dark green leaves • White blooms • Resembles sweet pepper	• Seed • Sow after ground is warm	• Plant late • Needs water, sun, shelter • Space 25 cm (10 in.) apart • Pinch out tops of branches to prevent bloom, producing more leaves	• Cut stalks when starting to flower • Dry for 2 weeks • Can be frozen, but drying preferred
SWEET MARJORAM *Majorana hortensis*	• Ornamental grey foliage used for colour contrast in garden • Leaves used fresh or dried as seasoning for meat dishes • Oil used in perfumes	• Annual or tender perennial • Velvety leaves • Very fragrant • Low-spreading and bushy to 30 cm (1 ft.) high	• Seed, stem cuttings or crown division • Sow early inside or in coldframe	• Shade seedlings until established, then full sun • Space 20–25 cm (8–10 in.) apart • Can be taken inside in winter	• Cut stalks when starting to flower • Hang to dry
SUMMER SAVORY *Satureja hortensis*	• Suitable as a border hedge 20 cm (8 in.) high • Leaves used fresh or dried as seasoning in soups, egg dishes, sauces	• Annual • Weak stems with mauve flowers • 40–45 cm (16–18 in.) high • Leaves pungent and spicy	• Seed • Sow 30–35 seeds per m (10–12 per ft.) • Do not thin	• Medium-rich soil in sun • Make several sowings 3 weeks apart • Space 15 cm (6 in.)	• Cut stalks when starting to flower, or cut leafy tops when plants are in bud • Hang to dry • Freezing not recommended
TARRAGON *Artemesia dranunculus*	• Fresh or dried leaves in sauces and seafood • Ingredient of tartar sauce • Young leaves flavour vinegar	• Hardy perennial • Doesn't set seed • Grows to 60 cm (2 ft.) • Many branched • Narrow, twisted leaves	• Division of root crowns	• Needs cold period each year (roots frozen) for continued growth • Divide plant every 3 years	• Young leaves and stem tips are best used fresh • Some flavour is lost in drying
THYME *Thymus vulgaris*	• Fragrant ground cover for rock garden • Fresh and dried leaves usually blended with other herbs to season meats, vegetables, soups, sauces	• Perennial • Shrubby, woody stems • 15–20 cm (6–8 in.) • Leaves highly aromatic • Can be potted and grown indoors in winter	• Stem cuttings, division • Sow seeds early	• Full sun • Well-drained non-acidic soil • Space 25 cm (10 in.) apart • Cut back each spring • Mulch over winter	• Cut leafy tops and flower clusters when plants are blooming • Hang to dry

Begonias in a hanging
basket

GARDENING OFF THE GROUND

Container Gardening for Decks and Balconies

The popularity of growing plants in containers is higher than ever before. In addition to apartment and condominium dwellers, many house owners with tiny shaded lots that have been paved over and owners of cottages in "rock" country have joined the parade. The choice of what will grow in containers is wide indeed, and ranges from summer annuals to trees.

LOCATION Where your containers are placed is the most important consideration in deciding what and when to plant. You can control the type of soil and the amount of moisture, but you may not be able to control the amount of sunlight or exposure to wind. South or west-facing locations get the most sun, and during the long days of late spring and early summer, you can grow such sun-lovers as tomatoes and roses.

If at all possible create a sheltered and protected area out of the wind. Wind tends to dry out container plants much quicker than those grown in the ground. High winds also tend to injure plants by break-ing off tender buds, stems and, in extreme cases, by knocking over or uprooting whole plants. For those who live in tall apartment buildings, wind protection becomes increasingly important and difficult, the higher in the building the apartment is located. Some tall building complexes create their own jet-stream by funnelling wind around the building in a way that actually increases wind speed. The best thing to do is to create a wind screen without casting too much shade. A solid wall does not really stop or control the effect of high winds. It is much better to build a barrier which allows air to flow through, such as a slat fence, hedge or small,

FLOWERS, HERBS, VEGETABLES, SMALL SHRUBS AND DWARF TREES CAN ALL BE GROWN IN CONTAINERS. GOOD DRAINAGE IS VITAL. WITHOUT IT, ROOTBALLS WILL BECOME WATERLOGGED.

sturdy trees. A tightly woven lattice or trellis is also effective and useful for hanging plants and climbers.

It is also good to have a partial overhang of some kind. An overhang neutralizes the effect of radiant freezing (the leaking of heat from plants and adjacent surfaces during cold, clear nights) and can greatly extend the growing season. One of the problems with a cozy, warm, protected deck with a southerly exposure, is that though plants can be set out very early in the spring, they tend to suffer from the extremes of temperature between daytime heat and nighttime cold. This is especially true of frost-sensitive plants like tomatoes. Rather than having to carry your plants indoors every night in the spring and fall, it is better to have some sort of overhanging cover. This could be a temporary or retractable awning, or something permanent like a trellis or plastic panels. Again, any covering is a compromise between protection from wind and cold and not creating a shade barrier that prevents plants from receiving adequate sunlight.

CONTAINERS AND SOIL Plant containers come in many shapes, sizes and materials. Anything that is non-toxic, can hold soil and will not disintegrate when wet can be used. Most important is good drainage. Without it, the root ball of the plant will become waterlogged and rot. If you have a deck or balcony, make sure the surface is porous or that there is somewhere water can runoff or drain. Otherwise, you will have a wet, muddy mess every time you water your plants. Drainage is also a consideration when you are placing hanging plants. They have to drip somewhere.

Soil selection for containers depends on what you want to grow. Start with a supply of clean topsoil or light loam as well as a bag of clean sand and large selection of different sizes of stones. If soil has been heat-treated, it might be fairly inert, and lack active organic ingredients. For this reason, it is recommended that you also add a fertilizer with an even mix of elements such as 7:7:7 or 10:10:10. Always start with a clean container and make sure the drainage holes on the bottom are open. Cover the bottom with stones and then add a layer of sand. This will insure good drainage and give roots a well aerated space to develop. With big containers and plants that have deep roots, fill one-third of the container with stones, broken brick or earthenware pot pieces to reduce your soil requirements. Adding other potting material, such as brown peat moss, helps retain moisture and bulk up the soil mixture. For containers that have a large surface area, such as those that hold trees, cover with a mulch of wood chips or plant low-flowering annuals. This will prevent hardening of the surface soil caused by baking heat and drying winds, and will also retard weeds from developing.

HANGING BASKETS Growing plants in hanging baskets is attractive and increases growing room. It allows you to view plants either from below or at eye level, and is the only satisfactory way to grow some plants, such as pendula or hanging begonia, ivy geranium or cascading petunias. Baskets can be made of many materials from steel wire to plastic mesh.

The problem of how to keep soil in place can be overcome by lining the inside of the basket with uncut sphagnum moss. Overlap the pieces of moss using a double thickness for water retention. Soaking the moss first makes it more malleable. A good soil mixture for basket planting combines two parts standard topsoil, one part brown peat moss and one part either leaf mould or worked compost. Small woody chunks

Basket-grown azalea

should be retained. Plant so that the stem and roots sit at the same height, relative to soil surface, as they did previously. Since drainage is so fast, and since the moss in the basket is exposed to drying air all around, you will have to water much more frequently than you would plants in a solid container. It is best to unhook the basket and bring the plant to a basin where you can water it from below until moisture appears on the surface.

Some plants suggested for hanging baskets may not drape themselves over the edge of the basket on their own. Some begonias and fushias tend to be upright growers. If you let the basket dry to the point of wilting, then nudge the stems down to the basket's edge before rewatering, you'll probably solve the problem. If light comes from only one side resulting in uneven growth, rotate the basket a partial turn each time you remove for watering. Hanging baskets can be placed outdoors as soon as they are planted, as long as the air temperature is above 10°C (50°F). Light ground frosts will not harm them, but cold air will slow their growth.

Cascading plants can also be grown in solid containers. When preparing soil for a solid container, you do not require as much humus as in a basket planting. Superior drainage is a necessity in a solid container. To achieve this, place a wad of sphagnum moss over the drainage holes before filling with the soil mixture. Water from the top until water runs out the bottom. You can plant almost any summer flower and many vegetables in hanging baskets as long as they are dwarf-growing varieties. The higher the garden, the more dwarf-like the plants should be, in order to stand up to winds.

WINTER PROTECTION Unless they are very large and protected, only the hardiest perennials will survive our southern Ontario winters in a container. Some trees, shrubs and well established woody bushes can do well if properly treated. The problem is that the soil used in containers is purposely constructed to retain more moisture then normal soils. This is because the container is raised above ground and, exposed to more air, tends to dry out rapidly. In winter, the combination of exposure to colder temperatures and lots of moisture often causes the container to freeze solid. For hardy container plants that you want to survive the winter, cover the plant and move to the most protected spot available. If possible, cover the soil surface area with a platform to deflect rainwater or melting snow away from the container. Protect from direct winter sun, which causes daytime thawing and could temporarily activate the plant's growing cycle.

PLANT SELECTION Containers can be used to plant annual flowers, vegetables, herbs and some shrubs and small trees. You can plant almost any annual in a container, though it is best to select smaller, more compact, continuously blooming plants for a better show. Your bouquet can be a combination of just about anything that grows well in your local climate. To get that bursting-at-the-seams look, cram the plants in much closer than you would in a normal garden bed. To encourage flower production over a long period of time, remove faded blooms before they go to seed.

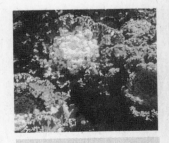

Container-grown plants often tend to be showy or unusual like these flowering kale, which features large green, pink and white blossoms.

Container Gardening

CONTAINER CARE

Q: I have a number of plants in containers on an uncovered deck. These include a tamarisk about 75 cm (30 in.) high, a dwarf peach planted in a half-barrel, a Colorgreen juniper and a few Japanese quinces. I would like to know if I can keep them safely outside in the winter without further protection. Also I have some Siberian wallflowers that were started indoors earlier. They began to bloom in late July. I am not sure if they are biennials or perennials. What do I do next?
– C.B., Newmarket

A: There is a possibility that one or more of your container plants will survive above ground in containers in a winter that is very mild and/or has few high winds and not much sun while the earth around the roots is frozen. Alternate freezing and thawing is one problem with winter survival, but worse is wind that dries out bark and leaves or needles when roots are unable to replace moisture.

A wise course of action with container plants is to plant them container and all in your garden before the ground freezes. Then mulch. Of all the plants you mention, the juniper may be the likeliest survivor; the peach the unlikeliest. It may not survive even regular garden planting in Newmarket.

The Siberian wallflower is a North American native and is also known as the prairie rocket. It is related to true wallflowers and best treated as a biennial. Your approach seems best: start seeds indoors very early for bloom that year, or outdoors in July/August for bloom the following year.

OVER-FERTILIZED PINE

Q: Last July, a mugo pine that grows in a container on our sundeck began to turn brown. By August it was dead. This tree was at least 15 years old and measured 10 cm (4 in.) at the base of the trunk, but as its needles had been pinched back annually, it had achieved a bonsai effect, measuring only 60 cm (2 ft.) high.

There is no evidence of insect infestation. I fertilize by boring 25 mm (1 in.) holes with a 15 cm (6 in.) stake and filling with lawn-type fertilizer, grade 7:7:7 in spring and 12:6:4 in fall. Also, in summer I use a soluble grade 30:10:10 every three weeks.

What do you think killed my pine?
– C.C., Waterloo

A: Your fertilizing habits sound overly enthusiastic. Holes punched right in and through the root system and filled with chemical fertilizer pellets can only result in some root damage at the very least.

It seems to me that your soluble 30:10:10 solution would be more than enough, used perhaps once a growing season. Its ratio (3:1:1) is inappropriate for needle evergreens, which do not need a blast of nitrogen to grow a crop of new leaves each year.

Compact evergreens like this dwarf Alberta spruce make excellent container-grown plants.

GARDEN INSECTS AND DISEASES

Your garden is naturally attractive to both harmful and beneficial insects. Every healthy garden has an insect population, but if insect pests become numerous enough to damage your crops, control procedures are necessary.

Many insect problems can be avoided by good housekeeping around the garden. Remove all debris from corners of your yard. Dark, damp undisturbed areas are breeding grounds for insect pests. Ample sunlight, weeding and good drainage all have a part to play in pest control.

Using Insecticides

Agriculture Canada has this comment about the use of insecticide in home gardens: "Use…only when pests are numerous enough to cause serious damage to your crops."

If you decide to use an insecticide, always read the label and follow the instructions on it. This sound obvious, but is so important that it bears repeating. Take special note of any information regarding the interval between use of the product and your garden harvest. Do not apply any insecticide on a windy day. To protect bees and other pollinating insects, do not apply to crops in bloom. If a long-flowering ornamental requires treatment, apply in the evening when bees aren't visiting its flowers. Rotenone and *Bacillus thuringiensis*, an organic insecticide, do not harm bees.

Handle insecticides with respect. They are powerful and must be used carefully. Pay attention when measuring and use a separate set of funnels and measuring cups. Never use a kitchen utensil. Wear gloves and a dust mask. Avoid skin contact and do not inhale fumes. Wash thoroughly after using.

Dispose of surplus or old insecticides in a way that will not damage the environment. Contact your local department of public works for

WHEN USING INSECTICIDES OR FUNGICIDES, TAKE SPECIAL NOTE OF ANY INFORMATION REGARDING THE INTERVAL BETWEEN USE OF THE PRODUCT AND YOUR GARDEN HARVEST.

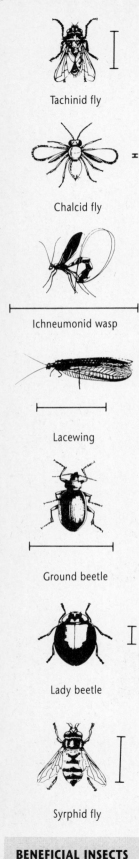

Tachinid fly

Chalcid fly

Ichneumonid wasp

Lacewing

Ground beetle

Lady beetle

Syrphid fly

BENEFICIAL INSECTS
(Note: line beside each illustration represents actual size.)

advice on disposal. Many cities and municipalities have designated pickup days or special receptacles for paints, old oil and insecticides. Use the opportunity to clean out your garage and tool room, ridding yourself of half-cans of paint and other leftovers from home and garden projects.

BENEFICIAL INSECTS Garden insects are usually thought of as pests, but many are helpful to both nature and the home gardener. Bees and wasps, of course, pollinate both wild and garden plants. In addition, predatory insects catch and consume insect pests. Other beneficial insects are parasites, living on or in the bodies of insect hosts.

Lacewings, ground beetles and lady beetles are predators, consuming aphids, caterpillars and scale insects. Lady beetles – also called ladybugs – also eat the eggs of aphids and other soft-bodied insects.

Parasites include tachinid flies, which lay their eggs in caterpillars, and chalcid wasps, which lay their eggs in the midst of the eggs of many moths, flies and other insects. These eggs hatch to become parasitic larvae.

OCCASIONAL PESTS Insects that can damage your garden but do not always do so are called occasional pests. They need only be treated if damage is detected.
Onion thrips are tiny insects that can pierce onion tops, causing them to turn grey and speckled. If detected, dust with malathion.
Blister beetles can eat leaves of garden plants. When adult beetles are detected, spray or dust foliage with malathion. If foliage is to be eaten (lettuce, spinach, etc.), use pyrethrum or rotenone instead.
Spotted asparagus beetles destroy the seed pods of asparagus plants, feeding on tender shoots in spring. Dust or spray with rotenone.

Red turnip beetles eat the leaves of cabbage, turnips and similar plants. They rarely require control measures. If necessary, dust or spray with rotenone.
Cucumber beetles, both striped and spotted, eat flowers and foliage of cucumbers, squash and melon. They rarely cause much damage. Control with rotenone.
Spider mites can damage the leaves of beans, eggplants and peppers. Spray with malathion or diazinon.
Greenhouse whiteflies are tiny winged insects that suck sap from tomato and cucumber leaves. Spray with carbaryl, malathion or diazinon.
Tomato hornworms eat the leaves of tomato, pepper and eggplant. Hand-pick and destroy.
Wireworms are six-legged, hard-skinned orange worms that feed on many plant roots, including potato tubers. If planting in newly-dug sod, apply diazinon, carbaryl or chlordane.

HARMFUL INSECTS The threat posed by some insect pests requires immediate action on your part. All the work you have put into your garden can seemingly evaporate if it is infested by destructive pests. A detailed guide to the most harmful garden insects follows.

Diseases

Many plant diseases affect specific varieties of plants. If you have a unique problem, contact your local Ontario Horticultural Association representative. The Master Gardener Program at the Civic Garden Centre in Toronto also operates a free information hotline that is staffed by qualified volunteers seven days a week from noon to 3 p.m. The horticultural hotline number is (416) 445-1552 which is a local call in the Toronto area. They will try to solve your problem and give you suggestions on how to prevent further occurrences. As well, the staff at your local nursery or garden centre can always help.

Here are seven of the most common plant diseases, with symptoms and recommended treatments.

CANKER *Symptoms* Diseased areas on twigs and branches causing dieback. *Remedy* Cut out all diseased branches. Use systemic fungicide paste on fresh cuts.

DAMPING-OFF *Symptoms* Seedlings die after emerging from soil. Caused by soil fungus. *Remedy* Use sterilized soil. Use bulb and soil dust.

DOWNY MILDEW *Symptoms* White or yellowish patches on the upper side of leaves. Caused by cool, damp weather. *Remedy* Use fungicide, powder or spray. Use tomato and vegetable dust.

LEAF SPOT *Symptoms* This is the most common plant disease. Brown or black spots appear on leaves. *Remedy* Use regular or systemic fungicide.

POWDERY MILDEW *Symptoms* White powdery growth on leaves, stem, buds. Caused by hot, humid weather. *Remedy* Use systemic fungicide, powder or sprays. Use garden liquid, lime sulphur.

RUST *Symptoms* Brown, orange to red spores on the underside of leaves. *Remedy* Spray with protective fungicide in spring. Use garden liquid, lime sulphur.

SCAB *Symptoms* Dark spots on leaves or fruit. Commonly found on fruit trees. Caused by cool, humid weather. *Remedy* Use fruit tree fungicide. Use garden liquid, lime sulphur spray.

Onion thrip

Blister beetle

White grub

Spotted asparagus beetle

Red turnip beetle

Striped or spotted cucumber beetle

Spider mite

 **Pests and Diseases**

EUROPEAN PINE SHOOT MOTH

Q: Each spring our Scotch pine trees have 6 mm (½ in.) worms appearing at the previous year's growth. They devour the needles and, after a few days, disappear. The worms are light green with a double row of black spots along their backs. Can you tell me what they are? — *B. M., Palgrave*

A: It seems likely that your Scotch (Scots) pines are infected with the destructive European pine shoot moth. The larvae of this moth feed inside the buds in May and early June. Young shoots developing at that time are deformed or killed. Austrian, red, mugo and Scots pines are susceptible. Spray thoroughly in late April and again in June. Recommended spray materials include diazinon or dimethoate.

It is hard to deal with overwintering larvae as they are located inside the buds unless you spot a mass of sticky pitch. Prune out and destroy any buds with this sticky coating. Like the elm bark beetle that spreads Dutch elm disease, this pest came over from Europe. It was first discovered in New Jersey in 1914 and has spread widely since.

OCCASIONAL PESTS
(Note: line beside each illustration represents actual size.)

Leaf miner

Greenhouse whitefly

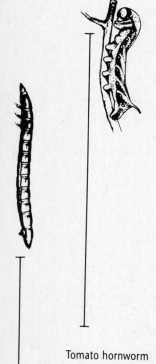

Tomato hornworm

Wireworm

 **Pests and Diseases** CONTINUED

HOLLYHOCK PEST

Q: What would eat hollyhock leaves? — *A.M., Toronto*

A: The hollyhock pest may be the leaf skeletonizer. A combination insecticide/fungicide spray may help not only with insects but with rust (a plant fungus). Your hollyhock pest is cyclical, having parasites of its own.

NATURAL INSECTICIDE

Q: Can you recommend any organic or natural insecticides? — *Y.P., Kitchener*

A: There are several products on the market that contain a natural insecticide called *Bacillus thuringiensis*, usually called B.T. for short. B.T. is a form of parasitic bacteria that activates as insect eggs hatch. As a parasite, B.T. either kills insects or renders them ineffective. It offers the home gardener a reasonable insect control, but does not result in 100 per cent protection. It is harmless to humans and is useful in the vegetable garden as well.

DAMPING OFF DISEASE

Q: On two occasions I have planted western red cedar from seed. In both cases seeds germinated, showing a nice green colour. But within a few days the plants shrivelled up and died. They were planted in clean soil with lots of light. Any ideas? — *H.S.M., Washago*

A: It sounds like post-emergent damping off disease. Tree seedlings are particularly susceptible to these soil-borne organisms. Was your soil sterilized before planting? At planting time, did you use utensils, including your fingers, that had been in contact with unsterilized soil? Never use old soil from other plants or unsterilized soil from the garden. Moist conditions at the soil surface can also bring on this problem.

It is wise to take further precautions. Use dampened soil to begin with so you don't have to water again after seed is planted. Water early in the day and only as necessary. Be sure your soil mix drains well. You can also drench the soil surface with a fungicide containing oxine benzoate.

Harmful Insect Guide

INSECT	LENGTH	PLANTS ATTACKED	TYPES OF INJURY	CONTROL	NOTES
GRASSHOPPER	22 mm 7/8 in.	• All vegetables	• Eats leaves	• malathion • carbaryl • diazinon • chlorpyrifos	• Eggs overwinter • Hatch in spring
LEAFHOPPER	3 mm 1/8 in.	• Potatoes • Carrots • Lettuce • Celery • Other vegetables	• Pierces plant to obtain sap • Brown tips, edges on potato leaves	• malathion • carbaryl • diazinon • pyrethrum • rotenone	• Adults carried into Canada on southerly winds • Inserts eggs into foliage • 2–3 generations each year
APHID	2 mm 1/16 in.	• All vegetables	• Sucks sap from stems and leaves • Deformed buds and flowers • Curled, withered leaves • Transmits fire blight bacteria • Transmits mosaic virus	• rotenone • pyrethrum • malathion • dimethoate • insecticidal soap • beneficial insects	• Most are bright green, though some are black, pink, yellow, red, brown or grey • Immature stages are wingless
TARNISHED PLANT BUG	6 mm 1/4 in.	• Most vegetables	• Sucks sap from stems and leaves • Feeding causes various distortions	• malathion • carbaryl • diazinon	• Overwinters under debris • Eggs laid in plant tissue in early summer • Probably more than one generation per year
COLORADO POTATO BEETLE	9 mm 3/8 in.	• Potatoes • Eggplants • Tomatoes	• Eats leaves	• carbaryl • diazinon • rotenone	• Overwinters beneath soil surface • Orange-coloured eggs laid in clusters on the underside of leaves • Adults have black and yellow stripes on wing covers
FLEA BEETLE	2 mm 1/16 in.	• Potatoes • Eggplants • Tomatoes • Cabbage • Cauliflower • Radishes • Turnips	• Eats tiny holes in leaves	• malathion • carbaryl • diazinon • rotenone	• Overwinters beneath soil surface • Eggs laid on soil in spring • Larvae feed on roots of host plant
IMPORTED CABBAGE-WORM	30 mm 1 1/4 in.	• Broccoli • Cabbage • Cauliflower • Turnips • Brussel sprouts	• Larvae eat large holes in leaves, bore into heads and leave greenish-brown droppings	• rotenone • *Bacillus thuringiensis* • diazinon	• Larvae big, slow-moving • Adult is white butterfly seen April through October • Single eggs laid on the underside of leaves in summer
CUTWORM	33 mm 1 3/8 in.	• All vegetables • Seedlings • Transplants	• Larvae cut off seedlings just below soil surface • Plants fall over	• prepared cutworm dust • malathion • carbaryl • chlorpyrifos	• Eggs overwinter in soil • Feeds at night • Late May and first three weeks of June most likely times for infestation • One generation per year

INSECT	LENGTH	PLANTS ATTACKED	TYPES OF INJURY	CONTROL	NOTES
EUROPEAN CORN BORER	25 mm 1 in.	• Sweet corn	• Larvae damage all above-ground parts of corn plant by feeding and boring	• carbaryl • diazinon	• Larvae overwinter in stalks • Eggs laid in July
CORN EARWORM	40 mm 1¾ in.	• Sweet corn	• Larvae eat kernels in the tips of ears of corn	• carbaryl • diazinon	• Adult moths invade from south in July • Eggs laid in July
BEET WEBWORM	30 mm 1¼ in.	• Beets • Cabbage • Alfalfa • Most vegetables • Weeds	• Larvae skeletonize leaves	• pyrethrum • rotenone	• Larvae overwinter underground in cocoons • Spin webbing in infested leaves
MAGGOT (*various*)	8 mm ⅜ in.	• Onions • Rutabagas • Turnips • Cabbage • Cauliflower • Radishes • Parsnips	• Lives in and destroys roots and bulbs	• prepared maggot killers containing diazinon	• Pupae overwinter in soil • Adults resemble house flies • Lays eggs on soil beside growing onions • To control, put diazinon in row when planting
SLUG	30 mm 1¼ in.	• Most vegetables	• Eats foliage and fruit at night • Leaves slimy trail	• prepared slug bait	• Often found in backyard gardens if damp • Ripe tomatoes often severely damaged • Lay boards between garden rows for slugs to hide under. Turn boards over daily; remove and destroy slugs
EUROPEAN EARWIG	20 mm ¾ in.	• Fruits • Flowers • Vegetables	• Eats foliage and fruit at night • Invades houses in July	• carbaryl • diazinon • chlorpyrifos • propxur • traps and bait	• Ground crawler that moves in great numbers • Has forceps-like pincers at rear of body • Fish oil in a shallow pan buried in soil is an effective bait • Use poisons in dry, warm weather in late June

GLOSSARY

Acid Soil
Soils are either acidic, alkaline or neutral. Neutral soil has a pH factor of 7. A pH factor lower than 7 indicates acidity, above 7 indicates alkalinity.

Aerate
To expose to or supply with air. Most plants must have access to air through their root systems. When soils are compacted or water-logged, plants suffer because their roots cannot breathe.

Alkaline Soil
Referred to as sweet soil, alkaline soil is the opposite of acid soil and has a pH factor higher than 7.

Annual
A plant which grows from seed, flowers, sets seed and dies within one year.

Arbour
A framework designed to provide a shaded or sheltered area when covered with vines. Most commonly used in home gardens to support grapevines.

Balled and Burlapped (B and B)
A term applied to a method used by nurseries to prepare trees or shrubs for transplanting or moving. A large ball of soil around the roots is wrapped in burlap to hold the soil in place.

Bedding Plant
A plant used in beds for mass effect. Often refers to a plant that has been started in a greenhouse and is set into the ground after the last frost is past.

Biennial
A plant that completes its life cycle in two years. In most examples, seed is planted and the plant grows in its first season, but does not flower until the following year. It then sets its seed and dies. Many biennials are regarded as perennials because they self-seed, sending up new plants each year.

Bolt
To quickly flower and go to seed when the rest of the plant is not yet fully developed. In vegetables, bolting usually occurs when strong summer heat accelerates growth.

Border
This term originally was used to describe plantings around the perimeter of a yard or along driveways or walks. It is now commonly used to describe any bed of garden flowers, either annual or perennial.

Broadcast
To scatter seed by hand over the surface of the ground.

Broad-leaved Evergreens
A shrub or tree that retains its leaves during winter, has flat, wide leaves and is not coniferous (needle-bearing). Many varieties of rhododendrons and azaleas are examples.

Bulb
A plant that grows from a globular underground structure at the base of a stem. A true bulb (such as tulip or onion) is made up of scales or layers. It is rounded, with the stem emerging from the slightly pointed top and the roots emerging from the slightly flattened bottom. In addition to true bulbs, other types are corms, rhizomes and tubers.

Cane
In trees, canes are woody branches that start at or below ground level. In grapevines and roses, the term is used to refer to woody, flexible growth of any kind.

Cold Frame
An enclosed or covered frame, the top covered with glass or plastic and situated so that it catches the rays of the sun. Used to adapt or harden plants to cool, early season temperatures.

Compost
A loose material high in organic content formed by decayed leaves and vegetable matter usually mixed with soil.

Conifer
A shrub or tree that has needles, is usually evergreen, and produces seeds in cones.

Corm
A bulbous, underground fleshy stem that is solid. Generally referred to as a bulb.

Crown
The part of a plant where the roots join the stem or trunk.

Cultivar
A selected clone or variety of a plant type. Cultivar names are distinguished by being preceded by Cv., which replaces the old term "cultivated variety".

Cuttings
Parts of the root or stem of a plant which, under the right conditions, will form new roots and develop into new plants.

Deciduous
A plant that goes into a dormant stage during the winter and drops its leaves.

Deadhead
To pinch back or snip off spent flowers before they go to seed and thus encourage further growth and more blossoms.

Division
A method of propagation. Any plant (including some bulbs) that forms clumps of stems with rooted bases can be divided and spread by replanting.

Double Flower
A flower that has two or more layers of petals, often clustered so that they cover the centre.

Evergreen
A tree, shrub or other plant that retains its foliage all year long. Encompasses both coniferous and broad-leaved plants.

Fix
The ability of certain plants to assimilate nitrogen or carbon dioxide by forming a non-gaseous compound.

Harden Off
A process in which plants that have been started inside a protected shelter are slowly exposed to outdoor temperatures, both hot and cold. This process helps the plant adapt and strengthens its resistance to transplant shock.

Hardy
A plant that is adapted to local winter temperatures. A hardy plant can survive the extremes of the local climate.

Herbaceous
A non-woody plant that dies back to the ground every year. "Herbaceous perennial" is the term commonly used to refer to a flower or other plant that dies back in the fall of each year and grows new stems the following spring.

Humus
Partially decayed plant material that is produced by bacterial action or decay. Humus holds moisture, separates soil particles and improves soil condition.

Hybrid
A plant produced by cross-breeding two or more species. Hybrids are usually more vigorous and productive than inbreds.

Invasive
Refers to a plant that tends to invade or encroach upon the territory of other plants. An invasive plant can become a weed if you accept the definition that a weed is any plant growing where you don't want it.

Layering
A method of propagation. With certain plants this can be achieved by covering a portion of the stem or branches with soil. After new roots have formed and a new plant has established itself, the connecting branch or stem can be cut.

Leader
The central trunk of a tree or shrub from which side branches develop.

Legume
Any plant that takes nitrogen from the air by nitrifying bacteria that live upon its roots.

Lime
A compound, usually natural, containing a large portion of calcium in a form that will neutralize soil acids. Most commonly used in the form of ground limestone.

Loam
A grade of soil between a clay and a sandy soil. It has a good humus content, drains well, and does not compact easily.

Manure
Animal excrement used to fertilize and enrich the soil. Must be fully decomposed, as fresh manure is usually too strong to apply to plants directly. The best is cow manure. Horse manure is much stronger, while poultry manure is not safe to use unless it is well-aged.

Mildew
Common term for fungi that attack garden plants when days are warm and nights are cool. Gives the plants a downy covering which later turns them black and wrinkled. Controlled through use of sulphur.

Mulch
Name applied to various materials (straw, wood shavings, plastic sheeting, etc.) used to moderate soil temperatures, reduce evaporation, and control weeds by being spread as a layer over the ground.

Narrow-leaved Evergreen
A shrub or tree that retains its leaves during winter and has foliage that may be flat and fern-like (e.g., arborvitae), or scale-like (false cypress), or dense soft needles (yew) or hard pointy needles (pine).

Native Plant
A plant that originates naturally in a given region or locale. In southern Ontario, the sugar maple is a native plant.

Neutral Soil
Soil that is neither alkaline nor acidic, having a pH factor of 7.

Oil Spray
A compound of mineral and vegetable oils used to control scale insects on trees and shrubs.

Perennial
A plant which under suitable conditions lives for three or more years.

Pinnate
Having leaflets arranged on each side of a common stalk.

Propagation

The growing of new plants from seed, from cuttings (slips), or by budding, grafting or layering.

Pruning

The deliberate cutting of branches or twigs from a living plant, designed to shape the plant, remove dead wood and/or strengthen the plant by encouraging new and diverse growth.

Resistance

Refers to a plant's ability to resist diseases or to withstand unfavourable weather conditions.

Rhizome

A kind of bulb with an underground stem that is thickened and root-like and can grow new plants from its joints.

Root Pruning

The deliberate cutting of roots designed to stimulate compact top growth and/or keep the roots within bounds.

Runner

A long trailing stem that may take root and develop into a new plant.

Scale

Sucking insects, usually with hard shells, that may be found on stems and branches. Can be controlled by oil sprays.

Set

A small bulb cluster used for planting. Pickling and storage onion varieties are commonly planted from sets.

Shrub

A woody plant of low to moderate size. Generally differs from trees in having more than one stem instead of a dominant single trunk.

Specimen

A tree, shrub or flower positioned to be a prominent focal point in a garden. Often used to refer to any tree or shrub that is of particularly high quality.

Sterilization

The killing of insects, diseases, and, in some cases, weed seeds in soil or plant material through the use of chemicals, steam or heat.

Stone Fruit

A plant with fruit that contains a pit or stone that is its seed.

Subsoil

This term refers to the layers of soil below the topsoil, usually found 15–30 cm (6–12 in.) below the surface.

Sucker

A stem that rises from the roots or comes from a bud along the stem of a plant. Usually grows very rapidly and is often unproductive, causing a crowding of branches.

Sweet Soil

A soil that is alkaline in nature. (See **Alkaline Soil**, above).

Systemic

A chemical that is absorbed into a plant's system to kill either harmful organisms or the plant itself (when used as a weed-killer). Most non-systemic insecticides, fungicides and weed-killers are not absorbed by the plant. Instead, these products coat the external surface of the plant.

Tender

A plant that is sensitive to the cold weather and low temperatures of the region. The opposite of hardy.

Topdress

To apply compost, fertilizer or other materials to the top of the soil. The food must be carried down into the soil by rain or watering.

Transplant

A seedling or starter plant that must later be transplanted to an outdoor location.

Tuber

A kind of bulb with a swollen underground stem or root that stores food and from which a new plant can grow. In some cases, new growth occurs at eyes (potato). In other cases, it occurs at the point of attachment to the stem (dahlia).

Whip

Central leader of a young tree. Often used in reference to newly-planted fruit trees.

Wind-firm

Firmly rooted and capable of withstanding strong winds.

ACKNOWLEDGMENTS

Special thanks to Peter Rice and colleagues, Royal Botanical Gardens, Hamilton; Judy Wanner, Horticultural Research Institute of Ontario, Vineland Station; Tanya Kroiter; Susan Main.

CREDITS

Front cover: tulip, saucer magnolia and tomato plant courtesy of the Horticultural Research Institute of Ontario, Vineland Station.

Reproduced courtesy of Agriculture Canada: 11, 120, 121, 123, 179, 180, 181, 182.

Horticultural Research Institute of Ontario: 14, 15, 32, 33, 37, 55, 56, 60 bottom, 80, 84, 86, 88, 89, 92, 94, 95, 96, 99, 100, 101, 102, 103, 107, 108, 114, 124 bottom, 132 top, 146, 147, 151, 156, 157, 161, 162, 163, 165.

Tom Main: 12, 132 centre, 134 bottom.

Reproduced courtesy of Ontario Ministry of Agriculture and Food: 45, 46, 47, 48 top, 49, 51, 69, 70, 71, 72, 73, 75, 91, 93, 94 top, 104, 105, 151, 171, 172, 173.

Royal Botanical Gardens: 17, 39, 41, 42, 44, 47, 50, 54, 55, 57, 58, 59, 60 top, 61, 63, 64, 66, 67, 68, 74, 75, 76, 81, 82, 83, 106, 109, 110, 114, 116, 119, 122, 124 top, 125, 126, 129, 130, 131, 132 bottom, 133, 134, 135, 136, 137, 139, 140, 142, 143, 145, 146, 147, 150, 154, 155, 158, 159, 160, 164, 170, 174, 175, 176, 178.

Jeanette Sobczuk: 21, 22, 27, 28, 29, 31, 53, 54, 57.

Toronto Star: 6, 8, 26, 34, 52, 65, 85, 90, 118, 144, 152, back cover.

INDEX